A Metaphysics Primer
Changing From The Inside Out

Michele Doucette, M. Ed.

A Metaphysics Primer: Changing From The Inside Out

Copyright © 2013 by Michele Doucette, St. Clair Publications

All rights reserved. No part of this publication may be reproduced or transmitted in any form or by any means, electronic or mechanical, including photocopying, recording, or by any information storage and retrieval system, without written permission from the author.

ISBN 978-1-935786-39-9

Printed in the United States of America by

St. Clair Publications

PO Box 726

McMinnville, TN   37111-0726

http://stclairpublications.com/

Table of Contents

Author's Note 1
Creation 4
The Image 16
The Great Philosophical Questions 24
The Lessons, Part 1 37
The Lessons, Part 2 310
The Rhythm of Life 417
The Walls Come Tumbling Down 435
5 Keys to Staying Positive 442
The Heart People 451
Changing From the Inside Out 460
Further Contemplation 461
A Final Note 469
Offerings to the Creator 471
Michele's Life Lessons for 2013 481
The Crux of the Matter 493
Addendum 501
Tools for Creation 508

Bibliography 534

About the Author 589

If you want to find the secrets of the Universe, think in terms of energy, frequency and vibration.

Nikola Tesla

Author's Note

Meta means *after* or *beyond* and physics means *matter, material things* or the *physical*.

Metaphysics, then, literally pertains to the study of the true nature of reality (meaning the spiritual force behind physicality).

It was Aristotle who first coined the term; it was also Aristotle who said that *thoughts are the creative elements within us that make our life what it is*.

The principles of metaphysics are based on the perception that we are not simply physical bodies; there is also a spiritual basis to our physical existence, for we are a merging of Universal Mind (shared spiritual consciousness) with Physical Mind (physical matter).

Metaphysical principles, then, enable one to look at situations with more clarity and objectivity.

A Metaphysics Primer

This is not something that happens instantaneously, nor does it happen overnight; metaphysics is a life-long discipline that spans years.

In experiencing and applying metaphysical principles, you gradually (and quite gently, at that) learn to alter your thinking, your emotions, your lifestyle; thereafter, it can be said that you have *become a metaphysician.*

In the course of my ongoing studies, I have learned that a Metaphysician is someone who is able to make changes in the physical world through *meta*-physical principles, meaning that they make use of the principles of mind (and beyond) to create powerful and lasting change in their own lives; henceforth, so, too, would they be able to instruct and guide prospective clients in the same manner.

With an upbringing within the Roman Catholic Church, focused on the personage of Jesus, it is my personal belief that Jesus had been both a master metaphysician as well as a great teacher of metaphysical principles, with a ministry that had been based on positive thinking, love, harmlessness, brotherhood and the healing of body, mind and soul; hence, the front cover image of this book. As a dear friend has shared, *this gorgeous, simple, and yet elegant, image beautifully reflects the subject matter: the opening of the inner self to blossom into a metaphysical form of existence.*

Jesus also saw man as creator, within the metaphysical realm; so, too, did he know that it was the mind that controls (creates) each individual reality; meaning that *if you think it, it is so.* This also means that if one exudes positive thinking, so, too, will increased positivity manifest in their life.

This book is a *continued work* of personal experience. As such, I am suggesting that it be used solely as a primer (an introductory guide) to the topic of study; in this case, metaphysics.

Please take the time to watch Validation, [1] a monumental video clip, for the simple reason that *we all need* to be validated from time to time.

---

[1] https://youtube.googleapis.com/v/Cbk98ojV7Ao%26hl=en_US%26fs =1%26

Creation

When one ponders the term creation, many think of the God of their religious upbringing; hence, we are a *creation* of God. In this light, then, God took the initiative and created us. From this same standpoint of eternity, we have always been a part of God, meaning that so, too, are we eternal.

In keeping with metaphysics, *we are also creator*, meaning that we have the power, and free will, to manifest that which we choose (to believe, to respond to) in this life.

In knowing that we are both creation, and creator, of this physical existence (within the confines of the realm into which we were born), so, too, does this mean that we have been assigned the role of *co-creator*, with God.

→ All is consciousness

→ Consciousness expresses itself through creation

→ Creation is *materialized* thought

A Metaphysics Primer

As participants completely immersed in, and totally responsible for, this creative process (a process that dictates, daily, the outcome of our individual, and collective, lives), we come to learn that there is a significant difference between conscious creation and unconscious creation.

It also becomes imperative to be able to understand that "everything that we can see in form, from our human vantage point, first proceeds from the invisible spiritual realm: our thoughts. Spirit encompasses form; form is encompassed by spirit. Creation is the movement of spirit into form, the progression of the invisible to the visible, the progression of thought to form." [2] Our physical world exists, as it does, because of this materialized thought creation process; hence, we must learn to *watch what we think* and *watch what we say* because both thoughts and words are things.

---

[2] *We are Creators and the Law of Creation* article accessed on March 21, 2011 at http://www.awakeningpath.com/articles/latest_peter_an_040627_we_a re_creators_and9.htm

A Metaphysics Primer

There exists a pre-requisite for conscious creation; namely, we must believe, and accept, that we are powerful and effective creators, able to "create forms and outcomes. When we know this, we can proceed to consciously create a world we want" [3] for ourselves; a world of unity, a world of forgiveness, a world of love, a world of peace, a world of compassion, a world of empathy.

There are choices to be made in every mindful and waking moment; we are always free to choose what we wish to create. As we make decisions to act in a more harmonious nature, we also begin to receive more positive feedback from the unified field (cosmic consciousness); increased positivity always leads to increased synchronicity (a grouping of events by meaning), a term first used by psychologist Carl Jung.

---

[3] *We are Creators and the Law of Creation* article accessed on March 21, 2011 at http://www.awakeningpath.com/articles/latest_peter_an_040627_we_a re_creators_and9.htm

A Metaphysics Primer

In the astute words of Michael Jackson ... *Consciousness expresses itself through creation. This world we live in is the dance of the creator. Dancers come and go in the twinkling of an eye, but the dance lives on. On many an occasion, when I am dancing, I have felt touched by something sacred. In those moments, I feel my spirit soar and become one with everything that exists. I become the stars and the moon; I become the lover and the beloved; I become the victor and the vanquished; I become the master and the slave; I become the singer and the song; I become the knower and the known. I keep on dancing, and then it is the eternal dance of creation; the creator and the creation merge into one wholeness of joy. I keep on dancing until there is only ... the dance.*

Are you ready to learn to transcend the holographic illusion considered, by the collective, to be the reality?

If so, change is but one thought away.

As further shared by the Navajo ... *Speech is the outer form of thought; thought is the outer form of knowledge; knowledge is the awareness of the primordial constituents of the universe.*

In acknowledging that I, too, am a powerful creator, I do my utmost, on a daily basis, to uphold the knowledge that I need to change my way of thinking, my way of living, and my way of acting, all in accordance with what I wish to create in my life; randomness simply does not exist.

When you take the time to observe the happenings in your life, so, too, will you experience yourself as creator.

In knowing, and believing, that we are individuated aspects of God (the infinite consciousness), so, too, does this mean that an infinite amount of knowledge already exists within us; a knowledge that can begin to be accessed if we take the time, every day, to turn our senses inward, venturing toward the point of stillness that exists within.

A Metaphysics Primer

Any technique that allows you to take the time to center (such as meditation or prayer) brings you closer to the singularity (the infinite consciousness, the oneness) that exists, thereby allowing you to tap into the infinite wisdom that exists within.

As has been proven through quantum physics, we are now beginning to understand that, as observers, we also have the ability to affect our reality "by how we observe it." [4]

Such can be demonstrated, with relative ease, when we choose to observe, and respond, in the most positive, and loving, way(s) possible.

As we come to own both our creating abilities as well as our creations, we become empowered; hence, we are better able to "take our power back from the illusions that once distorted our thoughts about life." [5]

---

[4] *Infinite Creators See Through Illusions* article accessed on March 21, 2012 at http://www.infinite-manifesting.org/infinitecreators.html
[5] Ibid.

Reality, then, is "a co-creation of everyone, everything, everywhere, since beginningless time, interdependently co-creating the Great Mystery in which we all find ourselves." [6]

Knowing that we are what we think and experience, the outer world becomes our mirror, our feedback, our final proof of confirmation, if you will.

I so appreciate the words of Cari Murphy when she shares that "we are the artists (creators), molding the clay (Source), to create the masterpiece (our reality). To wake up each morning *choosing to be happy* allows us the opportunity to set our own conditions for the events of each day. In this way, *we* mold our circumstances instead of being molded by them. The real beauty of life is known when we take accountability and responsibility for the creation of our daily

---

[6] *Do We Really Create Our Own Reality* article accessed on March 22, 2012 at http://www.realitysandwich.com/do_we_really_create_our_own_realit y

experience. Contentment is realized when we choose to celebrate the quiet victories of the soul as it makes its way through the process of expansion, growth, and learning with each purposeful twist and turn in the spiritual journey of our lives." [7]

In the end, when all is said and done, I can only control my little segment of reality. If however, enough individuated consciousness beings find themselves working toward the same goal, such will become the newest co-created reality.

Activation of Energy [8] (Pierre Teilhard de Chardin)

Are Quantum Physics and Spirituality Related? [9]

Awakening the Impulse to Evolve [10]

---

[7] *We Are Powerful Artists Creating Our Own Reality* article accessed on March 21, 2012 at http://carilmurphy.wordpress.com/2010/04/30/molding-our-experience-as-powerful-artists-of-our-own-reality/
[8] http://archive.org/details/ActivationOfEnergy
[9] http://www.theisticscience.org/talks/qps1/slides.htm
[10] http://evolutionaryspirituality.com/

A Metaphysics Primer

Beyond Theology [11]

Co-Creation: The Ultimate Responsibility of Authentic Spiritual Growth [12]

Co-Creative with the Divine: Simple Steps for Manifesting Miracles [13]

Conscious Evolution as a Context for the Integration of Science and Spirituality [14]

Consciousness: The Bridge Between Science and Spirit [15]

Deep Wisdom: The Marriage of Science and Spirituality [16]

---

[11] http://ktwu.washburn.edu/productions/BT/#
[12] http://www.stonyhill.com/newsletters/co-creation-and-spiritual-growth.htm
[13] http://vitalitymagazine.com/article/co-creative-with-the-divine-simple-steps-for-manifesting-miracles/
[14] http://ervinlaszlo.com/forum/2010/07/30/conscious-evolution-as-a-context-for-the-integration-of-science-and-spirituality/
[15] http://ervinlaszlo.com/forum/2010/11/28/consciousness-bridge-science-spirit/
[16] http://ervinlaszlo.com/forum/2011/05/30/deep-wisdom-marriage-of-science-spirituality/

A Metaphysics Primer

Designing a Multiperson Planetary Consciousness [17]

Dr. Fred Alan Wolf and Quantum Spirituality [18]

Evolutionary Spirituality [19]

Infinite Thoughts for Evolving Expanding Experiences [20]

Kryon: Co-Creation Explained [21]

<u>Le Phénomène Humain</u> [22] (Pierre Teilhard de Chardin)

Mystic Mamma [23]

Positive Co-Creation [24]

---

[17] http://ervinlaszlo.com/forum/2010/07/12/designing-a-multiperson-planetary-consciousness/

[18] http://suprememastertv.com/bbs/board.php?bo_table=featured&wr_id=804

[19] http://evolutionaryspirituality.wikia.com/wiki/Main_Page

[20] http://www.infinite-manifesting.org/InfiniteThoughts.html

[21] http://www.kryon.com/k_chaneltoronto.html

[22] http://www.archive.org/details/phenomenon-of-man-pierre-teilhard-de-chardin.pdf

[23] http://www.mysticmamma.com/

[24] http://www.greatdreams.com/creation.htm

A Metaphysics Primer

Quantum Physics Demystifies the Process of Manifestation [25]

Quantum Spirituality Trumps Newtonian Politics [26]

Science and Spirituality: Observations from Modern Consciousness Research [27]

Spirituality and the Meaning of Mysticism for Our Time [28]

Synchronicity is Being in Flow [29]

The Gospel of Co-Creation (Brian Piccolo) [30]

The Holographic Universe [31]

---

[25] http://www.abundance-and-happiness.com/quantum-physics.html
[26] http://peoplesgeography.com/2007/04/01/quantum-spirituality-trumps-newtonian-politics/
[27] http://ervinlaszlo.com/forum/2010/07/30/observations-from-modern-consciousness-research/
[28] http://ervinlaszlo.com/forum/2010/06/15/spirituality-and-the-meaning-of-mysticism-for-our-time/
[29] http://www.infinite-manifesting.org/Synchronicity.html
[30] http://www.lulu.com/shop/brian-piccolo/the-gospel-of-co-creation/ebook/product-17534203.html
[31] http://www.crystalinks.com/holographic.html

A Metaphysics Primer

The Observer Effect [32]

The Real Secret of How We Create Our Reality [33]

Vision for a New Earth Spirituality [34]

Vision for a New Earth Spirituality: Part 2 [35]

Vision for a New Earth Spirituality: Part 3 [36]

Vision for a New Earth Spirituality: Part 4 [37]

Words of Encouragement [38]

---

[32] http://www.infinite-manifesting.org/ObserverEffect.html
[33] http://ervinlaszlo.com/forum/2010/11/28/secret-create-our-own-reality/
[34] http://vitalitymagazine.com/article/vision-for-a-new-earth-spirituality/
[35] http://vitalitymagazine.com/article/vision-for-a-new-earth-spirituality-part-ii/
[36] http://vitalitymagazine.com/article/vision-for-a-new-earth-spirituality-part-3/
[37] http://vitalitymagazine.com/article/new-earth-spirituality-part-vi/
[38] http://www.daily-inspiration-quotes.com/encouraging.php

The Image

Made up of the elements of the universe, so, too, were we created in the image (likeness) of the Gods.

Genesis 1:26 reads *And God said, Let us make man in **our** image, after **our** likeness: and let them have dominion over the fish of the sea, and over the fowl of the air, and over the cattle, and over all the earth, and over every creeping thing that creepeth upon the earth.*

Psalm 82:6 reads *I have said, Ye are **Gods**; and all of you are children of the most High.*

John 10:34 reads *Jesus answered them: Is it not written in your law that ye are **Gods**?*

Might these cited passages refer to our physical appearance?

Is it not also conceivable that they could refer to our ability to be creative, via mind (thought), will and emotion?

Might they also refer to our ability to make moral and ethical judgments?

In the noteworthy words of Pierre Teilhard de Chardin, a French philosopher and Jesuit priest, who trained as both a paleontologist as well as a geologist, as penned in his 1955 publication, Le Phénomène Humain [39] ...

We are not human beings having a spiritual experience; we are spiritual beings having a human experience.

In essence, this means that we are not human beings on a spiritual journey; rather, we are spiritual beings on a journey into what it means to be human.

I totally concur with Ramtha in that we are a melding of *God-man* (the mind of God expressing in human form) and *man-God* (physical man expressing the God within); a combined merger of spiritual and physical that serves to

---

[39] http://www.archive.org/details/phenomenon-of-man-pierre-teilhard-de-chardin.pdf

continue the expansion of God (the infinite consciousness) into forever.

Likewise, so, too, are we *continually evolving and changing* as per our own individual experience(s); a process that adds to both the greater collective experience as well as the totality of God, which means, of course, that God is also continually evolving and changing.

How could it be otherwise for this loving energy that is ongoing and forever?

Long have we been taught to believe that God is perfect.

In viewing life as a continually evolving and changing process, can we say that perfection exists?

In keeping, I am ready to offer a completely different perspective; one that many may not be ready for.

→ God is *not* perfect, for perfection is naught but a limitation; God simply is.

God loves us so grandly that we have been allowed, through choice and free will, to create our vast illusions of perfection and imperfection, good and evil, positive and negative.

Quite simply, this means that God, being the totality of All That Is, is the wrong *as well as* the right, the vile ugliness *as well as* the alluring beauty, the unholiness *as well as* the divinity, the illusion *as well as* the reality.

Surely, there can be no greater love than this.

We have been entrusted with the power(s) to create that which will enable us to *expand in our knowingness*.

God allows us to express as we choose, without judgment.

We, alone, determine how, and to what degree, we progress along our evolutionary path, moving past our illusions of limitation to the freedom that lies beyond.

A Metaphysics Primer

In creating the life opportunities of our choice, we determine and select which path(s) to take.

As well, it is to be remembered that the primary tool for this journey is naught but life itself.

95 Thesis or Articles of Faith for a Christianity for the Third Millennium [40]

A Path Forward: Embracing our Creative Imagination [41]

Consciousness and the End of War Between Science and Religion [42]

Creation Spirituality (Matthew Fox) [43]

---

[40] http://www.matthewfox.org/index.php/2010/10/chapter-v-95-theses-or-articles-of-faith-for-a-christianity-for-the-third-millennium/
[41] http://ervinlaszlo.com/forum/2011/03/25/path-to-creative-imagination/
[42] http://ervinlaszlo.com/forum/2010/06/18/consciousness-and-the-end-of-the-war-between-science-and-religion/
[43] http://www.matthewfox.org/

A Metaphysics Primer

Earth and Spirit Council [44]

Extended Awareness [45]

Geoesthetics: The Spiritualization of Art and Science in the Noosphere [46]

Guiding Our Inner Evolution [47]

Inspirational Articles [48]

Let's Stop Trivializing God, The Universe and Our Role in Evolution [49]

Living Our Spirituality [50]

---

[44] http://earthandspirit.org/
[45] http://ervinlaszlo.com/forum/2010/06/13/extended-awareness/
[46] http://ervinlaszlo.com/forum/2010/09/12/geoesthetics-spiritualization-art-science-noosphere/
[47] http://ervinlaszlo.com/forum/2011/03/25/guiding-our-inner-evolution/
[48] http://www.transformationalarts.com/inspirational-articles/co-founder-vitality-articles/aligning-to-source
[49] http://www.thegreatstory.org/trivializing.pdf
[50] http://vitalitymagazine.com/article/conscious-living/

A Metaphysics Primer

Passionate Curiosity: the Stance of the Scientist, the Seeker, and the Journalist [51]

Quantum Consciousness: The Way to Reconcile Science and Spirituality [52]

Reciprocity Foundation: Transforming Youth from Within [53]

Reclaiming Science and Spirituality from the Ego [54]

Spirituality, Healing and Science [55]

Spiritual Practices for this Time of Crisis [56]

The Attitudinal Healing Connection [57]

---

[51] http://ervinlaszlo.com/forum/2010/09/12/passionate-curiosity-scientist-seeker-journalist/
[52] http://ervinlaszlo.com/forum/2010/07/12/quantum-consciousness-the-way-to-reconcile-science-spirituality/
[53] http://www.reciprocityfoundation.org/about/whole-person-approach/
[54] http://ervinlaszlo.com/forum/2010/11/28/reclaiming-science-spirituality-ego/
[55] http://ervinlaszlo.com/forum/2010/07/30/spirituality-healing-and-science/
[56] http://ervinlaszlo.com/forum/2011/05/30/spiritual-practices-for-crisis/
[57] http://www.ahc-oakland.org/

A Metaphysics Primer

The Direct-Intuitive-Nonlocal Mind: Another Foundation for Knowledge? [58]

The Real Issue [59]

The Role of Spirituality in a Worldshift [60]

Twelve Principles of Creation Spirituality [61]

Worldshift: We Are Learning to Live in a Living Universe [62]

YELLAWE [63]

---

[58] http://ervinlaszlo.com/forum/2010/11/28/direct-intuitive-nonlocal-mind/
[59] http://ervinlaszlo.com/forum/2010/07/12/the-real-issue/
[60] http://ervinlaszlo.com/forum/2011/05/30/role-of-spirituality-in-worldshift/
[61] http://originalblessing.ning.com/page/twelve-principles-of-creation
[62] http://ervinlaszlo.com/forum/2011/05/30/learning-to-live-in-living-universe/
[63] http://www.yellawe.org/YELLAWE/Welcome.html

The Great Philosophical Questions

Who am I?

Where did I come from?

Why am I here?

What is my purpose?

What happens when I die?

These are the existential questions that everyone, at some point in their lives, will ask. The way you answer them depends upon your belief paradigm (your view of the world).

Who am I?

As shared earlier, consciousness (God) wanted to occupy a physical form in order to experience the totality of the human condition.

A Metaphysics Primer

This combined merger of spiritual and physical allows us to take on form, thereby experiencing the reality of that form; an experience that allows us to forget our true identity.

Having individual preferences, goals, ideas, beliefs and philosophic points-of-view, each of us, initially, believe ourselves to be the ego personality.

In keeping with the first question, the challenge becomes in answering *without* reference to one's job, social status, material possessions, gender, nationality, religion, health situation, personal appearance and sexual orientation, as we are not any of these components.

Where did I come from?

As Science tells us, everything is energy; so, too, is infinite consciousness a form of energy. It must be remembered that we are all individuated aspects of this *same* energy.

Albeit a smaller individualized version, so, too, do we have all of the power, and all of the information, of the original version, meaning God.

A Metaphysics Primer

Why am I here?

As we continue to learn and grow, from experiences we deem necessary, we begin to understand that *we just are*; that everything, and everyone, while all part of the same (because I am you and you are me) are merely *appearing to be different* so as to be able to experience ourselves fully and completely.

In essence, this is what ascension means; it is a process whereby we learn to become one, once again, with Source.

What is my purpose?

The *real* you can be equated to that which is your propensity, your knowingness, your enthusiasm and your passion, for this is what constitutes your inner purpose.

In visiting the Kabalarian Philosophy website, [64] I was able to discover that I am what they refer to as a 3 birthpath.

The words shared therein rang true for me.

---

[64] http://www.kabalarians.com/cfm/articles/what-is-my-purpose-in-life.cfm

A Metaphysics Primer

My role is to use the power of the word to inspire and lift others to see a happier, objective, perspective of life.

These are the very words that resonate with me; they have a special energy, one that is unique to me. It is this same energy that I feel surge within my soul, whenever I contemplate the meaning of these very words.

I love to orchestrate the written word. In the course of my writing, I want to empower, motivate and inspire others to live happier (more fulfilled) lives.

On the flip side, so too, is it my daily mission to live a genuine authentic, conscious, and honest life, resonating with love, empathy, exuberance and compassion for the oneness of life that exists.

Discovering your purpose is, by far, the easiest part. The daily challenge involves working on yourself (as cited in the preceding paragraph) until you become that very purpose.

In this finding of yourself, so, too, can it be said that you are also re-creating yourself.

A Metaphysics Primer

What happens when I die?

It is my belief that the soul abides within the physical body. When the physical vehicle has completed that which it initially set out to do, the soul crosses over to the other side, of the veil, for a temporary rest, eventually coming back to live out another lifetime; a process that has continued for many millennia.

So, too, was this a belief held by Jesus.

In 553 AD, reincarnation was condemned by 165 church officials; prior to this time, it had existed as a fundamental teaching. [65]

In having addressed these deep philosophical questions, I was quick to find that they served to create another; namely, **who do I really want to be(come)?**

---

[65] http://www.facts-are-facts.com/magazin/6-reincarnation-the-churchs-biggest-lie.ihtml

A Metaphysics Primer

Just as there are laws that govern "physical events in this reality, so, too, are there laws that govern consciousness (spiritual or non-physical entities). Plato, Christ, Buddha, Lao Tsu, [along with] many [other] sages and yogis, in the past (and present) and also the teachings of most secret societies indicate an awareness of our true identity and also profess methods for remembering who it is that we really are (i.e., pure consciousness temporarily [housed] in a physical context)." [66]

There exists a philosophical problem regarding both mind as well as consciousness, in that "Western investigators examine consciousness as it operates externally to the conscious being; as such, these Western investigators, are going the wrong way.... they are going outwards rather than turning inwards and having consciousness examine itself, and its source." [67]

---

[66] http://www.the-unorthodox-life-coach.com/whoami.html
[67] Ibid.

A Metaphysics Primer

I know that I am a spiritual being (infinite consciousness) on a journey into what it means to be human; so, too, is it a journey with which we find our way back to God, meaning that as we shed the ego personality, we are better able to rediscover our true identity.

It is at this point that one can say they have been awakened to the true reality of existence.

In the words of Jean Klein [68] ... *The seeker will discover that he is what he seeks and that what he seeks is the source of the inquiry.*

In truth, we are like gamers in that we, the players, get to engage in an adventure; an adventure whereby we have forgotten our truest selves and must, therefore, find our way back. It is only on a temporary basis, therefore, that all relate to themselves as the ego personality; known by a given name, we express preferences, goals, notions, ideas and philosophic points of view.

---

[68] http://non-dualitypress.org/pages/jean-klein

A Metaphysics Primer

It is here that we describe ourselves, courtesy of such components as job, possessions, gender, nationality, health situation, personal appearance, religion and sexual preference; the very means through which consciousness is able to occupy a human form (physical vehicle) in order to experience the temporal human condition for experience, challenge, investigation, learning and pleasure.

There is, however, a far more profound reality that exists.

In actuality, we are pure consciousness. As individuated aspects of this same consciousness, while we are here to experience ourselves in all ways human, so, too, are we here to rediscover our true identity in the process, thereby living as an actualized human.

At one point, Mohandas Karamchand Ghandi (commonly known as Mahatma Gandhi) was asked about his religion. His response was profound in its simplicity.

The way I live my life, the things I do every day, this is my religion.

A Metaphysics Primer

Actuality and Reality [69]

Awakening to the Dream [70]

Between Light and Dark [71]

Divine Consciousness for Everyone [72]

Guided Meditations [73]

Have Confidence in Your Own Spiritual Potentiality [74]

Helping the Daughters of Buddha [75]

How to Discover Your Life Purpose [76]

---

[69] http://www.crcsite.org/actuality.htm
[70] http://www.awakeningtothedream.com/
[71] http://vitalitymagazine.com/article/between-light-and-dark/
[72] http://vitalitymagazine.com/article/divine-guidance-for-everyone/
[73] http://www.chopra.com/library/guidedmeditations
[74] http://thebuddhistblog.blogspot.ca/2006/06/have-confidence-in-your-own-spiritual.html
[75] http://accessnewage.com/articles/mystic/BUDHADTR.HTM
[76] http://www.stevepavlina.com/blog/2005/01/how-to-discover-your-life-purpose-in-about-20-minutes/

A Metaphysics Primer

Living Your Spiritual Potential [77]

Maslow's Traits of Self-Actualized People [78]

Mind and Body United [79]

Psyche and Spirit [80]

Quantum Consciousness [81]

Spiritual Enlightenment [82]

The Birthing of the Sacred Human [83]

The Power of Intention [84]

---

[77] http://www.aquarius-atlanta.com/articles/?issue=02-2012&i=1420&article=living_your_spiritual_potential
[78] http://www.tribalmessenger.org/headlines/maslow-self-actualized-traits.htm
[79] http://www.who-am-i-question.com/mind-and-body.html
[80] http://www.tparents.org/Library/Unification/Books/Psyche/Psyche-06.htm
[81] http://www.who-am-i-question.com/quantum-consciousness.html
[82] http://www.who-am-i-question.com/spiritual-enlightenment.html
[83] http://vitalitymagazine.com/article/the-birthing-of-the-sacred-human/
[84] http://www.who-am-i-question.com/power-of-intention.html

A Metaphysics Primer

The Power of Thinking [85]

The Road to Self-Actualization [86]

The Sacred Human: From Ego Driven to Soul Guided [87]

The Secret of Success [88]

The Seven Spiritual Laws of Success [89]

The Seven Universal Laws [90]

The Universal Law of Right Action [91]

Transformational Arts College of Spiritual and Holistic Training [92]

---

[85] http://www.who-am-i-question.com/the-power-of-thinking.html
[86] http://www.trans4mind.com/mind-development/maslow.html
[87] http://vitalitymagazine.com/article/the-sacred-human-from-ego-driven-to-soul-guided/
[88] http://www.who-am-i-question.com/secret-of-success.html
[89] http://www.chopra.com/library/laws
[90] http://www.who-am-i-question.com/laws-of-attraction.html
[91] http://www.who-am-i-question.com/do-the-right-thing.html
[92] http://www.transformationalarts.com/

A Metaphysics Primer

What is My Purpose? [93] [94] [95]

Who Am I? Blog [96]

Who Do You Think You Are? [97]

---

[93] http://divinecosmos.com/online-store/what-is-my-purpose
[94] http://timefindersmagazine.com/articles/jennifer-chandler/482-what-is-my-purpose
[95] http://thespiritscience.net/spirit/2012/03/11/what-is-my-purpose/
[96] http://www.who-am-i-question.com/life-blog.html
[97] http://www.who-am-i-question.com/who-am-i.html

A Metaphysics Primer

This antique engraving of Thinking Man was published in Tables of the Encyclopedia 1762 to 1777 by Denis Diderot (French philosopher, art critic, writer); a prominent figure during the Enlightenment, he is best known for serving as co-founder, chief editor of and contributor to the Encyclopédie.

The Lessons, Part 1

[1] The Nature of the Universe

At the most basic level, everything is comprised of energy. Energy is held together to create matter (which is really energy condensed to a slow vibration). There is one underlying field of energy (the Zero Point Field or ZPF) that pervades everything, thereby giving purpose and unity to our world.

In addition, everything is vibration (the result of energy in motion), which means that every object, every being, every thought, every action, every word and every psychological mood, has its own unique vibrational energy.

It can be said, therefore, that energy equals vibration.

Simply put, *energy and vibration are what life is all about.*

A Metaphysics Primer

As a force, energy consists of two opposing forces, that which we think of as positive and negative, each of which acts upon the other to cause a vibration. Without these two opposing forces, there would be no life. What this essentially means is that the totality of life acts (cause) and reacts (effect) because of this pull.

As you and I create our reality from these two forces, we do our best to try and reach a balance within each lifetime; this also demonstrates how the principle of sowing (the seed) and reaping (the harvest) becomes both a scientific and spiritual law, called karma.

Knowing that negative karma weighs the soul down and hampers one's personal evolution, it becomes the goal of every soul to enter into its next incarnation with as little negative karma as possible.

As stated by Hollywood Actor, Keanu Reeves ... *The recognition of the law of cause and effect, also known as karma, is a fundamental key to understanding how you*

create your world, with actions of the body, speech and mind. When you truly understand karma, you realize you are responsible for everything in your life. It is incredibly empowering to know that your future is in your hands.

Thoughts like fear, greed, hatred, revenge, jealousy, anxiety and frustration are often referred to as seeds of disease.

When the body is at *ease* (as in mental, emotional, and spiritual harmony), so, too, is it healthy.

By comparison, when the body is at *dis-ease* (meaning mental, emotional, and spiritual disharmony), illness follows.

If one feels inadequate, insecure, and lacking in self esteem, this results in an inward withdrawal. These are the very individuals that tend to become engulfed in a negative inner dialogue; one that is embodied by self-pity.

It is also this very negative vibration that emanates outward. In accordance with the Law of Attraction, this negative energy *will only attract more of the same.*

No matter how much they seek happiness and success in their life, they continue to feel more and more like a dismal failure, at anything and everything, primarily because they may not understand that it is *the inner world that must ultimately be changed before such can be duly reflected in the outer world* (of which they are a part).

Focus and concentration are major keys with respect to the changing of one's inner world.

It is your energy vibration that attracts corresponding circumstances (be they people, places, things or events) into your life. By the same token, it is your energy vibration that can ultimately change your reality.

We are constantly projecting our thought patterns.

If one is *conscious* of these thought patterns, they are *creating by deliberate intent*.

If one is *unconscious* of these thought patterns, they are *creating by default*.

Quite simply, the higher, lighter and purer one's energy vibration frequency, the more that individual is able to tap into the spiritual energy of who they *really* are.

[2] You Are Everything: Everything Is You

Scientists are well aware that the universe has exploded into existence, not just once, but repeatedly in endless cycles of death and rebirth; a process that is referred to as the cyclic universe theory.

Theoretical physicist, Paul J. Steinhardt, proposes, courtesy of this theory, that [1] space and time may have always existed in an endless cycle of expansion and rebirth; [2] the expansion of the universe is accelerating, as astronomers have recently observed; and [3] after trillions of years, expansion stalls, new matter and radiation is created, and the cycle restarts anew. [98]

The cyclic universe theory postulates that the universe has no beginning and no end, in the traditional sense, given that the universe has been exploding into existence, repeatedly over time, extending far into the past as well as into the future. It is quite conceivable, henceforth, that the universe has existed forever.

The cyclic universe theory also states that *matter and energy*, albeit finite, *are infinitely recycled* (meaning that energy continues to change form).

The implications of this theory, therefore, are many.

[1] It is quite conceivable that the universe is possibly many times older than we think. [99]

---

[98] *The Endless Universe: Introduction to the Cyclic Universe* article accessed on March 17, 2011 at
http://www.actionbioscience.org/newfrontiers/steinhardt.html

A Metaphysics Primer

[2] All finite resources (such as matter and energy) within the universe can be indefinitely recycled through the resetting event. [100]

[3] We finally have an explanation for how the universe continues its expansion. [101]

Based on the first law of thermodynamics, a fundamental dictum of physics, we know that energy cannot be destroyed, that it can only be transferred to a new form.

It can be concluded, therefore, that the universe was not created in the manner in which we understand creation, but that it was merely recycled from energy that cannot be destroyed; likewise for the continual cycles of death and rebirth that are experienced with each new (recycled) incarnation.

---

[99] *Cyclic Universe Theory* posting accessed on March 15, 2011 at http://www.eve-search.com/thread/1375175/author/Charles%20Baker
[100] Ibid.
[101] Ibid.

A Metaphysics Primer

Matter can be defined as being anything made up of atoms and molecules; in addition, matter is anything that has mass.

While there is no proof that matter is made of energy, all that can be proven is the fact "that matter can be converted into energy and vice versa. In fact, you need to have matter to be able to define energy … one without the other is an oxymoron." [102]

I chanced across a theory referred to as Ducheneism; an argument that uses a recycled energy theory to explain the happenings of the universe.

Believing in the idea that God is not one single person (force), Ducheneism states that while *everything is God, God is also everything*.

To put it simply, God is the energy that creates, circulates and becomes recycled.

---

[102] Philosophy Forums accessed on March 15, 2011 at http://forums.philosophyforums.com/threads/matter-is-not-created-or-destroyed-33846.html

Even though the term recycled is not an overly adequate one, it simply refers to the fact that energy is constantly changing form (which is *exactly* what we know continues to happen).

When a war has been started, negative energy is created. Knowing that lives are lost and widespread famine may prevail, such further results in increased poverty levels.

These particular offshoots clearly demonstrate recycled negative energy (as initially caused by war).

By means of a different example, on the flip side, if a person says something nice to you (positive energy), this makes you feel happy (recycled positive energy).

Any further complimentary actions that stem forth from the initial positive energy, as a domino effect that you may have set in motion, can also be referred to as recycled positive energy.

A Metaphysics Primer

According to Ducheneism, with God viewed as the energy that is distributed throughout the universe, Jesus was most likely a prophet, a man "who understood that we must feed the Earth positive energy, so that it can distribute positive energy to its subjects." [103]

Ducheneism denotes that while Jesus "may have existed, and was more connected with the earth and its energy, through meditation and so forth, he was not the son of God, as God is not a specific being, or object, and cannot, therefore, actually have a son." [104]

Ducheneism also states that "it is believed that every living thing is an energy source. When a person dies, it mostly is a positive event, as much as it is a natural one [in that] ... the energy that powers the person leaves the body, and is

---

[103] Ducheneism's Views on Jesus Christ posting accessed on March 15, 2011 at http://www.facebook.com/note.php?note_id=168025806574272
[104] Ibid.

recycled ... with this death comes life; with this positive energy, comes positive effects ... as the energy makeup that is you, is recycled as a different form of energy." [105]

Knowing that energy is incarnate, that energy is constant, that energy is cyclical, that everything emanates from the same source, I am everything and everything is me. Likewise, you are everything and everything is you; hence, the aptness of the name associated with this lesson.

Likewise ……

→ God is pure energy

→ God is universal energy

→ God is *conscious* (fully aware, deliberate and intentional) energy

→ God is *infinite* (boundless and endless) energy

---

[105] Views on Afterlife posting accessed on March 15, 2011 at http://www.facebook.com/note.php?note_id=168037566573096

A Metaphysics Primer

If we come to understand, and believe, that I am you and you are me, despite the fact that *we appear to be separated only in order to experience individuality*, surely this gives one pause to think things through, with clarity and intent, before uttering threats, before uttering words of defamation, before displaying actions of ill intent, toward another.

Each of us needs to begin thinking of ourselves in this same light: we are every bit as big as the sun, the earth, the stars, the planets and all the universes combined, simply because we are made of the same stuff.

The unified field, according to modern physics, is "the deepest, most powerful level of Nature's functioning, and the source of the infinite creativity and intelligence within every individual and displayed throughout the universe." [106]

---

[106] The Unified Field: The Key to Enlightenment, National Invincibility and World Peace website accessed on March 16, 2011 at http://www.america.unifiedfieldconferences.org/

A Metaphysics Primer

Gregg Braden, in <u>The Divine Matrix</u>, talks about the universe as having been founded on four characteristics; namely, [1] that there is a field of energy that connects all of creation (discovery 1); [2] that this field takes on the role of a container, a bridge and a mirror, for the beliefs as held by the individual (discovery 2); [3] that this field is nonlocal and holographic, meaning that every part of it is connected to another, with each piece mirroring the whole on a smaller scale (discovery 3); and [4] that we communicate with this field through the language of emotion (discovery 4). [107]

Gregg Braden is not the first to suggest that coherent emotion is the language that this field of energy understands; Esther and Jerry Hicks, through the words of Abraham, feel the same way.

---

[107] Braden, Gregg. (2007). *The Divine Matrix: Bridging Time, Space, Miracles and Belief* (page xxi). Carlsbad, CA: Hay House, Inc.

A Metaphysics Primer

"Coherent emotion happens when what we are thinking, feeling, and expressing are all in alignment," [108] which means that, on the flip side, incoherent emotion can be described as "the kind of emotion we experience when we are feeling one way, thinking another way, and expressing something different from either our thoughts or our feelings." [109]

When you think about something, further coupled with feelings and emotions, you are sending out powerful vibrations.

We have already concluded that everything is connected.

This means that *your vibrations affect everyone* else, directly or indirectly. Everything you do (what you think, what you feel, what you say, how you behave) is vibrated

---

[108] *Oneness and The Unified Field* article accessed on March 16. 2011 at http://www.escapetheillusion.com/blog/2008/10/oneness-and-the-unified-field-gregg-braden/
[109] Ibid.

A Metaphysics Primer

into the universal field (universal consciousness) of which you are a significant particle of source energy.

Knowing that each is affected by the other (directly or indirectly, as mentioned previously) is what demonstrates the interconnectivity (transpersonal consciousness) that exists between all of us.

In keeping with the unified field (with other names being Consciousness, Consciousness Grid, Source of Creation, Oneness, Unity, Nature's Mind, Mind of God and Quantum Hologram, to cite but a few), you are part of God.

God is in you, as well as everywhere.

This means that "we are not simply a part of the Earth; we *are* the Earth. We are not simply a part of the Force that governs all Creation; we *are* that Force." [110]

---

[110] Bolsta, Phil. (2009). *Gregg Braden on Prayer and the Unified Field* posting accessed on March 16, 2011 at
http://bolstablog.wordpress.com/2009/12/06/braden-video/

[3] The Nature of Who We Are

Many are familiar with the words... *we are not human beings having a spiritual experience; we are spiritual beings having a human experience.*

These words belong to Teilhard de Chardin (1881–1955), a philosopher, and Jesuit priest, who was also trained as both a paleontologist as well as a geologist.

We are spiritual beings immersed in a human experience.

As spiritual beings inhabiting a physical body, each of us has our own vibratory signature, the quality of which depends on both our thoughts and our inner mental (feeling) world.

In addition, harmonic resonance between fields of consciousness (meaning the minds of people) can be realized when their rates of vibration are similar.

A Metaphysics Primer

I am the proprietor of my soul, just as you are the proprietor of your own, and yet there exists a shared destiny within all of us: to sincerely identify with the fact that the *peaceable kingdom exists within* each and everyone.

How does one advance towards this peaceable kingdom?

One begins by opening up and saying yes to life.

A word of significant power, it is imperative that you take the time to say the word yes in your mind, making sure that you say it several times, getting louder with each utterance.

Are you able to feel the energy shift?

Are you able to feel the energy expanse?

When I say yes to life, I feel more joyful, more exuberant, more alive.

It now becomes imperative that you take the time to make a comparative between saying yes in your mind with saying yes, with strength and conviction, out loud to the Universe.

A Metaphysics Primer

If it is your intent to open up on a wonderfully energetic level, this is the best way to begin to do so.

The Universe continues to offer a multitude of opportunities and experiences in which to say yes. Not only that, but every time you both welcome and are open to what shows up in your life, your energy field shifts to a yes vibration.

Saying yes to life positions you in a completely different venue. You will find that you are now *open to experiencing the totality of all that life has to offer*.

The more one is able to remain open to a given experience, relaxing and embracing the situation at hand, doing their best to learn from the event itself, the easier it becomes to transcend, thereby allowing one to move beyond the experience in question.

Whatever you resist will persist, as the saying goes. It was Carl Jung who uttered these words. Here was a man who clearly understood that what you think about recreates itself within your own life experience(s).

Negative energies, then, will only begin to dissipate in the welcoming, accepting and embracing of that which you want to change.

It is essential that you allow this wisdom to guide you toward embracing the totality of all life.

Most are familiar with the saying that *the outer world is your mirror*, always reflecting yourself back to you; this simply means that your outer world is a direct reflection of your inner world.

If you embrace, and feel, love, peace, unison and truth, vibrating such throughout the entirety of your being, you will experience people (places, things or events) who feel and reflect the same.

If, on the other hand, all you experience in your outer world is disharmony, aggression, hate, separation and falsehood, so, too, will you experience people (places, things or events) who feel and reflect the same.

Much inner healing (often times connected with the false sense of self, meaning the ego) is needed in order to correct the imbalances that exist.

As you are traversing this new and unexplored territory, it is important that you make a conscious effort to be *gentle with yourself* while asking the following questions.

What do I love about myself?

What is it that I wish to change?

It is as equally imperative that you take the time to practice the Golden Rule, *treating yourself as you would have others treat you.*

Accepting the premise that you, and you alone, are 100% responsible for the changes that you wish to impart, upon your being, is also critical.

A Metaphysics Primer

I am here to tell you that it is possible to transcend situations in your outer world, all through the shifting of your inner terrain.

Not something that happens overnight, this is a process that requires work, effort and diligence on your part, of that you can be sure.

While it is not known to whom the following words can be attributed, they are well worth citing herein.

The good you find in others, is within you as well.

The faults you find in others, are your faults as well.

After all, to recognize something in your outer world, you must have a reference point in your inner world.

The world around you is a reflection, a mirror showing you the person you are.

To change your world, simply change yourself.

See the best in others, and you will be at your best.

A Metaphysics Primer

Give to others, and you give to yourself.

Love others, and you will be loved.

Seek to understand, and you will be understood.

Listen, and your voice will be heard.

Teach, and you will learn.

Clearly, this is the wisdom that needs to understood, internalized and lived.

We live in a world of infinite possibilities; that having been said, this array continues to take form based on one's thoughts, feelings and emotions.

Unfortunately, our 3D minds struggle with the truth that we are limitless beings, unable to fathom that we are connected to a Source of infinite power and consciousness.

Quite literally, this means that we have the ability to manifest that which we desire.

A Metaphysics Primer

As one learns to let go of the limiting mind, one begins to experience what it means, as an awesome spiritual being, to have access to infinite possibilities.

While this seems to be a case of far easier said than done, it *does* take time and it *does* get easier. Approaching it from the standpoint of one day at a time is how you begin to experience the precise unfolding that is needed.

In order to fully embrace who you really are, it becomes imperative that each individual must throw off the yoke of repression, the yoke of separation, the yoke of illusion, for they are all interconnected.

Limits exist only in the mind, a mind that has been programmed to believe in repression, separation and illusion.

Given that all souls are sparks of the divine, all of humanity is an expanded form of God.

Possessing both divine intelligence and freedom of will, we, too, are forever expanding. This means, quite simply, that God is forever expanding through us.

Ramtha says that it is only in becoming God-man and God-woman, by becoming a part of humanity, that we are God realized in the form of matter.

Mind you, most of us have a hard time accepting that we, too, are Gods.

In the deepest of realities, we are infinite beings; as a result, we have access to infinite experiences and manifestations, all of which can be found through the transcending of the mind.

In summation, *when one embraces humanity* in the physical form, *one is wholly experiencing God* meaning that <u>the physical body is the experience</u>.

A Metaphysics Primer

It must also be stated that the physical body, is not the personality; while the personality is also part of the physical experience, it is not who we are.

→ We are infinite consciousness

→ Infinite consciousness has no body

→ Infinite consciousness has no form

→ Infinite consciousness simply is

As creators of our own reality, there are but two options open to each and everyone.

One is based on fear, guilt and control; the other is based on love, empathy, compassion and understanding.

What I am here to experience may not be what you are here to experience, and, yet, all experiences are valid.

A Metaphysics Primer

In the course of my experience(s), I have been able to come to the conclusion that everything I need already exists within.

I am also of the firm belief that opportunities do not happen by chance.

Even though an opportunity may present itself, many still are doing their best to deal with the limiting thoughts and beliefs that may stop them from forging ahead.

This is why it becomes so imperative to *learn to become aware* of the thoughts and beliefs that may be limiting your experience(s). In this regard, everyone must work toward resolving and changing.

Negative feelings, negative thoughts and negative emotions are like toxins that, if suppressed (held onto) for long periods of time, will manifest in physical form.

This is why it is so important to learn how to release negativity.

Learning how to change negative self talk into positive self talk takes time, especially considering that we are only consciously aware of about 10% of the thoughts that buzz about in our heads.

For many years, too numerous to count, I found myself existing in a state of worry, stress, fear and guilt, both at home and in the workplace.

Watching the news on the television kept me in a controlled state of restless anxiety.

I had no idea that the media was so biased in their news coverage, that it was their job to saturate us, to have everyone view the same news, thereby orchestrating all of us to respond in the same manner.

This meant that there was a great propensity for millions and millions of people to broadcast similarly negative responses (vibrations).

Like a sponge, when surrounded by other negative minded people, I would sink deeper and deeper into altering depressive states. I was being controlled by that voice in my head.

It was almost impossible to achieve and maintain a positive outlook on life when my mindset was governed by such negativity.

As soon as I became aware that my thoughts, my words and my actions were energy based, I knew that I had no choice but to work towards reconfiguring the wiring of my brain.

I had to learn to think and respond from a more positive outlook. I was no longer willing to allow my ego to reign supreme.

This was *a stance* that, in the beginning, *took considerable time and monumental effort.*

How does one begin to go about understanding how they think?

A Metaphysics Primer

How does one begin to examine, without criticism, the belief system(s) that they are privy to?

The easiest way to start is by *observing your actions and reactions* to people, to things, to situations.

As much as possible, you need to detach yourself from your subjective responses.

You must also remain as objective as possible, under the circumstances of the time (and it does get easier), for your primary goal is to understand *why* you think the thoughts that you do and *why* you respond to people and situations in a specific way.

Once you begin *questioning your programmed beliefs and ideas,* you need to be ready to *replace them* with beliefs and ideas that resonate with you.

In so doing, you begin to embark on an internal and personal mental shift.

As you begin questioning, thereby experiencing this necessary internal shift, your energy signature, your vibration, changes.

If the Zero Point Field (ZPF) is free and boundless, then, so, too, are we.

Everything is interconnected within this life force that flows through the Universe.

Truly, what we have elected to experience here on planet Earth is both holy and divine.

[4] We Are Consciousness

Consciousness can be said to originate from the very fabric of this unified field. It is this experience of consciousness, then, this utilization of what consciousness and the unified field means, that leads to increased intelligence, increased creativity, better health, decreased anxiety, increased self actualization and better job performance, all of which serve to further enhance continued, and increased, successfulness in every avenue of one's life.

A Metaphysics Primer

If these same experiences were to take place on an ever increasing collective level, such would lead to enhanced coherence and harmony (meaning that there would be less instances of domestic, as well as international, conflict) among nations. [111]

In 1960, Maharishi Mahesh Yogi predicted that one percent of a population practicing the Transcendental Meditation technique would produce measurable improvements in the quality of life for the whole population.

This phenomenon, known as the Maharishi Effect, first noticed in 1974, was reported in a paper published in 1976.

---

[111] *Unified Field of All the Laws of Nature* article accessed on March 17, 2011 at
http://worldpeaceendowment.org/invincibility/invincibility7.html

The findings were such that "when 1% of a community practiced the Transcendental Meditation® program, the crime rate was reduced by 16% on average." [112]

The basis of the Maharishi Effect is the rise in collective consciousness, meaning "the wholeness of consciousness of any specific group. For example, when we talk of community consciousness, we merely put together the consciousness of all the individuals who make up the community; for national consciousness, we put together the consciousness of all the citizens of a nation." [113]

Since the theory and the phenomenon are so new to modern science, "the methodology of a study is subjected to rigorous

---

[112] Maharishi University of Management website. *Research on the Maharishi Effect* article accessed on March 28, 2011 at http://www.mum.edu/m_effect/
[113] Maharishi Vedic University (1999) website. *The Maharishi Effect* article accessed on March 17, 2011 at http://www.vedicknowledge.com/Maharishi_effect.html

analysis by the journal review boards before a paper on the Maharishi Effect is accepted for publication." [114]

Dr. David Edwards, Professor of Government, at the University of Texas, has been referenced as saying ... "I think the claim can be plausibly made that the potential impact of this research exceeds that of any other ongoing social or psychological research program. It has survived a broader array of statistical tests than most research in the field of conflict resolution. This work and the theory that informs it deserve the most serious consideration by academics and policy makers alike." [115]

In this sense, we very much operate like radio transmitters and receivers, sending out signals (vibrations), courtesy of the electromagnetic field that surrounds us.

---

[114] Maharishi Vedic University (1999) website. *The Maharishi Effect* article accessed on March 17, 2011 at http://www.vedicknowledge.com/Maharishi_effect.html
[115] Maharishi University of Management website. *Research on the Maharishi Effect* article accessed on March 28, 2011 at http://www.mum.edu/m_effect/

A Metaphysics Primer

In returning to the words of Gregg Braden, as per Lesson 2 (You Are Everything: Everything Is You), as individuals, we are constantly creating effects on every part of creation, primarily because it is consciousness that permeates every aspect of the unified field.

Many of us have taken the time, at some point in our lives, to throw a stone into a pond. It is this motion that creates ripples that spread outward.

As miniscule as many believe themselves to be, it is in a fashion similar to this that we are actually able to transform the cosmos.

Since collective consciousness "is created by the individuals within it, as individual consciousness grows, collective consciousness rises; and as collective consciousness rises, individual consciousness grows. In other words, as one individual regularly experiences self-referral consciousness and enlivens it in his own awareness, the levels of collective consciousness in which he participates (family, city, province, nation, etc.) are simultaneously improved. This higher value of collective consciousness, in turn, effects, in a positive way, every one of the individual members of that level of collective consciousness." [116]

The unified field of consciousness is "the essence and source of creation of everyone, regardless of race, age, gender, background, richness or poverty, place and time. Whatever we individually think, experience, or believe, we are all conscious beings, sharing the same essence." [117]

It becomes the beliefs that we have about ourselves, however, the beliefs to which we have become ingrained and attached, that create the sense of separation that is felt.

Clearly, *we are the source of our own perceived limitations.*

---

[116] Maharishi Vedic University (1999) website. *The Maharishi Effect* article accessed on March 17, 2011 at http://www.vedicknowledge.com/Maharishi_effect.html

[117] The Unified Field – The Consciousness of All Creation website accessed on March 17, 2011 at http://www.anunda.com/paradigm/unified-field.htm

A Metaphysics Primer

The language of this energy field, shared earlier, appears to be coherent emotion, which is what creates a chemical shift in the pH levels within our bodies. In addition, the hormonal levels in the body are also changed.

For example, "the life-affirming hormone precursor DHEA increases over 100 percent in our bodies, in the space of only six hours, while in the presence of coherent emotions, like appreciation and gratitude." [118]

By comparison, "life-depleting hormones like cortisol, the stress hormone, decrease over 23 percent in that same six hours, while in the presence of coherent emotion." [119]

Measureable statements such as these are truly indicative of the body having the potential to heal itself; as a result, there is much to be said for emotional energy.

---

[118] *Oneness and The Unified Field* article accessed on March 16. 2011 at http://www.escapetheillusion.com/blog/2008/10/oneness-and-the-unified-field-gregg-braden/
[119] Ibid.

A Metaphysics Primer

We are privileged to live in a world that has been infused with vital, living, conscious, infinite, fluid (malleable) energy.

As vital, living, conscious and infinite beings, capable of change, so, too, are we this same energy.

Life experiences are created by beliefs, imaginations, and emotions, all of which work together as one system. Emotions (the same as energy in motion), however, are the link that exists between the body, mind and spirit; an affiliation that must now be forged anew.

It is imperative that you learn to analyze (in a detached way) and challenge your beliefs.

It is equally as important that you learn to completely detach yourself from the hardened belief systems that continue to generate superstition, bias, discrimination, bigotry, intolerance, chauvinism, prejudice, ignorance, irrationality and premature (and sometimes perverse) conclusions.

Learning to release yourself from these negative outcomes is what shall begin to transform your inner world.

As you work toward attaining the inner peace (emotional freedom) that is needed, you are achieving self-healing.

Remembering that as individual consciousness grows, so, too, does this affect the collective consciousness in a positive way, this means that anything one does to enhance their own lives, in the here and now, can only serve to also benefit the unified field to which we are all connected.

The term universal mind is often a generic term used to imply a higher consciousness wherein the nature of this universal mind is omniscient (all knowing), omnipotent (all powerful), omnificent (all creative) and omnipresent (always present).

In essence, the universal mind is where everything exists; a rather fitting description for God, wouldn't you say?

A Metaphysics Primer

There is an aspect of ourselves that exists beyond this current physicality, often referred to as the Higher Self (which appears to be one's self in a different dimension).

The Higher Self, it is said, acts as a guide, attempting to communicate in a variety of different ways: with intuition and hunches, as well as with sudden and unexpected life changes.

In choosing to follow the guidance that has been received, the potential to become a physical manifestation of one's Higher Self exists, whereby wholeness can only "be maintained by living out the laws of wholeness in one's actions." [120]

In order "to receive the benefits of a peaceful and happy life, we have to take ourselves in hand, and, by patient

---

[120] Elade. (2006). *Joyful Living* (page 13). The School of Universal Mind. Located for free distribution at http://www.schoolofuniversalmind.com/joyful.pdf

persistence, transform our whole outlook, follow[ing] this up by practicing what we believe." [121]

If we "radiate, from within ourselves, happiness and harmony, then it is returned to us from all those we meet around us, in a greater or lesser degree." [122]

To experience harmony (love, peace, understanding), we must become harmony (love, peace, understanding).

The joy we "produce in the lives of others is automatically balanced from within into your own [lives]. Balance occurs from within outwards and has nothing to do with that which appears in the world of effects." [123]

We must become that which we seek, for it becomes through this very practice that we will be able to heal ourselves.

---

[121] Elade. (2006). *Joyful Living* (page 13). The School of Universal Mind. Located for free distribution at http://www.schoolofuniversalmind.com/joyful.pdf
[122] Ibid, page 7.
[123] Ibid, page 8.

A Metaphysics Primer

In demonstrating "the exercise of understanding, love and compassion, laughter and joy, we [are able to] tone up the cells of our bodies [so that] health and peace ensue." [124] On the flip side, it can be said that "a person who easily argues, resents, worries and hates, is altogether an unhappy person because he eventually suffers, by his own hand, the world he has created for himself." [125]

When we are in perfect control from our own center (meaning our Higher Self), we radiate harmonious (spiritual) energies that produce the same results: peace, harmony, wholeness, joy, love, compassion, acceptance and understanding.

Praying "for peace and harmony, or perfection, is to deny its all-presence, and this attitude of mind [also] prevents one

---

[124] Elade. (2006). *Joyful Living* (page 15). The School of Universal Mind. Located for free distribution at http://www.schoolofuniversalmind.com/joyful.pdf
[125] Ibid, page 17.

from enjoying *that which is already there* just to be lived out" [126] and experienced.

The inner sanctuary of yourself "is motionless, its activity is manifest in its radiation. By placing your whole reliance on this centre, the radiation extends more efficiently through your bodily organism; thus, you radiate from within, instead of clamoring for sustenance from without. This radiation, from within outwards, will inform you, sustain you and motivate your actions. When calamity occurs in worldly conditions, you will either not be there or by some means be protected, because that which has no power over you possesses no substance. The effects have no power over the source." [127]

---

[126] Elade. (2006). *Joyful Living* (page 34). The School of Universal Mind. Located for free distribution at http://www.schoolofuniversalmind.com/joyful.pdf
[127] Ibid.

A Metaphysics Primer

Knowing that our real nature is universal mind (spirit), "we cannot, then, be affected, in any way, by conditions appearing in our realm of effects. We are indestructible, permanent, beings, living to gain experience and the ability to mould our own environment according to the pattern we, as Gods, desire." [128] We suffer only because we allow ourselves to become identified with the illusion.

When you can honestly say that you are living each day according to your own true nature, under all circumstances, life appears in its correct perspective, meaning that "you have found yourself and all will work out according to the pattern." [129]

Life is to be lived and expressed from within; as you radiate your authentic self into the physical world of matter, you will find true balance and joyful living.

---

[128] Elade. (2006). *Joyful Living* (page 36). The School of Universal Mind. Located for free distribution at http://www.schoolofuniversalmind.com/joyful.pdf
[129] Ibid.

[5] Nonduality

To me, the words *to be, or not to be,* serve to highlight the duality of the cosmos, the inevitable existence of interconnected opposites: male and female, Yin and Yang, good and evil, day and night, life and death, happiness and sadness, new and old, spirit and body, same and different.

Such is the harmony of two opposite, yet complimentary parts, that integrate into a whole; the natural law that governs the whole of creation and life as we know it.

In keeping, then, with this 3D duality existence, so, too, does there exist both light as well as dark.

Long have we been conditioned to think of these opposites in comparative terms, meaning that light(ness) is good and dark(ness) is evil; a clear cut example of linear thinking, this could well have been how different world mythologies were created.

A Metaphysics Primer

We can either attribute all of the darkness on this majestic planet of ours as having been created by evil entities from another planet (or another galaxy) or we can take full ownership and responsibility in collectively having created the darkness ourselves.

It is important, to denote here, that my definition of darkness involves components such as greed, hatred, jealousy, anger, resentment, regret, fear, guilt, skepticism, cynicism, failure to be true to one's self, negativity, nagging anxieties, revenge, slander, doubt, condemnation, disappointment, insecurity, arrogance, ignorance, aggression, disharmony, illusion, resentment, perfectionism, chronic victimhood and selfishness.

Darkness (a term that simply refers to the absence of light) is so very easy to manifest. In truth, there is no need to attribute this energy to a creature of mythology; as humans, we are more than powerful enough to have manifested it ourselves.

In retrospect, we are here to learn how to reach, and maintain, a balance between light and dark.

Just as we can create dark energies for the planet, so, too, can we create light; such translates to components such as love, compassion, empathy, harmlessness, selflessness, happiness, contentment, trust, generosity, calmness, joy, peace, good will, responsibility, accountability, assurance, confidence, optimism, adherence to one's truth, forgiveness, kindness, certainty, encouragement, success, wonder, humility, respect, knowledge, wisdom, competence, elegance, grace, friendship, harmony, enjoyment, gratitude and cognizance.

In essence, it all comes down to the level of human consciousness, meaning that a change in the energy of the planet, a change which also encompasses the paradigm shift, must first begin with each of us.

A Metaphysics Primer

We are here to create a new balance for ourselves and Mother Gaia.

As difficult as change can be, we now find ourselves at a spiritual crossroads, so to speak; a choice must be made as to how we want to live our lives.

It is also imperative that we come to understand that as long as we are broadcasting energies of the light, wearing and living the love and compassion of God, the dark energies cannot interfere.

If you find yourself voicing words like *I can't do it* or *I'm not worthy*, however, then you will always find yourself moving backwards; something most of us have experienced.

In reference to drama, anger and frustration, most of us have, at some time in our lives, experienced how you can be manipulated in order to control the emotions; a prime example being the media.

A Metaphysics Primer

I am here to state that *you are the only one who can decide*, for yourself, how much of it you are going to participate in.

Many people enter into the drama, anger and frustration most readily. If you become engaged, because they have succeeded in pushing your buttons, they have gained control over you, emerging the victor.

When you are able to demonstrate being in control of your emotions, no matter what is happening around you, this is when you can say you have reclaimed your power.

So, too, will other changes be discernible, meaning that while you may still find yourself in the same situation(s), it is now completely different because [1] you are no longer controlled by frustration, [2] you are no longer controlled by anger, and [3] you have acquired the wisdom to refrain from the drama.

This is where you are able to demonstrate living the peace that you have found within.

A Metaphysics Primer

According to Rumi ... *No opposite can be known without its opposite.*

If duality did not exist, how would we know enough to yearn and strive for wholeness, for completion, for unity?

In remembering our divine nature, we are both the whole and the parts of the whole, the interconnected totality of all life; this, my friends, is where duality begins to blur, changing to nonduality.

This is where we begin to comprehend that we must strive to find the oneness, the unconditional love, the peace of mind, and the true understanding, that exists beyond the duality of this experience.

Nonduality allows us to see that all is connected, that all is unified; that all share in a divine Oneness. We are no longer separate. All that exists is in the here and now. The question, then, becomes how do we get from here to there?

A Metaphysics Primer

Jerry Katz is the author of *One: Essential Writings on Nonduality*, a work, explained from an impressive and diverse range of perspectives, that greatly increased my understanding.

Katz has a website dedicated to the subject, aptly called Nonduality: The Varieties of Expression [130] as well as a Nonduality Blog [131] for further exploration.

He also monitors a Nonduality Salon [132] yahoo email list, and publishes a daily letter, called Nonduality Highlights, [133] that one can subscribe to.

Katz, himself, states that "if you have ever had a sense of something deeper and more meaningful that lies beyond the everyday you, yet that is you in some way, you have had a

---

[130] Katz, Jerry. *Nonduality: The Varieties of Expression* website located at http://www.nonduality.com/
[131] Katz, Jerry. *Nonduality Blog* located at http://nonduality.org/
[132] Katz, Jerry. *NondualitySalon* yahoo email list located at http://groups.yahoo.com/group/NondualitySalon/
[133] Katz, Jerry. *Nonduality Highlights* located at http://groups.yahoo.com/group/NDhighlights/

A Metaphysics Primer

taste of nonduality. The taste of nonduality is the sense of unity, peace, something vaster than the everyday you." [134]

In continuation, "if you have ever felt deeply dis-satisfied, intensely unhappy, psychically imprisoned, it might be said that you can only feel this dis-satisfaction because part of you knows there is a place of freedom; that freedom is the experience of nonduality." [135]

What he shares next is something that should resonate with all of us.

"After experiencing the taste of nonduality, you may begin *to pursue nonduality*; since you are not separate from the something that is deeper, vaster, more meaningful than the everyday you, it follows that this pursuit is *the discovery of who you really are*." [136]

---

[134] Katz, Jerry. *Nonduality*. Retrieved April 27, 2008 from http://nonduality.net/
[135] Ibid.
[136] Ibid.

A Metaphysics Primer

Nonduality is a word, that, at one time, "was essentially unknown to the public; a word belonging only to philosophers, scholars in comparative religion, Buddhists, and Hindus." [137]

Its pursuit, as I have come to discover, can be experienced through mediums such as books, crystals, meditation, teachers, transformational tools, spiritual practices and retreats.

Over the course of this last decade, we have seen "the coming together of world teachers and the Internet, the wide dissemination of the teaching of nonduality in a variety of forms, the waking up of many, and the entry of the words nondual and nonduality, in numerous languages, into the spirituality mainstream." [138]

In living the truth associated with nonduality, there is no need for words because "love will say it all." [139]

---

[137] Katz, Jerry. (2012) *The word nonduality* email posting [NDhighlights] #4595 - Friday, May 11, 2012 - Editor: Jerry Katz
[138] Ibid.
[139] http://www.gurusfeet.com/blog/living-non-duality

[6] The Power of the Mind

There is only one universal mind and we are it.

As we are born into the world of physical matter, we pass through the Veil of Forgetting, remembering nothing. This is why we must regain, on our own, the consciousness of both whom and what we really are; hence, we have embarked on a voyage of both self rediscovery and self actualization.

Ultimately, it is our destiny to achieve oneness, once again, with universal mind.

As you progress from a lower frequency dimension to a higher frequency dimension, entering deeper into the true self (of universal mind), time and space exerts less of an influence due to the fact that you are leaving the denseness of this physical world behind.

This simply means that as you develop a deeper relationship with universal mind, you will demonstrate the ability to create all that you wish to experience.

When vibrating at the highest levels, thought manifests quickly, sometimes instantly.

By comparison, when vibrating at a much more dense level, as is the case here on Earth, "the unit of energy that you created through intention has to step down through lower and lower forms until it fully manifests in your reality." [140]

This tells me that the time it takes to manifest something could well depend on the connection one has with universal mind.

---

[140] Tan, Enoch. *Godlike Manifesting from a Place of Being* article (August 2008).

A Metaphysics Primer

The stronger "your connection to the source, the greater your energy levels will be. This gives you more power to alter reality and manifest what you desire. All intention takes energy to manifest, and the more energy there is, the faster it can manifest. When you are so strongly connected to the source, your energy level is so great that it results in near instantaneous manifestation of intent which is what others might define as a miracle. *Your connection to the source is your consciousness of the source.*" [141]

From time to time, negative thoughts and doubts will emerge.

When this happens, you will feel "noticeably weaker in your posture, actions and physical being as a whole. It can also happen unconsciously through subliminal means. That is why whenever you feel yourself being weakened in some way, [you need to] reaffirm your strength by thinking a

---

[141] Tan, Enoch. *Godlike Manifesting from a Place of Being* article (August 2008).

A Metaphysics Primer

strong positive thought and strengthening your physiology [so that you] ... keep returning your state of being to one of power." [142]

You must believe in the power that you wield. When you take action "while believing in the action you are taking, your action has greater power. The same goes with intending. When you know that you are a creator and are exercising your power as one, you manifest from a place of being." [143]

It is the metaphysical mind that demonstrates the ability to heal the body, to create or deny peace, and to bring one into conscious awareness; the very same beliefs as held true by Jesus.

---

[142] Tan, Enoch. *Godlike Manifesting from a Place of Being* article (August 2008).
[143] Ibid.

A Metaphysics Primer

In the embracing, and living, of metaphysical principles, courtesy of awareness of personal thought, every individual has been accorded a free-will opportunity to discover that they are not a victim of circumstance. Instead, each has the capacity to fully embrace, and acknowledge, that life actually follows a pattern according to conscious, and subconscious, thoughts. *Becoming consciously aware of this thinking process*, therefore, *is a fundamental principle of metaphysics.*

Despite the fact that there exists no scientific evidence to suggest that we use only 10% of our brains, I can only attest to my having believed this to be true; such meant that the remaining 90% of the brain was associated with untapped potential and unlimited possibilities.

Like a great many, I, too, have fallen into the New Age competition fray, wanting to further unlock the untapped hidden forces residing within my own mind, all courtesy of countless books, CDs and programs.

A Metaphysics Primer

We are conditioned to believe that what we are looking for exists outside of ourselves. This is the belief that has served to help enslave us. Truth be told, all that is needed to unlock the power of the human mind exists within, for the mind is incredibly dynamic and needs to be both recognized and acknowledged as such.

Learn deeply of the mind and its mystery for therein lies the true secret of immortality is the message put forth in <u>The Secret in the Bible</u>.

This sixteen-worded sentence "extracted from the ancient Book of God, a mysterious old document written on fabric of an unknown nature, and highly regarded by the Ancients thousands of years ago" [144] is what now serves to highlight my individual journey.

---

[144] Bushby, Tony (2003). <u>The Secret in the Bible</u> (page 6). Queensland, AU: Joshua Books.

A Metaphysics Primer

The so-called battlefield of the mind is merely the war that plays out between dark and light, a battle that everyone must conquer.

Such is the journey of every human soul, the pathless journey towards self realization, a journey in consciousness, a journey in metamorphosis.

This journey is also akin to the quest for self transformation, the journey of an observer, the journey to freedom.

We have all experienced and lived the ego.

In fact, the great enlightenment traditions "have long spoken about the enemy within and about uprooting the need to cling to a false and separate sense of self. Their teachings encourage us to tame, transcend and purify, or in some cases slay, this pernicious foe of the spiritual heart." [145]

---

[145] EnlightenNext Magazine (2008). *What Is Ego? Friend or Foe.* Retrieved April 30, 2010 at http://www.wie.org/j17/editorial.asp

Psychologists, however, define ego from a different perspective, claiming it to be "the command center of the psyche without which we could not function. Not only is the ego essential in human development … it is responsible for creating and sustaining the very civilization on which all of our lives depend." [146] So, while therapists tell us to develop the self the Buddhists say there is no self. [147]

Taking it one step further, psychologists explain to us how the ego is created as compared to religions explaining how the ego is transcended. [148]

Andrew Cohen, the publisher of EnlightenNext Magazine, has come to understand that "the way in which we understand and relate to the ego has everything to do with the way in which we understand and relate to all life, *including* spiritual enlightenment." [149]

Cohen also talks about the two different parts of the self.

---

[146] EnlightenNext Magazine (2008). *What Is Ego? Friend or Foe.* Retrieved April 30, 2010 at http://www.wie.org/j17/editorial.asp
[147] Ibid.
[148] Ibid.
[149] Ibid.

A Metaphysics Primer

[1] The *authentic self* is passionately interested in dynamic evolution. [150]

[2] The *ego*, by comparison, is deeply invested in its own narcissistic fears and desires (the one and only obstacle to spiritual enlightenment). [151]

One cannot be filled with, and directed by, both darkness and light at the same time.

You must tune into the spiritual energy of your choice, with only one of these facets taking over the so-called helm of the mind.

---

[150] Cohen, Andrew. (2009) Official Teacher of Spiritual Teacher and Founder of EnlightenNext magazine. *The Authentic Self: A Mysterious Compulsion to Evolve.* Retrieved June 7, 2010 at http://www.andrewcohen.org/teachings/authentic-self.asp
[151] Ibid.
http://www.andrewcohen.org/teachings/ego.asp

A Metaphysics Primer

What Is Ego? A Report from the Trenches [152]

When You Go Beyond the Ego You Become an Offering To The World [153]

The Enemy Within [154]

No Escape for the Ego [155]

Yoga, Ego and Purification [156]

Is the Ego an Illusion? [157]

The Man with Two Heads [158]

The 1001 Forms of Self-Grasping [159]

The Transpersonal Ego: Is There A New Formation? [160]

---

[152] http://www.enlightennext.org/magazine/j17/andrew.asp
[153] http://www.enlightennext.org/magazine/j17/amma.asp
[154] http://www.enlightennext.org/magazine/j17/dionysios.asp
[155] http://www.enlightennext.org/magazine/j17/sheng.asp
[156] http://www.enlightennext.org/magazine/j17/desai.asp
[157] http://www.enlightennext.org/magazine/j17/bannanje.asp
[158] http://www.enlightennext.org/magazine/j17/frager.asp
[159] http://www.enlightennext.org/magazine/j17/engler.asp
[160] http://www.enlightennext.org/magazine/j17/puhakka.asp

Self-Acceptance or Ego-Death? [161]

Was ist "das Ich"? [162]

[7] Paradigm Shift

The word paradigm refers to a conceptual framework, a belief system, an overall perspective, through which we see and interpret the world. As such, one's paradigm determines what they are able to see, how they think and what they do.

How one views the world, by way of a spiritual tradition, is part of the individual paradigm to which they adhere.

Paradigms are relative, subjective and personal.

We assume that the way we see things is the way they really are.

Our paradigms only become perceptible to us when we encounter one that differs from our own.

---

[161] http://www.enlightennext.org/magazine/j17/self_acceptance.asp?page=1

[162] http://www.enlightennext.org/magazine/j17/wasist.asp

A Metaphysics Primer

→ Do we see the world as a battlefield with good forces pitting against evil (an ancient tradition which takes us back to the Zoroastrians, the Manichaeans, and the Cathars)?

→ Do we see the world as a classroom (where we come to learn and are put through a multitude of tests)?

→ Do we see the world as a trap (whereby we attempt to disentangle ourselves, all in an attempt to ascend to a higher plane of tranquility)?

→ Do we see the world as a collection of inanimate objects (merely to accumulate, thereby stroking the ego)?

→ Do we see the world as a partner (whereby we attempt to commune more with nature in an effort to become more fully human)?

→ Do we see the world as self, as an interconnected whole (with each playing an important role in the overall script of life)?

A Metaphysics Primer

In an effort to glean a better understanding, there are several key questions that you must ask of yourself, namely;

[1] What are my paradigms?

[2] What set of structures, or belief system, do I operate from?

[3] How are these paradigms serving me in this life?

One way to know yourself, in the here and now, is to get to know the intricacies of your own operating system, which, again, leads to further insightful questioning.

[1] What do I value?

[2] What are my needs?

[3] What are my feelings?

[4] What matters to me?

[5] How do I fit into the grand scheme called life?

[6] How do I know what I know?

[7] What is truth?

The more you know about who you are, in the answering of these heady questions, the easier it is to respond (as opposed to react) to life.

Everything we do and say is the expression of our own beliefs about the world.

Finding the underlying beliefs can lead to insights and understanding.

As one would expect, paradigms shift when we change from one way of thinking to another way of thinking.

It can be compared to a revolution, a transformation, a sort of metamorphosis, if you will.

A Metaphysics Primer

Not something that happens out of the blue, a paradigm shift is driven by agents of change. Accordingly, change is often extremely difficult.

How is it, then, that paradigms shift?

World views emerge to solve problems. For an emerging new world view to take hold, the majority have to fully understand, aside from pure abstract intellect, that the current way of thinking is no longer adequate (suitable) to solve the problems that we are facing.

It is simply not enough to be passionate about the change that is needed, nor is it satisfactory enough to suppress the voices of those in disagreement, for neither, in truth, will bring about the changes that are needed.

As a result, we are currently being challenged to combine rational (logical) and non-rational (faith, intuition, spiritual insight, nature, body-based wisdom) ways of thinking.

Now is the best time for the dismantling of [1] mental, physical and emotional patterns, [2] conditioning, [3] belief systems, [4] attitudes, [5] institutions, [6] thought forms and [7] programming.

Books have always played a role of major significance in my life, serving to enhance my own understanding of a great many diversified topics.

Eckhart Tolle has written several books that have propelled others forward, namely; <u>The Power of Now: A Guide to Spiritual Enlightenment</u> and <u>Practicing the Power of Now: Meditations, Exercises and Core Teachings For Living the Liberated Life</u>. His most current book, <u>The New Earth: Awakening to Your Life's Purpose</u>, is an absolutely phenomenal read.

The message of Eckhart Tolle is a very simple one: *living in the now is the truest path to enlightenment and happiness.*

A first class teacher, Tolle has a way of writing, with clarity and simplicity, that one actually gets what he is trying to say.

A Metaphysics Primer

Tolle has allowed me to see, with additional clarity, that my role, my purpose, involves being able to sense my essential Being-ness, the I AM in the background of my life, at all times and in all situations.

It is so simple and yet so utterly profound; this, then, becomes my own personal ascension.

Not everyone will be ready for Jed McKenna and the books that make up The Enlightenment Trilogy. [163]

In <u>Spiritual Enlightenment: The Damnedest Thing</u>, McKenna carefully distinguishes religiosity from mystical experience (with neither having anything to do with enlightenment), which merely equates to abiding nondual awareness, meaning *no self*. McKenna states that the only way to get to enlightenment comes down to continually searching out what is true. Writing within his own experience from the nothingness of the Void, McKenna's

---

[163] http://www.wisefoolpress.com/

lean, mean and tough stance challenges anyone with a belief system.

Spiritually Incorrect Enlightenment, the second book in the trilogy, is a book about injunction, compelling an individual to refrain from thinking and engaging in the same old way, thereby invoking a negation process in the nondual tradition. As the reader will, by now, have surmised, McKenna's approach to enlightenment, and awakening, is anything but orthodox.

We finish the trilogy off with Spiritual Warfare wherein we are invited to fight in a war like no other; a war where loss is counted as gain, a war where surrender is counted as victory. Ultimately, the enemy you must face, an enemy of unimaginable superiority, is none other than yourself.

I hereby challenge you to challenge yourself.

In the dropping of resistance, in the dropping of density, we are discovering that the old programs no longer work.

This is where we will truly experience the meaning of *Let Go and Let God.*

It is time for the truth to be revealed.

Truth has power.

As the greater multitude gravitates toward similar ideas, such will bring forth the impending transformation that is needed.

The so-called second coming is actually the coming of humankind back to themselves; we are the very beings of whom the ancients spoke.

We are on the verge of a truly great period of illumination; a new renaissance, if you will. As a result, a new world view is in the process of arriving.

[8] Mindfulness

Mindfulness involves many different components; namely, [1] awareness of the present moment (participating in the now), [2] nonjudgmental observation (the ability to observe without criticism, condemnation or judgment), [3] impartial watchfulness (the ability to perceive without taking sides), [4] nonconceptual awareness (you do not get involved with thoughts, emotions, concepts; you merely observe without reaction), [5] non-egoistic alertness (everything takes place without reference to the self), [6] goal-less awareness (you accept the present moment for what it is, without trying to accomplish anything specific), [7] awareness of change (which becomes obvious in the course of the observation) and [8] participatory observation (you are both participant and observer at the same time; an alert participation in the ongoing process of living). [164]

Despite these constituent parts, mindfulness still needs to be experienced in order to be fully understood.

---

[164] *Sati* article accessed on July 17, 2011 at http://dharma.ncf.ca/introduction/instructions/sati.html

A Metaphysics Primer

A well rounded definition for mindfulness is *a state of active, open attention on the present* (the here and now) *without judgment.*

One of the simplest ways to achieving mindfulness is focused breathing (from your diaphragm as opposed to your chest).

You breathe in through your nose and out from your mouth. If you are able to focus on your breathing, in this manner, whenever you are stressed, agitated or upset, you will find the exercise both calming and grounding.

Listening to soothing music (classical, slow tempo, nature based sounds) and focusing on the sound (vibration) of each note, is also another wonderful way in which to experience mindfulness.

We allow ourselves so little time to practice stillness and calm.

A Metaphysics Primer

Taking the time to breathe, while placing your whole focus on the breath, is taking a much needed step in the right direction.

Believe it or not, cleaning the house, with an established positive mindset before beginning, can also assist one in experiencing mindfulness.

Whenever you become totally focused on completing an activity, whatever it may be, and enjoying what you are accomplishing, you have become a mindful participant.

A daily commitment to exercise can also work, especially if you take the time to focus on the muscles of the body and how they feel when to stretch, warm up, speed up, walk, run, jog, slow down, can assist in the achieving of mindfulness.

Of course, meditation still continues to be one of the most popular ways in which to achieve mindfulness.

A Metaphysics Primer

Taking the time to step back and observe your thoughts (feelings, emotions) is another way to achieve mindfulness. This might be a wise alternative for those who find meditation to be too much of a challenge for them, as is often the case with me.

Instead of trying to combat the voice in your head, you simply sit and take the time to observe your thoughts without reacting to them in any way.

You acknowledge them and then let them go, almost as if releasing a balloon to the wind.

Most of us "don't undertake our thoughts in awareness. Rather, our thoughts control us. *Ordinary thoughts course through our mind like a deafening waterfall,* writes Jon Kabat-Zinn, the biomedical scientist who introduced meditation into mainstream medicine. *In order to feel more in control of our minds and our lives, to find the sense of balance that eludes us, we need to step out of this current, to*

A Metaphysics Primer

pause, and, as Kabat-Zinn puts it, *to rest in stillness; to stop doing and focus on just being."* [165]

It was Buddha who shared …… *All that we are is the result of what we have thought. The mind is everything. What we think, we become.*

In truth, while we are not our thoughts, we have come to believe that we are.

What you are thinking and feeling (or vibrating) right now has a definite and direct impact on your immediate future.

That having been said, you are *not* your thoughts and you are *not* your feelings, despite the fact that they are an integral part of the physical experience.

---

[165] Dixit, Jay. (2008) *The Art of Now: Six Steps to Living in the Moment* article accessed on March 21, 2011 at http://www.psychologytoday.com/articles/200810/the-art-now-six-steps-living-in-the-moment

Transcending the mind is akin to watching your thoughts and feelings pass by, choosing which thought, or feeling, to entertain at any given moment.

Whatever influences the mind also affects the body. All diseases get into the body by way of the mind, courtesy of persistent and continued mental tension and worry. Unfortunately, most are unaware of this profound truth.

In keeping, it has been said that the mind can either be the cause of one's bondage or the cause of one's liberation.

By now, it should already been known, as well as understood, that negative thoughts beget bondage whilst positive thoughts beget liberation.

While stilling the chatter of the mind can aid in mental and physical relaxation, what is even more important is both recognizing as well as acknowledging that you are not your mind.

Transcending the dualistic mind is merely the battle of surrendering the bullying of the mind (ego dominated existence) to mindfulness (awareness of one's thoughts, actions and motivations).

Mindfulness means *being aware of the moment in which we are living*.

Mindfulness is *meditation in action*, allowing life to unfold without the limitation of prejudgment.

Mindfulness means *being open to an awareness*, whilst becoming an Infinite Possibilitarian.

Mindfulness pertains to existing in a *relaxed state of attentiveness*, one that involves both the inner world of thoughts and feelings, as well as the outer world of actions and perceptions.

Choosing at least one activity each day, to carry out in a mindful manner (by giving it your full and undivided attention), helps considerably.

If you are chopping vegetables, take the time to absorb the colors, the textures, the smells, the motions, the tastes.

If you are exercising on a treadmill, take the time to feel your muscles moving as you walk, run, jog, speed up and slow down.

As depicted here, one can learn to live the entirety of their day in mindful meditation.

There is no witness.

There is no judgment.

You have succeeded in becoming an observer without engaging the mind.

Thoughts and feelings are simply thoughts and feelings; they are not who you are.

Before one can work toward transcending the mind, with any degree of success, one must first reprogram (reconfigure) the subconscious mind.

This is what I had to do in order to eclipse a life filled with total negative media bombardment.

Everywhere you turn, one can easily read articles and books about the power of the subconscious mind.

Like the hard drive on a computer that stores all pertinent computer files, so, too, is one's subconscious mind comparable to this particular analogy.

The subconscious is where one locates everything that is not located in one's conscious mind, such as previous life experiences and memories; these are our original files, so to speak.

In order to gain access to this databank of information, in order to make changes to the original files, one must bypass the conscious mind. This, then, allows one to neutralize the negatives of the past (because memories cannot be changed) in order to gain the positives in the now.

Meditation is but one avenue open to the seeker who wishes to upgrade their operating system.

At first, you will hear your own thoughts forming in your mind. You may quickly come to realize that there tends to be much continuous repetition to your thoughts.

A Metaphysics Primer

Herein lies the greatest challenge, for there will be many thoughts that will arise as you are attempting to meditate.

In the very beginning, you will find yourself getting lost in them. Trying to remain unattached to the chatter in your head is the most difficult part.

You merely wish to become an observer, standing at the sidelines, if you will. As soon as you pass judgment on what you are observing, the thoughts will drag you down.

Pretend that you are outside, observing the clouds as they float across the sky. Now imagine your thought forms as the very clouds that are passing you by.

It is in coming to this realization that you can honestly say *I have become a witness to my own mind.*

There may also be pictures and images that begin to filter through. Try to become a witness to these visualizations as well.

A Metaphysics Primer

Do not engage with either the thoughts or the images. Simply accept them while remaining unattached. Do not judge them; remember, you are merely the observer.

You may also notice your body responding (emotional reactions) to specific thought forms that are filtering through. Once again, you must step out of the emotion.

One should not allow an emotion to control them while in the physical body. You are merely the observer. You may continue to be the witness, but only without judgment.

Becoming a witness, to thought forms, pictures, images and emotions, is not an easy task; however, it *is something that needs to be practiced* every day.

As you are able to experience success with this while in a meditative state, so, too, shall you be able to practice living a *waking meditation* throughout your entire day.

A Metaphysics Primer

While it is imperative that you become aware of what goes on in your mind when you are going about your daily life, it is important that you continue to step back, thereby maintaining the stance of an objective observer.

When you are able to experience this with considerable success, you can say that you are practicing a mindfulness type of meditation.

It is also important to realize that there is a monumental difference between you (as the observer) and the things that are observed by you.

As you become more of a witness to your own mind, your consciousness is becoming more aware of itself.

What this means is that the egoic mind will begin to quiet so that you can learn to reside, in a pure and nonjudgmental way, in what can be called the real Self.

A Metaphysics Primer

All of the varied forms of meditation have but one purpose: to introduce you to the experiencing of consciousness. With this, then, comes the realization that this is all there is.

As you dedicate yourself to this practice, on an intense and daily basis, you will begin to observe transformation on many levels, each as unique as the individual.

In addition to meditation, affirmations, affirmations and visualizations can also be used as transformational tools, a way of bypassing the conscious mind.

Affirmations are personal statements written in both positive and present tense terms. The more emotion one evokes upon saying these affirmations aloud, the more powerful they become.

Affirmations are positive statements, or directions, you make to yourself in order to bring about changes in your subconscious behavior patterns to whatever you will them to be.

For affirmations to be effective, <u>they must always be stated as positive</u>, <u>already accomplished</u>, <u>results</u>.

Wording them in futuristic terms, such as [1] I will be, [2] I am going to be, or [3] I would like to be actually *prevents the changes from ever taking place* because we are always in the now.

Therefore, *giving energy to the positive trait*, such as <u>I am always Unselfishly Loving</u> *always supersedes the negative*, (as in I will become Unselfishly Loving).

You need to *feel, mean* and *believe the words* as you say them, or the affirmation will not be an effective tool.

When you make the statement (affirmation) *I am happy* it is filtered, through your subconscious, as either true or false.

There are many people who struggle with affirmations, for the very reason cited above; truth, be told, there were times when I did as well, for the statement will *only* be accepted as

A Metaphysics Primer

truth when (if) the beliefs that you hold do not contradict the statement.

Joyce and Ken have succinctly put it this way ... I asked myself a logical question: "If the human mind is always asking and searching for the answers to questions, why are we told to repeat positive statements we don't believe? Instead, why don't we ask ourselves empowering questions; questions that will force us to change our thought patterns from negative to positive in order to answer them?" [166]

When you ask the question (afformation) *why am I so happy?* it does not have to be filtered as true or false. Instead, an answer or solution is immediately sought; likewise, evidence to support the answer is also sought. In other words, you mind is looking for reasons for *why am I so happy?*

In essence, the *question* becomes the answer.

---

[166] http://www.empowernetwork.com/joycelatimer/afformations-by-noah-st-john-asking-the-right-questions-to-grow-your-business/

The point of afformations, then, does not lie in finding the answer, but in asking better questions, more empowering questions.

With afformations, you take conscious control of the questions you ask.

Once you start gathering answers to your empowering questions, your internal beliefs begin to shift in a most powerful way.

This changes what the brain focuses on, which quite naturally changes how you think.

When you have been successful in changing how you think, your perspective has changed.

When your perspective has changed, this further changes your actions.

In changing your actions, you will have changed your life.

Here is a truly empowering way to change subconscious thought patterns (from negative to positive).

A Metaphysics Primer

We all know that the Law of Attraction is activated according to your dominant thoughts, feelings, and beliefs.

Almost everything we do is a question that has *already* been answered; there is a significant difference here.

Are you able to *see* the difference?

Better yet, are you able to *feel* the difference?

Mind you, I still make use of affirmations, but in combination with afformations.

AFFORMATION

Why does doing the things I love (updating my website and blog, operating as a Certified Law of Attraction Practitioner, researching (for books as well as genealogy), writing, editing, publishing, sending out long-distance Reiki and operating as a Crystal Healing Practitioner) bring me more abundance than I ever dreamed of?

AFFIRMATION

I expect only the best from my passions.

When it comes to visualization, yet another medium, I find it incredibly difficult to see the pictures while also trying to put myself in the image.

It is quite difficult to get emotionally excited about a specific impression when all my mind sees are some dark and fuzzy attempts at a new reality.

Having discovered Mind Movies,[167] which is an absolutely phenomenal metaphysical tool, I am able to visualize with increasing clarity. Mind Movies is a *multi-media tool* that allows you to create a vision of what you want, scored with your favorite song; the one that makes you feel good, the one that makes you want to dance, the one that makes you smile and sing along.

Freedom experienced on an inner level is the very freedom that all seek, for it is the *real freedom*; this is what you experience when you are able to still the mind.

---

[167] http://www.mindmovies.com/?10107

A Metaphysics Primer

A calm mind is a powerful mind.

Peace, contentment, happiness and bliss are to be found when one experiences this silence, this stillness, this sense of calm.

Accordingly, there are also additional benefits.

You will find that your ability to concentrate improves.

You will find that you have more patience, showing more tact in responding to difficult situations.

You will find that others do not hold as much sway over you (what they may think of you or say about you), as before.

You will find yourself responding to situations with less anxiety and worry.

As difficulties arise, you will demonstrate an increased ability to maintain a sense of inner poise and common sense.

You will find that you are sleeping better.

In addition, all of the above vastly improves your ability to meditate. Inner peace enables one to feel grounded, to feel balanced.

In these stressful times, this is what is needed by all.

Developing the inner ability to still the mind (through such tools as meditation, detachment, visualizations, affirmations, afformations and yoga) will take you a considerable distance towards attaining and maintaining inner balance and peace of mind.

Cultivating a "nonjudgmental awareness of the present bestows a host of benefits; mindfulness reduces stress, boosts immune functioning, reduces chronic pain, lowers blood pressure, and helps patients cope with cancer. By alleviating stress, spending a few minutes a day actively focusing on living in the moment reduces the risk of heart disease. Mindfulness may even slow the progression of

HIV." [168] In addition, "mindful people are happier, more exuberant, more empathetic, and more secure. They have higher self-esteem and are more accepting of their own weaknesses. Anchoring awareness in the here and now reduces the kinds of impulsivity and reactivity that underlie depression, binge eating, and attention problems. Mindful people can hear negative feedback without feeling threatened. They fight less with their romantic partners and are more accommodating and less defensive. As a result, mindful couples have more satisfying relationships." [169]

As Ellen Langer, a psychologist at Harvard and author of <u>Mindfulness</u>, *states ...... "When people are not in the moment, they're not there to know that they're not there.*

---

[168] Dixit, Jay. (2008) *The Art of Now: Six Steps to Living in the Moment* article accessed on March 21, 2011 at http://www.psychologytoday.com/articles/200810/the-art-now-six-steps-living-in-the-moment
[169] Ibid.

A Metaphysics Primer

Overriding the distraction reflex and awakening to the present takes intentionality and practice."[170]

Michael Kernis, a psychologist at the University of Georgia, says that *"when people are mindful, they're more likely to experience themselves as part of humanity, as part of a greater universe. That's why highly mindful people, such as Buddhist monks, talk about being one with everything."* [171]

How many times have you completely entangled yourself, either by worrying about the future or reliving the past?

As long as you continue to engage in such thoughts, you are unable to joyfully experience the now.

---

[170] Dixit, Jay. (2008) *The Art of Now: Six Steps to Living in the Moment* article accessed on March 21, 2011 at http://www.psychologytoday.com/articles/200810/the-art-now-six-steps-living-in-the-moment
[171] Ibid.

A Metaphysics Primer

It is imperative that you take the time to derive pleasure from whatever it is that you are doing in the present moment.

Taking the time to savor the feelings, the smells, the tastes and sounds, will allow you to experience more joy, more happiness and more gratitude in your life.

As well you know, most negative thoughts involve either the past or the future. It was Mark Twain who wrote ... *I have known a great many troubles, but most of them never happened.*

When you find yourself worrying about something that has not happened, and may not happen all, you become depressed and your anxiety increases.

In effect, worrying is a situation whereby you continue to torment yourself about the uncertainties of the future.

The moment you bring yourself into awareness of the present moment, you have been freed from worry.

Brooding about happenings of the past, situations whereby you are unable to let things be, also contributes to a troubled state.

The moment you bring yourself into awareness of the present moment, you have been freed from unnecessary agitation.

It is of the utmost importance that you begin to develop and cultivate an awareness of how you interpret and react to what is happening in your life.

In becoming the ever mindful observer, you have the opportunity to acknowledge the emotion that is being felt.

In stepping back to observe how you are feeling and responding, setting aside both anger and fear, you allow yourself additional time to counter the initial response(s) with mindfulness.

A Metaphysics Primer

Through the art of inhabiting your own mind more fully, not only does this affect you in a more positive way; it also has a powerful effect on your interactions with others.

By "being open to the way things are in each moment without trying to manipulate or change the experience; without judging it, clinging to it, or pushing it away, the present moment can only be as it is. Trying to change it only frustrates and exhausts you. Acceptance relieves you of this needless extra suffering." [172]

Working with the neediest students, as a Special Education teacher, provides me with countless opportunities from which to keep learning this acceptance.

As with life, there are certain things that are beyond your control; hence, you can only work within the confines of the

---

[172] Dixit, Jay. (2008) *The Art of Now: Six Steps to Living in the Moment* article accessed on March 22, 2011 at http://www.psychologytoday.com/articles/200810/the-art-now-six-steps-living-in-the-moment?page=4

situation while demonstrating nonjudgmental awareness. Suffice it to say that some days are easier for me than others.

While living a consistent mindful life takes time, diligence and effort, the mindfulness part is easy when you become focused on the present. Mindfulness "isn't a goal, because goals are about the future, but you do have to set the intention of paying attention to what's happening at the present moment. As you read the words printed on this page, as your eyes distinguish the black squiggles on white paper, as you feel gravity anchoring you to the planet, wake up. Become aware of being alive and breathe. As you draw your next breath, focus on the rise of your abdomen on the in-breath, the stream of heat through your nostrils on the out-breath. If you're aware of that feeling right now, as you're reading this, you're living in the moment. Nothing happens next. It's not a destination. This is it. You're already there." [173]

---

[173] Dixit, Jay. (2008) The Art of Now: Six Steps to Living in the Moment article accessed on March 22, 2011 at http://www.psychologytoday.com/articles/200810/the-art-now-six-steps-living-in-the-moment?page=5

A Metaphysics Primer

Taking the time to pay attention to your immediate experience, right here, right now, is what mindfulness is all about. So, too, however, is there a fundamental paradox associated with mindfulness.

Mindfulness is "the only intentional, systematic activity that is not about trying to improve yourself or get anywhere else, explains Kabat-Zinn. It is simply a matter of realizing where you already are. A cartoon from The New Yorker sums it up: Two monks are sitting side by side, meditating. The younger one is giving the older one a quizzical look, to which the older one responds: Nothing happens next. This is it." [174]

In quick summation, then,

→ Mindfulness is not about detaching from your experience

---

[174] Dixit, Jay. (2008) The Art of Now: Six Steps to Living in the Moment article accessed on March 22, 2011 at http://www.psychologytoday.com/articles/200810/the-art-now-six-steps-living-in-the-moment?page=4

→ Mindfulness is not about detaching from life

→ Mindfulness is not about disengaging on an emotional level

Instead, mindfulness allows you to engage more fully, with emotions and experiences, rather than simply reacting (which can also translate to over reacting).

Courtesy of the nonjudgmental awareness component, mindfulness is not the same as accepting whatever happens (including things of a harmful nature).

→ Mindfulness is not about becoming a passive bystander to life

Instead, *mindfulness allows you to respond* to events, people and situations *with enhanced awareness and thoughtfulness*.

The benefits to the practice of mindfulness are many; namely, [1] improvements in mood as well as health, [2] improved concentration (focus), [3] clarity of thinking, [4] enhanced (deepened) peace of mind, [5] significantly

reduced stress, [6] improved intuition (which, in turn, further enhances both insight and wisdom), [7] increased self confidence, and [8] a more insightful awakening to authenticity (the real you), to make note of a few.

Like wisdom, so, too, is the cultivating of mindfulness a lifelong endeavor.

The Peaceful Warrior is a movie that deals with mindfulness in the present moment. I highly recommend that each reader take the time to watch this movie.

[9] Knowledge versus Wisdom

Knowledge can be referred to as *information gleaned from a multitude of sources* (cognition) as well as through exoteric means (communicated to the general public: familiar, known and evident).

Wisdom, on the other hand, can be referred to as *applied* (lived) *information* (consciousness) as well as through esoteric means (understood by, and meant for, a select few who have special knowledge or interest: hidden, mysterious, mystical and arcane).

Ardriana Cahill puts it thusly … "Knowledge is but the messenger that calls you to wisdom, but it is not wisdom. One can gain knowledge, but one does not seek wisdom; one meets it when one often least expects it and recognizes it as kindred. Knowledge puts us in the way of wisdom, but wisdom is experiential; it is a truth one recognizes in the external world that already resides in the internal one. One cannot learn wisdom; one must awaken to it." [175]

Based on the comparative opening at the beginning of this chapter, knowledge is intellectually based when contrasted with wisdom (located within), which is divine.

In the words of our brother, Yeshua ben Yosef, the one we have come to know as Jesus, "Seek ye knowledge and ye shall find the truth that liberates. Seek ye discipline in the persisting with positive thoughts. Seek ye the joy of creating, the joy of learning, the joy of experiencing. Seek

---

[175] *Knowledge versus Wisdom* article accessed on July 17, 2011 at http://www.controverscial.com/Knowledge%20vs%20Wisdom.htm

ye the realm of infinite possibilities for therein ye shall find the all. Seek ye the seer that ye be." [176]

Would you define these words as knowledge or wisdom?

Knowledge and wisdom also make use of two completely different organs when needing to communicate with you: "one is known, the other felt. The divine speaks to us through the spirit, not the mind. When wisdom is revealed to you (it does not explain itself), it reveals itself full blown, like manna from heaven on a silver platter. It awakens within as an all encompassing flood of warm illumination or a bolt of lightning that shocks or stuns you. This is why the sages call it enlightenment. Wisdom does not need digesting, deliberating, debating or dissecting by doubt or reason; it breathes within you as calm surety and perfect peace. It is then that you recognize [on an intellectual level], that this [inner knowing] has always been with you, just

---

[176] Doucette, Michele. (2010) <u>Veracity At Its Best</u> (p 141). McMinnville, TN: St. Clair Publications.

waiting for you to find it. From head to toe, you have everything you need to become extraordinary." [177]

The Vedas are a large body of texts, long preserved in ancient India, that constitute the oldest authority of Sanskrit literature. They are also the oldest Hindu scriptures. While their exact date is controversial, it is quite possible that they were "first written around 3,000 BC." [178]

The metaphysical foundation of Hinduism, as expressed in both the Vedas and the Upanishads, is that "reality (Brahman) is One or Absolute, changeless, perfect and eternal. The ordinary human world of many separate and discrete (finite) things (which our mind represents by our senses) is an illusion. Through meditation and purity of mind, one can experience their true Self which is Brahman,

---

[177] *Knowledge versus Wisdom* article accessed on July 17, 2011 at http://www.controverscial.com/Knowledge%20vs%20Wisdom.htm
[178] *Ancient Eastern Philosophy* article accessed on July 17, 2011 at http://www.spaceandmotion.com/buddhism-hinduism-taoism-confucianism.htm

A Metaphysics Primer

God, the One infinite eternal thing, which causes and connects the many things. True enlightenment is self-realisation, to experience the supreme reality as Self." [179]

Hence, while you live, "you are the caretaker of the divine within you." [180]

It becomes through knowledge and wisdom that we are able to "eliminate fear, which produces understanding. We begin to understand who we are and why we are here. We recognize, with generosity, others stumbling while seeking their way, and develop a keen awareness and love for the miracle that is all Life, and that includes oneself." [181]

In essence, wisdom is a lifelong experience.

---

[179] *Ancient Eastern Philosophy* article accessed on July 17, 2011 at http://www.spaceandmotion.com/buddhism-hinduism-taoism-confucianism.htm
[180] *Knowledge versus Wisdom* article accessed on July 17, 2011 at http://www.controverscial.com/Knowledge%20vs%20Wisdom.htm
[181] Ibid.

While you must seek knowledge in order to reawaken wisdom, it soon becomes apparent that the more we know, the more we realize how much we really do not know.

Likewise, "the wiser we grow, the more wisdom we sense is yet to be discovered. With each step, we grow larger in each other's sight, we grow larger in the sight of the Gods, and, it follows, the Gods grow larger within us. Experiencing this knowledge, we find true humility and peace from the inside out." [182]

Knowledge changes over time.

Wisdom is timeless.

Knowledge, gathered from learning and education, is often referred to as one's intelligence.

---

[182] *Knowledge versus Wisdom* article accessed on July 17, 2011 at http://www.controverscial.com/Knowledge%20vs%20Wisdom.htm

A Metaphysics Primer

Wisdom is intuitive information (as in inner knowing, words that may come to you, visions and gut feelings). As such, wisdom is unlimited, coming together, courtesy of personal experience.

Knowledge (in the form of gathered data and pieces of information) does not exist merely to serve wisdom, given its correlation with lifelong experience.

Wisdom, on the other hand, can be further enhanced through knowledge.

It seems to me as if each is connected on an even deeper level in that ... *knowledge becomes wisdom only after it has been put to practical use,* [183] thereby requiring active participation and action.

Mind you, without wisdom, knowledge can become dangerous, leading to conceit and selfishness.

---

[183] http://www.indiadivine.org/audarya/advaita-vedanta/142414-some-quotes-knowledge-wisdom.html

A Metaphysics Primer

This is why it becomes essential to "use your intellect and your cognitive processes, as well as the wisdom that comes from your intuitive knowledge. The combination of these aspects is a powerful one, and will show you the truth that is right for you." [184]

In most cases, it will be your heart leading the way.

[10] Conscious Creation

As Anastasia of the Siberian tiaga has stated throughout the Ringing Cedars series, *Man is Creator*. In keeping, so, too, is God Creator.

It is my belief that God is thought; henceforth, thought is also Creator. After all, was not the beginning stated as being the word?

What was the word, then, if not thought?

---

[184] Bendriss, Lilli and Løken, Camillo. (2011) The Shift in Consciousness (page 13). Lightning Source UK Ltd: Milton Keynes, UK.

A Metaphysics Primer

Mankind creates his (her) own reality through thought (as well as belief and response).

It all comes down to *what does Man wish to create*, does it not? In that mindset, then, thought is tangible.

In keeping, all of my previous publications (resulting from thought) can be physically held by you, the reader, for they are materialized thought.

It is known that thought must first exist before manifestation of thought, also known as creation, can take place.

In that alignment, we have the ability to manifest whatever we wish, all for the sole purpose of enhancing the wisdom that we continue to accrue, life after life after life.

We create our lives through our own thought processes.

A Metaphysics Primer

Everything we think, we will feel; everything we feel, we will manifest; everything we manifest serves to create the condition(s) of our lives.

Every word we utter expresses some feeling within our souls; every word we utter also serves to create the condition(s) of our lives. This is a direct fusion of thought with emotion.

Many will have heard the phrase *like attracts like*, which means that what one gives thought to attracts, unto itself, the very same.

In the end, it is still a matter of choice and free will.

Thought is the true giver of life that never dies, that can never be destroyed.

All have used it to think themselves into life, for thought is your link to the mind of God.

We *get* what we speak.

A Metaphysics Primer

We *become* what we think.

We *become* what we direct our energies to.

We *become* that which we conclude ourselves to be.

Hence, we are neither slave, nor servant; by comparison, we are sovereign and masterful beings. We are both creator and director of our lives, writing the script and deciding who plays the assigned roles.

While many continue to accept limiting thoughts, of which there are a significant number (including fear, guilt, despair, unworthiness, failure, worry, unhappiness, pity, misery, hatred, dissension, denial of self), into their lives, it must be remembered that this is neither good nor bad.

Coming from a place of nonjudgment, it simply is.

In the end, we must summon into mind that *everything comes down to personal choice.*

A Metaphysics Primer

We are here because we want to experience the freedom and unlimitedness that God is.

→ We are *not* our successes

→ We are *not* our failures

→ We are *not* our poverty

→ We are *not* our pain

→ We are *not* our joy

→ We are *not* our fear

These are merely elements of the physical experience that we are here to partake of so that we can *know ourselves* in all ways.

I believe this to be what Jesus meant when he spoke of living in this world while not being part of the physicality of the world.

The path chosen by each individual is wholly unique to that person. Each path is a valid one, all leading to the same destination, all leading to their truest nature as guided by compassion.

This is why it becomes imperative to feel the feelings, to engage the emotions, and to think the thoughts, for they are what allows us to experience ourselves in all ways.

The source of all thought, as we know, is the conscious mind; the segment that also deals with logic, reasoning (inductive, deductive, analytic and synthetic) and judgment.

The source of all power, on the other hand, is the subconscious mind; the segment that deals with intuition, emotion, inspiration, memory and imagination.

In Lesson 8 (Mindfulness), I compare the subconscious mind to the hard drive on a computer that stores all pertinent computer files.

A Metaphysics Primer

I also address how you can reprogram the subconscious mind through such mediums as meditation, detachment, visualization, affirmation, affirmations, Mind Movies and yoga.

Having made use of *all* of these transformational tools, as well as others (natural hypnosis, brainwave entrainment and NLP or Neuro-Linguistic Programming), in order to bypass the conscious mind, I am a firm believer in their assistive abilities.

Most of us have been told that in order to succeed in life we have to work hard and struggle; likewise, many are familiar with the phrase no pain, no gain. As a result, life can be a long series of hardships for most people, until they realize that what they have been taught is a lie.

There exists a secret in this vast universe of ours.

If you can change the way you perceive any given situation, then each context, thereafter, will have changed.

A Metaphysics Primer

In essence, if you can change the way you look at things, the things you look at will change.

You must learn to *think only about what you want*, accepting it as part of your life. It is also imperative that you achieve vibrational harmony with what you are creating.

You will know that you have achieved (and are achieving) alignment with your thought(s) when you feel happy, contented, elated, peaceful, ecstatic, overjoyed, playful and upbeat.

The deeper the feeling(s) experienced, the closer the alignment.

If "you desire one thing while expecting another, you are sending out two intentions that conflict and oppose each other; to be completely intentional, it means you [must] think about your desire and expect it to happen. Having all your thoughts in alignment with a single direction will ensure that your desire manifests without complications." [185]

Knowing what you want gives you the clarity that is needed.

Repetition of a chant, a mantra, an affirmation ... all leads to belief. As soon as the belief has become instilled as a deep conviction, things begin to happen; therein lies the psychology, and power, of repeated suggestion (which can also be used wrongly, so please be careful in this respect).

Fearful thoughts create fearful situations and hard times.

By direct association, when all of the citizens of this planet stop thinking about war and destruction, so, too, will these perils cease.

---

[185] Tan, Enoch. *Power of Expectation* article (August 2008).

A Metaphysics Primer

We create by way of our emotional thinking.

Thought is the greatest force in the world, and, as stated earlier, *everything begins with thought.*

Whatever you fix your thought(s) upon (meaning whatever you steadily fix your imagination on) is what you shall attract.

It is imperative that you work to keep your dynamic vision alive, without being swayed by what you read, by what you see, by what you hear, by what you are told.

Pictures (as in vision boards) can be very instrumental. The more often you visualize your desire, the faster its manifestation shall be.

The world in which we are living is made up of molecules, which are, in turn, made up of atoms, which are, in turn, made up of sub-atomic particles.

These sub-atomic particles (nucleons) can become either a particle or a wave, depending on how they are measured.

Werner Heisenberg realized that "the wave-particle duality of nature implied that there was a natural tradeoff between knowing an object's position and knowing its momentum. The greater the uncertainty in an object's particle's position, the smaller the uncertainty in its momentum. It is impossible to predict, measure, or know both the exact position of an object and its exact momentum at the same time. In fact, an object does not have an exact position and momentum at the same time." [186]

Not surprisingly, this came to be called the Heisenberg uncertainty principle. By definition, "it is a natural consequence of the wave-particle duality of nature. Recalling that a particle's momentum is just its (mass) x (velocity), Heisenberg's uncertainty principle says that an object does not have an exact position and velocity at the same time." [187]

---

[186] Carroll, Bradley. (2005). *Wave-Particle Duality* article accessed on October 30, 2010 at http://physics.weber.edu/carroll/honors-time/duality.htm
[187] Ibid.

A Metaphysics Primer

This duality paradox also "deals a fatal blow to the Newtonian clockwork universe. The idea of a deterministic universe was that if we could know the exact position and velocity of every atom in the universe, then the entire history of the universe could be calculated, at least in principle. Heisenberg's principle demolishes that idea, because nothing in the universe has an exact position and an exact velocity. The future is not determined, not in fact and not in principle. Nature simply does not know how the future will unfold." [188]

While quantum physics does not explain the free will that we have as humans, it does free us from the restraints of a deterministic universe; a pertinent fact that helps to further substantiate the knowledge that we are the creators of our world.

---

[188] Carroll, Bradley. (2005). *Wave-Particle Duality* article accessed on October 30, 2010 at http://physics.weber.edu/carroll/honors-time/duality.htm

A Metaphysics Primer

We have long been conditioned to believe that what we are seeing is the reality; hence, we continue to live this way, observing the same things happening over and over again in our lives, often times wondering why things are not improving.

Here comes the shocker: *your conditioned reality is not reality.*

As soon as you come to the realization that *your own observation is the cause of everything*, you are in a powerful position to decide to create, and observe, another reality for yourself. Conscious creation, therefore, is akin to "the heightening of self-awareness to its greatest potential." [189]

Being a conscious creator means that you are the creator of your reality. This truth has only ever been understood by a few.

---

[189] Fox, Kristen and McNally, John. *RC 101 – Lesson One: What is Conscious Creation?* article located on the Conscious Creation website and accessed on November 1, 2010 at http://www.consciouscreation.com/central/Lesson-1.htm

A Metaphysics Primer

While everything that you will ever need to bring about these changes already exists within you, very few individuals are completely self integrated in such a way so as to be able to comprehend what this involves (hence, the possible need for transformational tools until you have been able to master a certain level of self mastery and they are no longer needed).

The manner in which "each of us creates our own reality is through our beliefs, whether we unconsciously accept the default beliefs we grew up with or consciously choose beliefs that support us more fully in our joy. The beliefs you hold about yourself, the people you love, the world, are all projected outward to literally form the world you perceive around you." [190]

There is another integral concept that merits understanding.

---

[190] Fox, Kristen and McNally, John. *RC 101 – Lesson One: What is Conscious Creation?* article located on the Conscious Creation website and accessed on November 1, 2010 at http://www.consciouscreation.com/central/Lesson-1.htm

A Metaphysics Primer

All separation is an illusion.

In truth, we have always been connected to the larger universal source.

Think of conscious creation this way.

You have written a novel in which you are the main character. In addition, there are many other characters that you have written into this novel, all of whom do their best to play the ever changing roles that you have assigned to them.

To Be (as you are) and to Become (who you truly are and have always been), one has to believe. Everything starts with *mastering the mind*.

Knowing that everything is made up of energy, thought is also a form of energy.

Things do not happen randomly, nor do they happen by accident.

A Metaphysics Primer

We attract that which we think about and give our energies to.

We are the creators.

You must make sure that the outer world (which may also be your conditioned reality) does not succeed in circumventing you from observing what it is that you want to witness in your own mind.

With certainty and clarity, you must create a vivid picture in your mind.

Knowing and believing that you have already created your desire(s) at the quantum level, you can relax and allow the universe to bring it to you.

It is also imperative that you take concrete action as opportunities arise, remembering to express your deepest gratitude.

A Metaphysics Primer

One of "the big differences between conscious creation, and many other systems of thought is that conscious creators recognize and celebrate their own motivations for the things they choose to do." [191]

Each individual is the true creator and controller of his or her life.

The purpose of life, however, is simply to be part of it.

The key is to *live life consciously*.

We are to *live fully* and *with intent*.

As we continue to expand in our knowingness and wisdom, we also expand the consciousness of all life, thereby acquiring a better understanding of the concept of God.

We are here to *live lives of unlimited love*.

---

[191] Fox, Kristen and McNally, John. *RC 101 – Lesson Two: Discovering Your Joy and The Importance of Self-Love* article located on the Conscious Creation website and accessed on November 7, 2010 at http://www.consciouscreation.com/central/Lesson-2.htm

A Metaphysics Primer

We are here to *live lives of unlimited joy*.

If we want to have these conditions in our lives, then we must first *become that which we want to experience more fully*.

We are here to express our joy (passion) in creative ways. We are here to show others, by example, what is possible.

Sometimes this means helping others. At other times, this may not be the case; there is nothing wrong with being selfish when you are following your bliss.

Being divinely selfish "means trusting that following your joy is the best possible thing you can do not just for you, but for everyone else as well." [192] In so doing, you become an important role model to those around you.

---

[192] Fox, Kristen and McNally, John. *RC 101 – Lesson Two: Discovering Your Joy and The Importance of Self-Love* article located on the Conscious Creation website and accessed on November 7, 2010 at http://www.consciouscreation.com/central/Lesson-2.htm

A Metaphysics Primer

It is a known scientific fact that, relative to quantum cohabitation, two atoms (mass) cannot occupy the same quantum space simultaneously; this is referred to as the Pauli-Einstein principle.

If you keep your mind filled with positive, creative and powerful thoughts, there will be little space left for that which is negative (fearful, doubtful and troublesome).

As individuals think and believe, this is what they become. Every person is an image of their own thinking and believing.

It must also be reiterated that the subconscious mind will automatically respond to the thoughts that dominate, so unless you successfully close your mind to negative thoughts, immediately counteracting them with positive ones, sooner or later even the most powerful will succumb to the destructive effects of these detrimental thoughts.

A Metaphysics Primer

You must decide which thoughts shall continue to reside within your own mind.

A mental picture is the same thing as a thought projection; just envision the movie projectors of old in order to achieve an operable visual.

If these thought projections remain steadfast and unwavering, it is with consistent practice and concentrated effort that you achieve that which you desire, all courtesy of the subconscious mind.

In short, you become energized action in motion.

The more interest you take in any initiative, the more attention and energy you naturally give.

Knowing that energy follows thought, it only makes sense that you continue to experience greater results in keeping with said initiative; the more absorbing the initiative, the better.

Possessing the right mental attitude, in combination with remaining firmly fixed on that which is your steadfast goal, is what creates the necessary ambiance to achieve.

It becomes through the cooperation of both the conscious mind and the subconscious mind that you can succeed.

You must also believe (earnestly, sincerely, strongly and completely), for it is belief that makes things happen.

---

[11] The Law of Attraction

In returning to Lesson 1 (The Nature of the Universe), we know that everything is comprised of energy, that everything is vibration. We know that energy is held together to create matter. We also know that matter is energy condensed to a slow vibration.

Given that every object, being, thought, action, word and psychological mood, has a unique vibrational energy, it is clear that energy also equals vibration.

A Metaphysics Primer

As spiritual beings inhabiting a physical body, so, too, do each of us have our own vibratory signature, the quality of which is very much dependent on both one's thoughts as well as their inner mental (feeling) world.

Focus and concentration are paramount with respect to the changing of one's inner world.

It is your energy vibration that attracts corresponding circumstances (people, places and things) into your life; likewise, it is your energy vibration that changes your reality.

While we are constantly projecting patterns of thought outward, whether consciously (creating by deliberate intent) or unconsciously (creating by default), the higher, lighter and purer your energy vibration frequency, the more you are able to tap into the spiritual energy of who you really are.

As you become more at peace with life, you attract less negativity.

While it is true that negative events take place at some point in everyone's life, the more you are able to remain open to the experience, relaxing and embracing the situation, doing your best to learn from the event in question, the easier it becomes to transcend, to move beyond.

In knowing that whatever you resist will persist, it becomes the welcoming, accepting and embracing of positive change that the negative energies begin to dissipate.

Too often we affirm the negative, over and over again, in our daily lives without even realizing that we are attracting more and more of the very same into our lives.

If we give our attention (attraction) to something while emphatically stating **I do not want this in my life**, we are merely *attracting what we do not want* because we are continuing to give our attention to that which we do not want.

This can railroad all of the positively inspired thoughts and aspirations that we need to move ourselves forward.

A Metaphysics Primer

I know this to be true because it happened to me, all courtesy of my teaching assignment for September 2012.

When we *stop giving attention to that which we do not want*, this becomes the time when we start attracting more of what we do want.

I know this sounds complicated, but it need not be.

As you become *more conscious about focusing on what you really want*, you begin to experience a sense of complete freedom.

The more you focus, the stronger your vibration becomes.

Most are familiar with the saying be careful what you wish for.

It is in knowing what we do not want that we can begin to place more emphasis, more energy, more effort, on that which we do want.

This dualistic dichotomy is of extreme importance, if only to serve as the much needed catalyst in giving less attention to that which we do not want.

What you focus upon is, of course, magnified. If there are many people focusing on the same thing, be it positive or be it negative, this is manifested multi-fold.

The more popular something is, the more it tends to flourish. By the same token, the more people reject something, the faster it fades away into oblivion.

What an amazing marketing ploy, yes?

The Law of Attraction brings your focus to you; to put it more succinctly, the Law of Attraction pulls together the quantum field to manifest it for you.

It is your direct and uninhibited focus that collapses the wave function into particles, allowing the universal sea of infinite possibilities to materialize into something that becomes both tangible and experiential.

A Metaphysics Primer

You always attract, into your experience, that which you are in vibrational resonance (alignment) with.

When your thoughts and desires are in vibrational resonance with the mindset of *already having attracted* the experience into your life, you are able to manifest that which you desire, for it is here that your inner world defines your outer world.

As you are able to find within yourself *what it already feels like* to have, be or do that which you desire, while, at the same time, being sure to express the gladness, the contentment, the joy, the happiness, the gratitude, the pleasure, the elation, you are in direct vibrational alignment with the manifestation process.

Feel it as you read these very words.

→ Give thanks for what you want, even before it manifests

→ Feel the joy of having what you want

As you feel this joy and elation, you continue to draw more of the same to you.

Having is about BEing ......

To have love, you must be love.

To have peace, you must be peace.

To have compassion, you must be compassion.

To have confidence, you must be confident.

To have acceptance, you must be accepting.

To have forgiveness, you must be forgiving.

It is as much a belief system about thought as it is a belief system about action.

It is only in changing who you are on the inside that the outer world changes accordingly to reflect the new you.

A Metaphysics Primer

What you embrace in your inner world gives birth to what you experience in your outer reality.

I think, therefore I am.

I am, therefore I have.

In summation, this is manifestation.

We attract that which we find vibrational resonance (alignment) with.

Your vibration is your feeling.

It is your feeling that attracts your experience(s).

The more you feel from a place of abundance, the more abundance will be attracted to you.

The more you feel from a place of lack, the more unfulfilled you will become.

Emotions, therefore, help you create your reality. When you believe in something so strongly, you will find that you are able to create that very same thing much more freely.

You have the power to manifest anything that you desire. Whatever you wish to create more of, you merely have to focus on it, become one with it, feel it already existing for you.

Whenever you feel good about something you desire, you are in vibrational harmony with your desire. Feeling good is of the utmost importance.

There are activities that you can engage in that will serve to strengthen and maintain these good feelings: listening to a particular song, watching certain television shows, or movies, reading a specific book, engaging in discussions of a synchronistic nature.

A Metaphysics Primer

It is important to be conscious of how you are feeling, always choosing to be positive. An individual with a higher vibration (positive) will create their desires more easily, more freely, more effectively, than someone harboring a low, dense energy (negative).

Should you find yourself in a less than positive state, simply bring yourself back into a thought that makes you feel positive.

Happiness, joy, bliss, appreciation, love, gratitude, peace, compassion, confidence, faith, excitement, success, awareness, freedom and trust are the feelings and attitudes that emit a higher frequency and attract people, places and situations of a positive nature.

By comparison, feelings and attitudes like condemnation, guilt, worry, disappointment, fear, revenge, insecurity, doubt, failure, hesitation and sadness emit a lower frequency, thus attracting people, places and situations of a negative nature.

A Metaphysics Primer

You control what you are feeling with your thought(s).

Positive thoughts and feelings create a higher vibration.

Keeping your vibrations high will allow you to manifest things more freely in your life.

You can choose to be happy by consciously focusing on what makes you happy.

Keep imagining the excitement and exhilaration, the gratitude and the happiness, associated with your desire, existing as a reality right now.

When your vibrations are consistently high, your desires will manifest more freely.

The more enthusiastic, the more pumped up, the more excited, the more emotionally charged, you are about something, and the better it feels, the faster it will show up in your life.

Keep thinking, talking and acting in the state where your desire is already a reality.

Manifestation occurs when energy takes form.

A higher rate of vibration means that energy is moving at a higher speed.

Remember that things take longer to manifest in the physical earth plane reality because it exists at a lower rate of vibration (as are we when we choose to be present in this physical form).

This is why it is so important to trust, to believe, to have faith.

Everything manifests first in the mental plane before showing up in the physical plane.

Manifestation works best when one has a strong intent. When you know something must happen, it will.

A Metaphysics Primer

However, every time your desire changes, you are, in essence, beginning anew with the creation process.

If you have spent weeks giving your attention and focus to a specific desire, picturing it, thinking about it, feeling it, and then you change your mind about what it is that you want, all of the previous creative energy ceases to be and you have to begin the whole process anew.

It needs to be emphasized, once again, that things take longer to manifest in the physical earth plane reality because it exists at a lower rate of vibration.

Most people are unable to create, either because they do not know what they want or they keep changing their mind.

This is why it is so important to get as clear as possible about what you want and stick with the plan that you have put into motion.

Keep focusing on it until it becomes a reality.

A Metaphysics Primer

A master of creation chooses something to manifest and does not move on to something else until he (or she) has manifested it completely.

→ Be committed

→ Be persistent

→ Focus on it with every fiber of your being

→ Expect it to manifest fully

→ Do not take no for an answer

When you are totally committed, the universe responds with synchroncities of all kinds; doors will open effortlessly for you.

Do not take any action in reference to people, places and opportunities until you feel positive emotion well up within you, for in that very moment, you will instinctively know what to do.

Continue to maintain the vision, in your mind, of what it is that you want.

→ Trust the universe

Believe in yourself, acting on your intentions when you feel inspired to do so.

Taking positive steps in the direction of your desire simply reinforces your claim that it already exists in your present reality.

The more you want something, the more focused you must be in your actions towards achieving it; continue to be appreciative of each and every moment.

As you already know, your beliefs create your reality. When conflicting beliefs exist, they serve to sabotage your reality creation; hence, you fail to manifest what you want. Doubt, worry and fear are the culprits.

A Metaphysics Primer

The moment you think *why isn't this working yet* or *why hasn't it happened yet* or *why is this taking so long*, you have started moving away from your desire.

This is when you simply stop and immediately re-focus on the desire in question.

Do not focus on your fear of not getting it.

If you doubt the fact that the universe is in a position to grant your every desire, you end up pushing these desires further and further away.

Visualizing and affirming are methods that can be used to assist one in maintaining their focus.

The more you focus on what you want, the more you are moving toward the reality of that desire and vice versa, meaning, that it, too, is moving toward you.

A Metaphysics Primer

When you are not thinking about what you want, your thoughts are in neutral, which is neither good nor bad.

The moment you start thinking about the opposite, while doubting and worrying, you have cancelled out the forward movement and are now traveling backwards (both mentally and physically).

Intend that your desire is your reality.

Believe that your desire is your reality.

Trust that your desire is your reality.

Express gratitude, knowing that you are being taken care of every step of the way.

Detach yourself from all doubt, worry and fear.

Having done so, you can leave it and move forward.

A Metaphysics Primer

The Law of Detachment says that in order to successfully attract something, you must be able to detach yourself from the outcome; having done so allows you to work from a position of serenity, trust and faith.

Many are familiar with the saying *Let Go and Let God*.

This sums up the Law of Detachment perfectly.

Several months after having done so, I had manifested a brand new Dell Inspiron 1501 laptop; let go and enjoy the process.

Detachment is a word that some people have a difficult time with because many believe it to mean that one feels nothing, that one is apathetic or indifferent.

While there exists a fine line between caring in a detached way, and being truly uncaring, it is a line of extreme significance.

A Metaphysics Primer

To feel detached is to feel a deep sense of freedom, knowing that we can trust in our greater good, knowing that we are taken care of, knowing that we are able to manifest that which we desire or something better.

Intentional creation means existing in a place of peaceful expectation.

Being able to sustain positive thought, on a consistent and consecutive basis, is the hardest work in the world. From my viewpoint, it continues to be a most significant challenge.

In the beginning, the monitoring of your thoughts, keeping them positive, focusing only on things you desire, requires constant attention.

Clearly, it is a moment to moment, hour to hour, day to day act of *conscious* and *deliberate* creation.

A Metaphysics Primer

Keep empowering your life with the vision(s) of what you desire, *for any individual who succeeds as a conscious and deliberate creator literally holds the key to mastering their world.*

Might this be the awakening, or the enlightenment, that all actively seek at some point in their physical existence?

Interestingly enough, enlightenment is also a state of non-attachment.

The more you remain unattached, the more you allow your Higher Self (or your Christ Consciousness) to flow through you.

As you let go and trust, not only do you feel different, but you radiate a different vibration to the world, allowing better things and experiences to come to you.

While the Law of Attraction allows one to acquire things, courtesy of their material needs and desires, it is also this same universal law that focuses on the spiritual needs of humanity.

When you are focused upon spiritual thoughts, you will find that you are not overly concerned with the physical burdens of life.

[12] The Power of Positive Thinking

Shaped by our thoughts, we become what we think, primarily because what we think about is where our energy goes. Put another way, "energy moves to whatever your consciousness focuses on." [193]

I am a firm believer in maintaining my own power.

That having been said, I am responsible for whatever I have created.

---

[193] Sharp, Michael. (2004) <u>Dossier of The Ascension: A Practical Guide to Kundalini Activation</u> (p. 60). St. Albert, AB: Avatar Publications.

A Metaphysics Primer

Being responsible also means that I have to watch what I think and watch what I say, all in an effort to make sure that I never, intentionally, give my power away.

There are but two choices: one can either maintain conscious control or unconscious control over their life.

It becomes my choice to choose the former, just as it becomes your choice to also choose for yourself.

While many people have very little understanding of the power that they wield (or not, should that also be their choice), it is true that *"the more you are interested in something, the more you think about it, and the more you focus intent on it, the closer you are to that thing.* The less you think about something and the less you focus, then the farther you are away from it." [194]

---

[194] Sharp, Michael. (2004) <u>Dossier of The Ascension: A Practical Guide to Kundalini Activation</u> (p. 63). St. Albert, AB: Avatar Publications.

Essentially, this means that, being the creator of your life, you can manifest something into physicality, into matter, with continued and concentrated effort, because energy always follows intent.

Buddha understood the universal law that dictates his words; namely, *we are shaped by our thoughts*, thereby becoming what we think.

While you may not yet accept such a law, such comes into manifestation, courtesy of your beliefs, your feelings and your thoughts.

It also needs to be stated that we are the creators of our own misery.

While we may have limited control over the situation(s) we find ourselves in, we still have the power to create by way of thoughts, feelings, intentions, actions or inactions.

A Metaphysics Primer

Even though this should offer compelling spiritual reflection, most imperative for self examination, such is not always the case.

Beliefs have a dominant and powerful effect on every aspect of one's life.

There have been individuals and powerful institutions, throughout history, all willing to kill for their beliefs.

As shocking and unbelievable as this may seem, it needs to be acknowledged that, even in our 21st century world, this mentality, unfortunately, still exists.

It is for this reason that every individual must be willing to scrutinize the beliefs that they hold dear, especially as these same beliefs ultimately serve to create the condition(s) of our lives.

In taking the time to analyze your beliefs, here are the key questions that need to be asked.

A Metaphysics Primer

→ Do my beliefs, thoughts, feelings, intentions and actions *prevent* the manifestation of unselfish love?

→ Do my beliefs, thoughts, feelings, intentions and actions *allow* the manifestation of unselfish love?

→ Do my beliefs, thoughts, feelings, intentions and actions *give rise* to anger, hatred and harm?

→ Do my beliefs, thoughts, feelings, intentions and actions *bring forth* tranquility, love and healing?

→ Do my beliefs, thoughts, feelings, intentions and actions *make for an improved world* for all, myself included?

→Do my beliefs, thoughts, feelings, intentions and actions *make for an abominable world* for others, myself included?

We live in a world that has long created the illusion of separateness from the Universal Spirit.

In believing ourselves to be separate, *we have created selfishness*.

A Metaphysics Primer

Knowing that we create our own reality by the very thoughts that we think, the very words that we verbalize, the very actions that we employ, *now is the time to learn to let go of fear* so that one can concentrate solely on the expansion of love and forgiveness.

We are here to heal ourselves of this affliction.

In working with thought forms, it is imperative that one stay positive.

It is only in thinking positive thoughts that we continue to attract more positive people, as well as positive events and happenings, into our lives. In this way we become ripples in a pond, creating a domino effect of increased positivity out into the world.

On the flipside, of course, the more we focus on the negative, the depressed, the dismal, the more negativity we bring into our lives; clearly, we must become more aware of our thoughts in order to eliminate the unnecessary and judgmental ones.

It is for this reason that I no longer watch the news (on television), read magazines, read newspapers, or listen to the news (on the radio).

I made the decision to eliminate all media negativity in my life because I found myself existing in a state of depression, unable to focus on the joys associated with life and living.

There is a way to manage a better sleep at night: stop watching the news before going to bed.

In keeping with the changes that we are trying to bring forth within, it is important to remember that for every action or non-action, there is a consequence.

When we give our minds and our responsibility away, we give our lives away.

Do you really want to keep living this way?

A Metaphysics Primer

It is important to remember that most of the media is controlled by a few.

It is imperative, therefore, that you take the time to use discernment, looking for the hidden agenda.

The following bullets (paraphrased from the work of David Icke) may well be the format utilized by those that control the media, so please take the time to reflect upon them.

→ Why is this information being presented to you?

→ What is their *real* agenda?

→ Is it a case of problem – reaction – solution, meaning that *they* create a problem so that we react as they intend, thereby asking for a fix?

→ Do *they*, then, offer a solution?

→ Might this *solution* be what *they* really wanted in the first place?

Do not allow yourself to be fooled; infinite power exists within every single individual. We have the power to decide our own destiny, but only if we do not give that power away.

When something happens that we do not like, why is it that we have a tendency to look for someone else to blame?

When there is a problem in the world, why is it that we have a tendency to wonder what they are going to do about it?

In retrospect, it is this non-action type of response that has resulted in the giving away of our power.

The same institutions and organizations that control the world on a global level want to control your mind because when they have succeeded in doing this (when you are no longer thinking for yourself), they have you where they want you; hence, the answer lies in taking our minds back, thinking for ourselves, questioning what we are being told in an attempt to redefine our own truth(s), while also allowing others to do the same, without judgment or ridicule.

A Metaphysics Primer

We create our own reality by our thoughts and our actions.

If we change both of these, we will begin to change the world, beginning with ourselves, first and foremost.

It really is that simple.

More people are waking up to the fact that, in making these necessary thought changes, they are also allowing their own frequencies to assist others in this much needed planetary change.

As already touched upon throughout the text, everyone lives in the world of his or her thoughts.

Thoughts are energy; hence, positive thoughts attract positive results, naturally, while negative thoughts attract negative results; like always attracts like.

Interestingly, body parts, including cells and organs, also have vibratory signatures, be they healthy or diseased. From a scientific standpoint, we also have the power to alter the vibratory signature of our body through thought forms.

A Metaphysics Primer

Our thoughts, beliefs, expectations, words and actions find their way to the electromagnetic field (aura) which surrounds us.

Monitor your thoughts as carefully as you can, being sure to think only about what you want. In making this thought your burning desire, your major purpose, it will be this very thought that shall manifest in form.

Remain determined to see each thought fully realized, while doing your utmost to work towards achieving them, even if in small steps.

Success comes to those who have, and demonstrate, success consciousness.

→ You get what you think about

→ You get what you focus on

→ You get what you talk about

→ You get what you believe

That having been said, continue to do your utmost to keep those thought forms positive.

It is also imperative that you learn to make the connection between positive thinking and positive living.

[13] Empowerment

Empowerment is a process whereby individuals and groups are able to make choices (be they spiritual, political, social, economic, workplace or gender related), based on accessible information, and then transforming those choices into desired actions (and, hence, desired outcomes).

As a result, empowerment is also synonymous with the ability to reclaim one's power.

Empowerment, then, becomes *knowing what you want* and *knowing what you do not want*.

A Metaphysics Primer

When you are able to express knowledge and understanding from both camps, clearly, succinctly and calmly (without engaging any degree of emotional attachment), you are able to detach from the outcome in a secure, loving and compassionate manner.

One who is truly empowered "would never interfere with another; one who is truly empowered would never seek to control another or impose his or her will upon another; one who is truly empowered would never judge another." [195]

This serves to constitute spiritual empowerment; the key to remembering the sacredness of all life.

The state that "you are in at any given time is completely up to you. We create our state of mind, relative to the state of our conscious awareness. The more conscious you become

---

[195] Manifest Messenger email series (as taken from *Journey Into Now* by Leonard Jacobson) received from Jackie Lapin on June 23, 2011.

A Metaphysics Primer

of how the vehicle, of your body and mind, works, the more control you will have over your senses and your life." [196]

The operative term here is *the more conscious you become* which is really what this existence is all about.

Being spiritually empowered means that you have taken back your personal power, meaning that you are now able to take charge of what you do, what you think, what you feel, and how you respond to whatever comes into your life.

Ultimately, spiritual empowerment means that you take conscious control of everything that matters to you.

To free yourself from entanglement on all levels, "you will have to bring to consciousness all the ways that you lose yourself in others. Each time you notice that you are seeking love, acceptance, or approval from another, you will

---

[196] Manifest Messenger email series (as taken from *The Awakening* by Steven S. Sadleir) received from Jackie Lapin on June 14, 2011.

have to own, acknowledge, and confess that you are giving away your power. If you are trying to please another to gain acceptance, [you must] own, acknowledge, and confess it without judgment." [197]

Spiritual empowerment begins with the realization that you are a spiritual being having a physical experience; that you are here to experience yourself in all ways.

It becomes this very belief that lends itself to the next phase, whereby you come to the realization that it is through the power of your mind (through the reconfiguring of your subconscious as well as the redirecting of your conscious awareness) that you are able to create the world that you wish to create for yourself.

Ultimately, the choice rests with you.

---

[197] Manifest Messenger email series (as taken from *Journey Into Now* by Leonard Jacobson) received from Jackie Lapin on June 27, 2011.

A Metaphysics Primer

As you awaken to your divine and infinite essence, you begin to live the qualities of love, respect, compassion, empathy and nonjudgment.

In knowing that you are everything and everything is you; in knowing that God is present in every thought, every word, every emotion, every action, and every deed, primarily because you *are* God, here to experience yourself in all ways, this is what further propels you to begin living a more conscious existence.

By direct association, the practices of meditation, prayer and contemplation become even more meaningful (insightful), further enabling you to discern that which ultimately is your truth.

Every thought, every word, every emotion, every action, and every deed is the result of either positive or negative thinking.

A Metaphysics Primer

It is only "through awareness of, and creatively working with, our thoughts, feelings and emotions that we manifest more positive qualities within. Through being increasingly aware of our actions and reactions, we become more spiritually responsible. Until we have awakened to self-awareness, we can never truly know who we are and fully trust ourselves. We see that self-awareness is not just about spiritual and psychic development, but the whole of what we are." [198]

Likewise, by "being aware of how we act in everyday life, we can grow into more centred and loving individuals, and by cultivating our minds and looking after our bodies, become more active forces for good. All are part of the process of discovering who we really are, and can be used as vehicles for transformation and expressing the true Self. With spiritual gifts, the more open and cultivated the mind

---

[198] Edwards, Gly and Santoshan. *Steps to Spiritual Empowerment* article accessed on July 30, 2011 at http://www.spiritualistresources.com/cgi-bin/articles/index.pl?read=40

is, the more receptive the individual will be to higher and refined influences." [199]

Knowing that we are an integral part of God, so, too, is everything derived from God.

All creative potentials and possibilities "are within this spirit that we are. We need to recognise that it is through our minds, emotions and individuality, that we develop the ability to be more Divinity-centred, and establish greater awareness of who we are and how we interconnect with all life. The more we are able to recognise this reality, the more receptive we will be to infinite qualities of good within us. This will give us the strength to free the mind and emotions, and embrace a greater Truth." [200]

---

[199] Edwards, Gly and Santoshan. *Steps to Spiritual Empowerment* article accessed on July 30, 2011 at http://www.spiritualistresources.com/cgi-bin/articles/index.pl?read=40
[200] Ibid.

A Metaphysics Primer

As you seek to understand the purpose of life, you learn that peace, joy and harmony reign supreme when you choose to live life from a higher spiritual viewpoint (embracing the essence, the totality, of who you are).

All of life is interconnected, in ways that we cannot even begin to fathom.

Knowing that we have "within us infinite qualities of good, love and compassion … every act, thought and expression can be reflected upon and used to unfold these qualities more purely. By doing this, we make our lives a constant meditation and uncover a sense of the inherent universal Self in everyday life; we become less self-centred and more in tune with life and our spirit." [201]

All of life is sacred. Knowing and believing this to be true, we should "seek to become one with this sacredness that exists in everything and everyone, and respect and care for all life, including ourselves. Anything that separates us from

---

[201] Edwards, Gly and Santoshan. *Steps to Spiritual Empowerment* article accessed on July 30, 2011 at
http://www.spiritualistresources.com/cgi-bin/articles/index.pl?read=40

others means separating ourselves from life and the creative Principle in all." [202]

Living by spiritual law means "taking responsibility for every area of our lives, our thoughts, our feelings, our actions, and being respectful of everyone and every form of life we come into contact with ... [in order to] become more caring, loving, centred and responsible human beings." [203]

→ Respect means coming to understand that you can only change yourself

→ Respect means that you must allow another to work their way through their own experience(s)

There will always be times when you find that you are unable to do something physically about a given situation.

---

[202] Edwards, Gly and Santoshan. *Steps to Spiritual Empowerment* article accessed on July 30, 2011 at http://www.spiritualistresources.com/cgi-bin/articles/index.pl?read=40
[203] Ibid.

A Metaphysics Primer

This is when you may only be able to work on the metaphysical level, assisting in other ways.

For example, "by discovering your inner truth, manifesting it as practical knowledge, and maintaining your frequency and confidence in what you know, you become a beacon broadcasting higher frequency and higher knowledge into your environment and into the lives of all who cross your path. You create ripple effects in reality, sending waves out through the lives of others. You throw seeds and they grow in those whose minds are fertile. You create a forward cascading effect into the future, in ways only the divine mind can grasp in its entirety because the future is nonlinear; small things can have HUGE effects if applied in the right way at the right place at the right time. It's not about *right* and *wrong*, but a matter of what needs to be done and the wisest way of doing it." [204]

This is what constitutes spiritual empowerment.

---

[204] *Maximizing Your Potential to Help Others* article accessed on July 30, 2011 at http://montalk.net/metaphys/59/maximizing-your-potential-to-help-others

[14] Compassion and Compassionate Allowing

The electromagnetic grid of the Earth has a strong influence on human consciousness, meaning that any change in the grid "will have a corresponding effect on the consciousness of mankind." [205]

Ancient cultures were amazingly aware that every 26,000 years or so, the Earth makes a rare alignment with the center of our Milky Way galaxy.

It is understood that "when these alignments occur, they offer spiritual renewal for humanity, a transformation or evolution of consciousness." [206]

Based on Mayan information, the most current alignment date was December 21, 2012, a time that the Mayan elders were able to see as the beginning of a new era.

---

[205] Rennison, Susan Joy. (2008) <u>Tuning the Diamonds: Electromagnetism and Spiritual Evolution</u> (page 69). Staffordshire, UK: Joyfire Publishing.
[206] Ibid, page 58.

A Metaphysics Primer

In accordance with the research of Dr. Valerie Hunt, all healing takes place in the electromagnetic field.

She also claims that as we come to "understand more of our electromagnetic nature and how to raise our frequency level, this will [also] hasten spiritual enlightenment, which is our evolutionary goal." [207]

This means that as we "acknowledge our electromagnetic field and learn how to enhance it, we can undergo an evolution of consciousness, creating health and healing in the process." [208]

Likewise, our energy signatures (based on our levels of vibrational frequency) are also directly related to our level of consciousness; in turn, such is reflected in both mind and body.

---

[207] Rennison, Susan Joy. (2008) <u>Tuning the Diamonds: Electromagnetism and Spiritual Evolution</u> (page 108). Staffordshire, UK: Joyfire Publishing.
[208] Ibid.

A Metaphysics Primer

The physical heart is the "most powerful generator of electromagnetic energy in the human body." [209]

In fact, the electrical field of the heart "is about 60 times greater in amplitude than the electrical activity generated by the brain. Furthermore, the magnetic field produced by the heart is more than 5,000 times greater in strength than the field generated by the brain." [210]

In keeping, it is the heart that governs the emotions, as well as the health of the physical body, as opposed to the brain.

Emotions that occur in the frequency band of love (which include terms like appreciation, wonder, joy, compassion, gratitude, elation, encouragement, exuberance, peace, bliss) possess "this unique, most powerful, oscillating ability. Therefore, a loving heart can, and will, entrain other hearts/minds and affect those in close proximity by virtue of the force of its energy output. This research highlights

---

[209] Rennison, Susan Joy. (2008) <u>Tuning the Diamonds: Electromagnetism and Spiritual Evolution</u> (page 124). Staffordshire, UK: Joyfire Publishing.
[210] Ibid.

[how] the power of being loving can affect our own well-being, and, it seems, those around us." [211]

The heart, then, demonstrates that, as an organ, it has a major balancing effect on the body. As a result, the emotions and states affiliated with love (denoted in the previous paragraph) vibrate at a higher calibration of consciousness.

This is paramount to health, healing and change.

Positive emotions create "increased harmony and coherence in heart rhythms and improved balance in the nervous system. The health implications are easy to understand. Disharmony in the nervous system leads to inefficiency and increased stress on the heart and other organs while harmonious rhythms are more efficient and less stressful to the body's systems." [212]

---

[211] Rennison, Susan Joy. (2008) <u>Tuning the Diamonds: Electromagnetism and Spiritual Evolution</u> (page 126). Staffordshire, UK: Joyfire Publishing.
[212] Ibid, page 129.

A Metaphysics Primer

In the esoteric tradition, the heart is considered "the gateway to higher consciousness."[213]

What became even more fascinating for me was learning that it was the philosopher, Aristotle, who taught that "the seat of human consciousness lies not in the brain, but in the heart."[214]

Science, it seems, is now able to demonstrate what the mystics have always known; namely, the fact that the heart is pivotal to the practice of real spiritual life.

In the words of the Hopi elders ... *When the heart of man and the mind of man become so distant that they are no longer one, Earth heals itself through the catastrophic events of change.*[215]

---

[213] Rennison, Susan Joy. (2008) <u>Tuning the Diamonds: Electromagnetism and Spiritual Evolution</u> (page 129). Staffordshire, UK: Joyfire Publishing
[214] Ibid.
[215] Ibid, page 161.

A Metaphysics Primer

Everything starts with consciousness. In fact, it has even been proposed that the electromagnetic field of the brain *is* consciousness.

Likewise, the field of science has also been able to prove that we are able to interact with energy, meaning the Zero Point Energy field.

It is now becoming more evident, courtesy of this knowledge, that space "was never an empty vacuum, but a vibrant mass of energy," [216] through which we are all connected, by way of both individual as well as planetary electromagnetic fields.

There is a solution to the issue of the current Earth changes and that means that we need "to teach people to change their consciousness." [217]

---

[216] Rennison, Susan Joy. (2008) <u>Tuning the Diamonds: Electromagnetism and Spiritual Evolution</u> (page 161). Staffordshire, UK: Joyfire Publishing

[217] Ibid, page 165.

A Metaphysics Primer

Our consciousness evolves when we "learn to develop our feeling nature without using judgment, so our feelings become just neutral reports of our awareness." [218]

Compassion is who you are. The keys to compassion lie in your ability to embrace all experiences as part of the one, without judgment.

This is the greatest challenge that all must face as they move towards greater states of personal mastery, which is the return to their truest form.

Demonstrating love through compassionate allowing means that *you must love others enough to allow the range of their experience.*

→ Compassion is your birthright

→ Compassion is your truest nature

---

[218] Rennison, Susan Joy. (2008) <u>Tuning the Diamonds: Electromagnetism and Spiritual Evolution</u> (page 184). Staffordshire, UK: Joyfire Publishing.

→ Compassion allows you to view from an equal standpoint (there is no judgment)

→ Compassion, then, is what you allow yourself to Become

All people express their own versions of compassion through the manner in which they conduct themselves in every waking moment.

Are you willing to forgive those who have wronged you?

Are you willing to see beyond hate towards those who oppress you?

It is only in answering yes to these questions that *you can choose* to Become more than the circumstances.

In breaking the cycles of collective response, you become the higher choice.

Mastery of compassion means redefining what your world means to you.

A Metaphysics Primer

It is not about forcing change upon the world around you.

You, and only you, choose how you respond.

As a being of compassion, you are offered the opportunity to *transcend polarity while still living within the polarity*. This is what enables you to move forward with life; a life filled with freedom, resolution and peace.

→ Compassion means living in trust

→ Compassion means living with joy

As your own vibrational level raises, so, too, are you adding to the increased vibrational level of the planet. By sending out "stronger, clearer messages in a loving, gracious way, we create a stronger, clearer reality." [219]

---

[219] Rennison, Susan Joy. (2008) <u>Tuning the Diamonds: Electromagnetism and Spiritual Evolution</u> (page 189). Staffordshire, UK: Joyfire Publishing.

A Metaphysics Primer

Balance equals order; hence, greater balance will bring greater internal order, all of which comes to be reflected in your outer world.

Despite what appears to be happening, you must continue to withhold judgment, keeping all negative thoughts, and feelings, at bay (as much as is possible), primarily for the betterment of yourself.

Knowing that your thoughts create what happens in your life, and in your world, knowing that everything you do affects everything else in this universe … this is why it has become even more imperative that you continue to believe in who you are, acting, always, on your convictions, your principles, your aspirations and innate experiences.

You must learn to adhere to your courage, your wisdom and your spiritual and moral integrity.

You must be willing to persevere against all unsightly odds.

A Metaphysics Primer

As you are able to keep your heart and consciousness in the right place, so, too, do you assist others in the same manner.

In knowing that you are here to learn your own lessons, so, too, are you here to respect that all Beings are here to do the same.

It becomes in demonstrating both compassion and compassionate allowing (which is far removed from pity), that you are able to help yourself.

As you help yourself, so, too, are you able to help another, purely by example.

The reciprocal is also true: as you help another, you are, in truth, helping yourself.

As compassion deepens, "we find ourselves developing a nobility of the heart. Increasingly, and often to our surprise, we respond to difficult situations with calmness, clarity and directness. A quiet fearlessness or confidence is present as we no longer fear that we will compromise our own integrity. We find, too, a joy, a joy which arises from the knowledge that our every act is meaningful and helpful to the world." [220]

In touching the lives of others, in caring, compassionate and considerate ways, can it not be said that we are all angels?

[15] The Holy Grail

When the two become as one, therein shall you find the true Holy Grail.

What does this mean?

Is it deliberately meant to be cryptic in nature?

Is it meant only for those who have eyes to see and ears to hear?

It is in the coming together of all duality (male and female, Yin and Yang, day and night, life and death, happiness and

---

[220] McLeod, Ken. *Awakening Compassion* article accessed on July 17, 2011 at http://www.unfetteredmind.org/articles/compassion.php

sadness, old and new, body and spirit, same and different), and the embracement and acceptance of the dual parts of the self (light and dark), that one begins to comprehend that nonduality, in truth, is the reality.

Ultimately, it is this that shall lead to the healing of all, including the patriarchal institutions of old.

The reading of <u>A Travel in Time to Grand Pré</u>, a previous publication of mine, will further serve to enlighten you, the reader, as to what I am endeavoring to share (refer to the chapter entitled *Message for the 21st Century*).

Every individual is on a journey of self, a journey of rediscovery, if you will.

In the integration of the dualistic parts of the self (light and dark, love and hate, masculine and feminine), we are able to revert back to our truest nature: one of compassion and compassionate allowing; thereby leading to the reestablishment of one's creative powers through the balance of the self.

It shall be in this *rediscovery of our true selves* that we will have found the Holy Grail.

While the Holy Grail is the same for everyone, the process and experience(s) for each individual shall be vastly different; hence, we all become the Grail.

In having identified that there is something great at work, every time you are at peace, so, too, are you enlightened.

Inner peace is probably the most important thing that can be attained.

When you experience inner peace, you are truly happy and content with your Self.

Your state of mind is a quiet mind and you are completely connected to God.

God and peace are synonymous. Inner turmoil is what suffocates your spirit, thereby preventing you from living from your higher self, unable to see life with a greater sense of clarity.

A Metaphysics Primer

Enlightenment (the Holy Grail) is a state of being whereby you are reunited with your true spiritual self.

It is this connectedness, the freedom of the Self, that leads us to the ultimate and definitive realization that we are all one, thus imbuing our bodies with a sense of inner peace that allows us to joyfully accept and live life as per our creation.

Was Yeshua ben Yosef (Jesus) of a royal bloodline? It is my belief and understanding that he was.

Did Yeshua marry and have children? Most definitely.

Is Yeshua the Holy Grail? Absolutely.

Is Yeshua showing us the way to the Holy Grail? Uneqivocally.

We must now take the time to revisit the message that he attempted to share with us 2,000 years ago, as opposed to that which has been corrupted, hijacked, fabricated and manufactured in his name, for therein lies the necessary truth(s).

Seek ye knowledge and ye shall find the truth that liberates. Seek ye discipline in the persisting with positive thoughts. Seek ye the joy of creating, the joy of learning, the joy of experiencing. Seek ye the realm of infinite possibilities for therein ye shall find the all. Seek ye the seer that ye be. [221]

[16] Transcendence

Transcendence pertains to being free, from limitations inherent in matter, while also having continuous existence above and beyond the created world.

Simply put, transcendence means the real Self, the fully conscious Self, the essence of who and what you really are; likewise, transcendence is also a self-mastery process that enables you to understand the differences between creating by conscious intent versus creating by default.

---

[221] Doucette, Michele. (2010) <u>Veracity At Its Best</u> (page 141). McMinnville, TN: St. Clair Publications.

A Metaphysics Primer

Transcendence pertains to living from a heart-based consciousness (love) instead of an ego-based consciousness (fear, guilt, power, control).

There are many different aspects that, in totality, add up to the definition of transcendence as shared herein.

[1] You must learn how to control your emotional responses, instead of having them control you; as long as you are being controlled, you are not in control.

[2] You must learn to recognize the negative (thoughts, feelings, emotions, beliefs) that dwells within, replacing all with positive.

[3] You must learn to become an observer (to your thoughts, feelings, and emotions) instead of a reactor.

[4] You must understand what balance means, applying this knowledge to your life on a daily basis.

A Metaphysics Primer

[5] You must continue to see the all-encompassing picture (shared consciousness) as you strive to acknowledge, and work toward, the greater good in your life.

[6] Upon experiencing a profound modification of Self, you must remain committed to living the new life experience(s).

To put it simply: *to know something, you must become it.*

In the words of John Roger, founder of the Movement of Spiritual Inner Awareness (MSIA) ... *All that you want to be, you already are. All you have to do is move your awareness there and recognize the reality of your own Soul.*

The purpose of The Movement of Spiritual Inner Awareness (MSIA) is "to teach Soul Transcendence, which is becoming aware of yourself as a Soul and as one with God, not as a theory but as a living reality. Your Soul is who you truly are; it is more than your body, your thoughts, or your feelings. It is the highest aspect of yourself, where you and God are one." [222]

Knowing that there is much joy and beauty in life, what is it that is keeping you from discovering this inner peace, this joy, this beauty, this total contentment?

Let's face it, we only have ourselves to blame when we worry and are fearful. It seems like I am forever reminding myself of this very fact.

If we were to embrace any given situation with the calm acceptance (without complaint, without a grudge, without surrendering or giving up) of truth, simply allowing the body to go with the flow (because it is what it is), we would have transcended the illusionary world of ego eons ago.

---

[222] http://www.msia.org/soultranscendence

A Metaphysics Primer

According to Debbie Ford, author of <u>The 21 Day Consciousness Cleanse: A Breakthrough Program for Connecting with Your Soul's Deepest Purpose</u>, transcendence involves stepping "into the enormity of what's possible for your life" [223] so that you may "live in the expansiveness of your future." [224]

There exists a simultaneous feeling, one that has often been described as "self-consciousness watching consciousness and consciousness arising as self-consciousness" [225] with no separation between the two, meaning that being human allows one to "be self-consciousness while swimming in the bliss of consciousness." [226] As your mind completely

---

[223] *Consciousness Cleanse Day 18 – The Light of Transcendence* article accessed on April 15, 2011 at
http://www.oprah.com/spirit/Consciousness-Cleanse-Day-18-The-Light-of-Transcendence
[224] Ibid.
[225] *Cosmic soup: The zero point field, transcendence-immanence, self-conscious consciousness and what was/is before words were/are?* article accessed on April 15, 2011 at
http://integrallife.com/member/ani-kowal/blog/cosmic-soup-zero-point-field-transcendence-immanence-self-conscious-consciousn
[226] Ibid.

A Metaphysics Primer

transcends thought, you experience a state of restful alertness and inner peace. This is what continues to be referred to as Transcendental Consciousness.

It has been said that the enlightened mind can attain and gain the true, transcendent type of free will, but only by emphatically rejecting the false, deluded type of free will. [227]

In knowing that everything, and everyone, is made of the same stuff, that all is a stream of consciousness, so, too, can consciousness be expressed in materialized (physical) form; while these forms may appear to be separate and distinct, this is not the case at all.

Our scientists have been able to observe that the entire universe is continually expanding, and at an accelerated rate. What, then, is it that drives this pace?

---

[227] *Transcending Determinism: Transcendent Freedom vs. Naïve Freewill Thinking* article accessed on April 19, 2011 at http://www.eGod(dess)eath.com/TranscendingDeterminismVsNaiveFreewill.htm

It certainly "cannot be a material force, for no such force exists. And thus, the only rational, logical explanation is that the real force that drives the universe is the fact that the universe is a stream of consciousness." [228]

Taking it one step further, "matter cannot transcend itself; matter cannot go beyond the state in which it was created. Yet consciousness has this ability; consciousness can reinvent itself, consciousness can transcend itself, consciousness can choose to let the old die and be reborn and be resurrected into a higher state." [229]

Just as the entire material universe is expanding at this ever accelerating rate, so, too, are you, as an individual, being "compelled by the very life force itself to expand your

---

[228] *The Stream of Consciousness* article accessed on April 19, 2011 at http://quantumunlimited.org/vem/articles-english-mainmenu-82/1599-the-stream-of-consciousness
[229] Ibid.

consciousness, in order keep up with what is happening to the universe." [230]

This expansion of consciousness "is what drives the material universe, the physical planets and galaxies, to move away from each other at an accelerated speed. The inhabitants of Earth are not expanding their state of consciousness at that rate; they are expanding it at a slower rate. And this means that the Earth is lagging behind the position in absolute space where it would have been, if it had followed the expansion rate of the universe as a whole." [231]

It is this lagging behind that creates the illusion of time as well as the "friction that creates so many problems on Earth that seem to have no solution. The reality is that the Earth is being pulled by the background expanding force of the universe to move through space at an ever increasing speed." [232]

---

[230] *The Stream of Consciousness* article accessed on April 19, 2011 at http://quantumunlimited.org/vem/articles-english-mainmenu-82/1599-the-stream-of-consciousness
[231] Ibid.
[232] Ibid.

In order "for the Earth to grow, there would have to be an ever increasing force [to resist the increased friction], and this is indeed what is currently the case. But there is an alternative to this scenario, for the ever-increasing force is necessary only to propel a body of the same density." [233]

Here is an interesting hypothesis for you.

If the Earth was "becoming less and less dense, so that it was propelled to move faster" [234] because there was less friction and less resistance, this could also mean that the Earth would be able to "effortlessly move through space at an accelerated speed without there being an increase in force." [235]

In reality, what makes this plausibility even remotely possible is the acceleration of consciousness, whereby you "let go of the old sense of identity that was at a certain level of density ... [knowing that] when this happens on a

---

[233] *The Stream of Consciousness* article accessed on April 19, 2011 at http://quantumunlimited.org/vem/articles-english-mainmenu-82/1599-the-stream-of-consciousness
[234] Ibid.
[235] Ibid.

collective scale, by all of humankind raising the collective consciousness, then the entire planet will become less dense" [236] which means it can then "move through space at an ever accelerated pace without the application of greater and greater force," [237] for this is what shall bring about a revolution, not only in human thought, but in society as a whole.

There will no longer be a need for this "physical, mental, emotional force to keep the old structures alive" [238] for they will have been "replaced, not by new structures, but by the willingness to flow with the stream of life ... for you do not gain any longer your sense of identity from the structure, you gain it from seeing beyond structure, beyond even the structure of the Earth itself." [239]

---

[236] *The Stream of Consciousness* article accessed on April 19, 2011 at http://quantumunlimited.org/vem/articles-english-mainmenu-82/1599-the-stream-of-consciousness
[237] Ibid.
[238] Ibid.
[239] Ibid.

A Metaphysics Primer

Jean-Paul Sartre was the author of an essay, written in 1937, called *The Transcendence of the Ego*.

Sartre refers to the fact that intentional objects are objects of consciousness, with their inherent value being their very consciousness.

As we are conscious of things, so, too, are we also "conscious of ourselves being conscious of things," [240] meaning that "things and our own consciousness of the things [in question], both evoke our own reflective consciousness." [241]

According to Sartre, the ego pertains to the states and actions that it supports, which is to say that "the material presence of things, in turn, proves the ontology of the object contemplating them. Ego is then nothing without something in which to contemplate, but is reliant on itself and its being; further, the flexibility of consciousness, for Sartre, is the

---

[240] http://en.wikipedia.org/wiki/The_Transcendence_of_the_Ego
[241] Ibid.

ability to contemplate something in its absence," [242] which appears to be his idea of reflection.

Sartre concludes that while people are able to contemplate the same thing, we simply cannot comprehend the intuitive apprehension of another, which means we are only able to perceive (experience) that we are responsible for our own doings.

In addition, while we are able to reflect on our own consciousness (of something), we are unable to reflect on the consciousness of another (of that same thing).

Interestingly, many philosophers believe the ego to be an inhabitant, as it were, of one's consciousness.

It becomes in transcending the ego that one is able to experience [1] increased rest and relaxation (from the questioning, analyzing, judging and scheming of the ego), [2] increased inner knowing (gnosis), [3] an enhanced sense

---

[242] http://en.wikipedia.org/wiki/The_Transcendence_of_the_Ego

of oneness with all creation, [4] increased creativity, stillness and clarity, and [5] a sense of liberation (from conflict and stress as well as from a sense of needing to defend the ego). [243]

The Bhagavad-Gita (the eternal message of spiritual wisdom from ancient India) talks about transcending the ego.

The word Gita means song and the word Bhagavad means God; often the Bhagavad-Gita is called the *Song of God*.

One can locate the Bhagavad-Gita in the historical epic Mahabharata (as written by Vedavyasa), a significantly voluminous book that covers the history of the earth from the time of creation (in relation only to India).

Composed in 100,000 rhyming quatrain couplets, the Mahabharata is seven times the size of the Iliad (as written by Homer).

---

[243] *Transcending the Ego: Healing Egocentricity via Soul Connection* article accessed on April 20, 2011 at http://www.brothermichael.org.uk/resources/soul.htm

A Metaphysics Primer

It was written to also include all of the people in the world (who are outside of the Vedic culture). The Mahabharata, then, contains the essence of the Vedas.

It is said that in studying the Bhagavad-Gita, one will gain "accurate, fundamental knowledge about God, the ultimate truth, creation, birth and death, the results of actions, the eternal soul, liberation and the purpose, as well as the goal, of human existence." [244]

Those that teach enlightenment (based on the information that stems from India, including the Bhagavad-Gita) all agree on one aspect: transcending the ego. If you want to advance on a spiritual level, this must be accomplished.

The ego is crafty "to the point of deluding the person that is in the public eye; that they themselves have transcended the ego and others have not. It is *impossible to transcend the ego being in the public eye.* The ego will take advantage of any open door of opportunity for attention, which includes

---

[244] http://www.bhagavad-gita.org/Articles/faq.html

feeling special, being number one within a group, having people follow you, having control over others, and playing the victim." [245]

The ego exists in the form of emotions, feelings, beliefs and desires.

To transcend the ego does not mean that we get rid of it; it simply means that you must learn to recognize it for what it is: an illusion (of separation) to which all are attached.

In knowing, believing and accepting that you are no different from anyone else, because everything exists in the oneness of creation (which means that you fully acknowledge and recognize that you are something much greater than the egoic self), you are already on your way to transcending the ego.

---

[245] *Transcending the Ego: Number One Priority* article accessed on April 20, 2011 at http://clearlyenlight.com/transcending-the-ego

A Metaphysics Primer

Disentangled from both prejudice and judgment, you experience a deep sense of complete freedom.

→ You are not here to destroy the ego

→ You are not here to dissolve the ego

→ You are not here to kill the ego

You are here to transcend the ego, which has a need to protect, defend and secure your physical identity (aka social status, reputation (which may also translate to having power over other people), nationality, religion, closed belief systems), so that both mind and spirit (heart) can merge together, thereby working in unison.

A Metaphysics Primer

We need to become "aware of our individual identities while simultaneously developing an expanded sense of global consciousness. Then we need to make sure both of these levels of awareness are aligned." [246]

The realization that you are more than just your ego (emotions, feelings, beliefs, desires, life experiences) is what allows you to begin to engage the world more fully, more completely, more consciously.

One successfully transforms (transcends) the ego by recognizing the fact that thoughts and behaviors at the individual (personal) level also impact thoughts and behaviors at the global (collective) level.

This is the central position from which one must begin this expansive work.

---

[246] *The War on Ego* article accessed on April 20, 2011 at http://www.stevepavlina.com/blog/2008/03/the-war-on-ego/

A Metaphysics Primer

As you come to realize that you are part of the macrocosm (the bigger picture, the same stream of consciousness to which all are connected), you will have reconciled yourself with the knowingness that "if you can live constructively as an individual, and if you can influence enough of the other cells to make similar changes, you'll have a positive impact on shifting the larger body [of humanity] to more constructive behaviours." [247]

When I continue to align my choices with the higher good, knowing and believing that my choices are also serving to help others, I find that I am mysteriously guided and directed to the right circumstances, the right people and the right situations.

It must also be remembered that when you help another, you are also helping yourself.

---

[247] *The War on Ego* article accessed on April 20, 2011 at http://www.stevepavlina.com/blog/2008/03/the-war-on-ego/

A Metaphysics Primer

In short, achieving global consciousness, one individual at a time, is central to this philosophy, the main caution being that "you have to stay focused on the overlap between your individual good and the good of humanity. This takes a bit of practice because it's a different way of thinking about life than most people are taught. We're encouraged to think about how our actions affect the people closest to us, but not the entire body of humanity. There is an effect though, and it does make a difference." [248]

Transcendence resides within. The spirit that exists within is both formless and eternal. It becomes in acknowledging and living this knowledge that the ego loses its power. Seeking and claiming the power within is the only way to transcend. It was Isaac the Syrian who explained *the purpose of silence* as *awakening the mind to God.* [249]

---

[248] *The War on Ego* article accessed on April 20, 2011 at http://www.stevepavlina.com/blog/2008/03/the-war-on-ego/
[249] http://www.theosophical.org/publications/quest-magazine/1432

A Metaphysics Primer

Interestingly, there are many who claim that Stonehenge is a center for this spiritual transcendence.

Given the proven acoustical properties, and knowing that sound equates to vibration, it is also a well known fact that altered states of consciousness can be reached "through beat tones and rhythmic sessions at certain frequencies." [250]

This is why "monks chant, those of Jewish faith rock back and forth (davening) while praying, and indigenous people incorporate drumming into their rituals. This is also why Rave participants are easily induced into trance-like states. These rhythmic actions actually produce a clinically measurable effect on the brain." [251]

It is through rhythmic sessions and beat tones (binaural beats) that the brain reaches what is referred to as a state of coherence.

---

[250] *Stonehenge: A Spiritual Transformational Tool* article accessed on April 19, 2011 at http://aphroditeastrology.com/2009/12/stonehenge-spiritual-transcendence-tool.html
[251] Ibid.

A Metaphysics Primer

Coherence is reached when "waves in phase and of one wavelength simultaneously are generated in the different parts of the brain. This synchrony between the waves make the brain run like an optimal brain and a deep state of altered consciousness can be achieved. The frequencies that generate these altered states of consciousness on the human brain are known as Alpha and Theta waves." [252]

Stonehenge researchers have noticed that "the side of the rocks facing the interior center of the circle were carved out somewhat to produce a concave dip in the face of the rock. This was done purposefully and for a reason. It appears that the acoustical qualities of Stonehenge are such that, when the proper rhythm is achieved through beat tones (drumming), Stonehenge actually begins to produce Alpha wave frequencies at 10 HZ," [253] frequencies that are "necessary to achieve altered states of consciousness that

---

[252] *Stonehenge: A Spiritual Transformational Tool* article accessed on April 19, 2011 at http://aphroditeastrology.com/2009/12/stonehenge-spiritual-transcendence-tool.html
[253] Ibid.

A Metaphysics Primer

allow for astral planing or astral projection (out of body experiences)." [254]

In addition, the researchers were able to reproduce the acoustical affects of Stonehenge using binaural beat tones. They "played them for research subjects and then studied their brain wave patterns. Beat tones that were played with the Stonehenge acoustical properties produced near perfect brainwave patterns conducive to producing altered states of consciousness for the individual." [255]

Imagine, if you will, "an ancient ritual at Stonehenge. The entire circle is literally ringing loudly in Alpha wave frequencies, producing binaural beat tones in the brain and beat vibrations in the physical body that can be felt. Your brain is entering a state of altered consciousness while you

---

[254] *Stonehenge: A Spiritual Transformational Tool* article accessed on April 19, 2011 at http://aphroditeastrology.com/2009/12/stonehenge-spiritual-transcendence-tool.html
[255] Ibid.

are dancing in rhythm with the flickering flames of the burning fires." [256]

According to quantum physics, we are all made up of subatomic particles. Given that subatomic particles "can bounce in and out of different dimensions ... then this means that, technically, human beings can do the same." [257] Theoretically speaking, does this not *suggest* that human beings possess the ability for inter-dimensional travel?

Knowing that Stonehenge appears to be "a perfectly composed mechanism for producing Alpha waves necessary to reach the altered state of consciousness for astral transcendence," [258] this begs the question ... what may have happened to the people of Stonehenge?

---

[256] *Stonehenge: A Spiritual Transformational Tool* article accessed on April 19, 2011 at http://aphroditeastrology.com/2009/12/stonehenge-spiritual-transcendence-tool.html
[257] Ibid.
[258] Ibid.

A Metaphysics Primer

Author David Darling refers to the pivotal moment, in awakening, as being the switchover from "normal dualistic mode of thinking to the selfless experience of transcendence." [259]

Known by a multitude of different names (satori, nirvana, Tao, enlightenment, zoning, bliss), this fundamental mystical feeling, *The Perennial Philosophy*, may come "after years of asceticism, study, and devotion to some particular religious or meditation system." [260]

For most ordinary folk, it may arrive "out of the blue; unbidden and unsought" [261] given that "the very act of seeking may block or hinder the experience of enlightenment." [262]

The feeling of transcendent unity "is the same for everyone when it happens, since there is only one reality. However,

---

[259] www.daviddarling.info/works/ZenPhysics/ZenPhysics_ch13.html
[260] Ibid.
[261] Ibid.
[262] Ibid.

problems ensue in translating this feeling into words. Even greater difficulties arise when others, who have not had the experience themselves, try to convey, second hand or third hand, what the fundamental teaching consisted of." [263]

From the reasonably clear and simple message of Gautama Buddha, "the vast and intricate system of religious philosophy that is Buddhism has sprung. Thousands of books and many millions of words have been set down on the subject, often in a style that only a lifetime devotee or learned academic could penetrate, but the irony is that language and symbolism are anathema to the basic message of Buddha, which is all about *direct experience and unadulterated being*. And the same is true of Christianity. The central teaching of Jesus, a flesh-and-blood human being like you and me, was to *forget yourself and get in touch with the real world*." [264]

---

[263] www.daviddarling.info/works/ZenPhysics/ZenPhysics_ch13.html
[264] Ibid.

A Metaphysics Primer

Mind you, there can be "no proof of transcendence without the necessary self-transformation. Adopting an attitude of humility, and recognizing one's lack of knowledge, in order to seriously consider a transcendental philosophy, can be a beneficial exercise in and of itself." [265]

In the words of Albert Einstein ... *there are moments when one feels free from one's own identification with human limitations and inadequacies. At such moments, one imagines that one stands on some spot of a small planet, gazing in amazement at the cold, yet profoundly moving, beauty of the eternal, the unfathomable: life and death flow into one, and there is neither evolution nor destiny; only being.*

Clearly, this was an individual who understood his purpose, both as a scientist as well as a human being.

---

[265] *Transition to Transcendence* article accessed on April 23, 2011 at http://www.cejournal.org/GRD/Wolff.htm

Ultimately, what needs to be transcended are the limiting beliefs, the ignorance, the victim consciousness and the anger, all of which hold us back from our true selves.

Once your consciousness transcends "into quantum realms, you will not be above others or better than others, but you will be much more present in the here and now, channeling into space/time the grace of your higher consciousness." [266]

It was also Albert Einstein who said ... *The intuitive mind is a sacred gift and the rational mind is a faithful servant. We have created a society that honors the servant and has forgotten the gift.*

[17] Gnosis

The spiritual exercise of attention is the same as (1) existing in the now, (2) living in the zone, and (3) the practicing of mindfulness.

---

[266] *Becoming Galactic: Presuppositions of Quantum Consciousness* blog article accessed on April 23, 2011 at http://www.becoming-galactic.org/presupp8.html

A Metaphysics Primer

While thusly engaged, you are able to acknowledge that this is the only time when you are really living.

Mindfulness allows us to make any activity, or exercise, a spiritual activity.

The exercise of attention "is exercising and developing consciousness of awareness itself. And, for every situation we can exercise attention in, it is another situation where we are now free not only to act, but to be. This is not only a basic skill and a place to start on the path to Gnosis, it is a very powerful tool in its own right, for it is the ability to focus, to shine, the light within." [267]

---

[267] Pierce, Rev. Troy W. (2007). *Following The Path of Gnosis: The Spiritual Exercise of Attention* article. Retrieved June 7, 2010 from http://gnoscast.blogspot.com/2008/03/following-path-of-gnosis-spiritual.html

A Metaphysics Primer

Although it is "a mistake to simply equate Gnosis with enlightenment," [268] it can be said that "Gnosis is the method (means) of liberation" [269] as opposed to the liberated state itself.

Gnosis, then, is "a way to refer to a fundamental spiritual growth, transformation, liberation process." [270]

Gnosis is "not what you think. It is not an idea; not a doctrine. It is not objective. It is not definable. It is not found inside of rigid limits, not outside of all considerations. It is not yours. It is not ours. It is something attained, and is a quickening of what we already have. It is a knowledge that you are, not a knowledge that you have." [271]

---

[268] Pierce, Rev. Troy W. (2007). *Questions: Practices for Gnosis* article. Retrieved June 7, 2010 from http://gnoscast.blogspot.com/2008/02/questions-practices-for-gnosis.html
[269] Ibid.
[270] Ibid.
[271] The Gnosis Institute. (2008) Retrieved April 27, 2008 at http://gnosisinst.org/

A Metaphysics Primer

If you are "looking for a label, Gnosis is not it. If you are seeking a path with answers, Gnosis is not it. If you are looking for a path that fits you, Gnosis is not it. If you are seeking what is real beyond yourself and your ideas, then you may already be on the path of Gnosis." [272]

Gnosis is "not something you will understand quickly. It is something you will come to know [so that you may] grow in that knowing." [273]

Scriptures tell us that "the truth shall make us free. In Greek, the word for truth is "un-hidden". The un-hidden, the unveiled, the examined shall set us free. This requires discipline and commitment, training and work. It requires an allegiance to the real that is higher than the allegiance to the ideal." [274]

---

[272] The Gnosis Institute. (2008) Retrieved April 27, 2008 at http://gnosisinst.org/
[273] Ibid.
[274] Ibid.

A Metaphysics Primer

In the earliest of my research, I had been under the impression that Gnosis was the Greek word for knowledge. I have since discovered that there are three essential Classical Greek words that speak to different types of knowledge: doxia, episteme, and gnosis, all of which Rev. Troy W. Pierce further discusses in his blog article entitled *Gnosis, Episteme, and Doxia, Oh My!* [275]

The path of Gnosis is an individual one.

This clearly means that *my path is my responsibility.*

For those who strongly adhere to a culture of collective religious identity, this concept is not easily understood.

From the perspective "of the Gnostic tradition, personal growth and transformation is what it is all about, expressed as Gnosis; a very deep and sure knowing, a knowing that you are, rather than a knowing that you possess. It is a true knowing that is liberating. Gnosis is this way of knowing,

---

[275] Pierce, Rev. Troy W. (2007). *Gnosis, Episteme, and Doxia, Oh My!* article. Retrieved June 7, 2010 from http://gnoscast.blogspot.com/2007/11/gnosis-episteme-and-doxia-oh-my.html

and with it comes a deep understanding of who we are, and where we are, and what sets us free." [276]

There is a website called **Imagination Awakened Ministry**, also denoted simply as **I AM**, that believes, as do I, that mankind is awakening into a new era whereby the human mind "is the vehicle in which consciousness enters into and experiences creation. One aspect of the mind is Thought, the other is Imagination, which is its natural evolution. Thought and Imagination are two sides of the same coin." [277]

In essence, one's imagination creates one's experience. One's world is an expression of their wonderful human imagination. We become what we think. Might it be that we can learn to understand thought enough to create something new for ourselves?

---

[276] Pierce, Rev. Troy W. (2007). *Questions: Approaching Gnosticism* article. Retrieved June 7, 2010 from http://gnoscast.blogspot.com/2007/08/questions-approaching-gnosticism.html

[277] *Universal Laws* article located on the **Imagination Awakened Ministry** website. Retrieved June 7, 2010 from http://www.i-am.cc/us/Ministry.htm

A Metaphysics Primer

Imagination allows one to live in the "freedom of limitless possibility, for all things in this world are imagination of which consciousness is the animating power in a world of shadows. It has been said that God is in all things." [278]

Imagination, ergo, is God.

One attracts what they believe to be true. This is why it is so important to *become aware of your unconscious programming*, your unconscious patterns.

In so doing, you become even more aware of the world around you, including the belief systems of others.

The only cure for all of the problems that we are faced with in today's world lies in losing separate consciousness and selfishness by regaining consciousness of our oneness with everything.

---

[278] *Universal Laws* article located on the Imagination Awakened Ministry website. Retrieved June 7, 2010 from http://www.i-am.cc/us/Ministry.htm

This can only be attained through unselfish love, looking to both Jesus and Buddha as important and living examples of what is representative of true spirituality: compassion, kindness, caring, giving, sharing and harmlessness.

We must see the illusions of self consciousness that we carry with us in our mind and break them.

While there are many different words (gnosis, satori, bodhi, nirvana, kensho and moksha) that can be used to describe aspects of enlightenment, *believing* something (perhaps because many others believe the same thing and it is more reassuring to be able to continue to do so) *is not the same as knowing* (and having experienced) something (for yourself), for therein lies your wisdom, your truth.

Gnosticism means "breaking free of the conformity set forth to us by religious dogma; the same dogma that, for centuries, has instilled unbelievable fear and guilt upon the masses. It means dispelling all the fear based untruths about

A Metaphysics Primer

God and our eternal Souls by bringing reasoning and intelligence into the equation."[279]

Gnosis, then, means self-knowledge; a knowledge that you glean as you come to understand that nothing is random or pointless.

To be open to gnosis requires the transcending of previously held beliefs, so that one can begin to experience their truest nature for themselves.

The most important concept in Gnostic philosophy is that which is called polarity. In this instance, polarity can be described as *the presence or manifestation of two opposite or contrasting principles or tendencies.*

Polarity, then, is simply a duality of opposites that are essentially, one, as in good/evil, night/day, yes/no,

---

[279] http://www.urbandictionary.com/define.php?term=Gnostic&defid=1802872

A Metaphysics Primer

masculine/feminine, black/white, life/death; comparable to the heads or tails of any given coin. In essence, you cannot have one without the other.

Philosophies that "adopt an either/or approach teach that we are either separate or all one." [280] Hmmmm; either completely separate or one, without any other possibility in between. Having seen through the illusion of separation, I think that I will pass on this outmoded definition of my existence.

By comparison, however, Gnostic philosophy is "based on an understanding of polarity, so it adopts a both/and approach, teaching that we are both one and many," [281] which simply equates to everyone being of the same energy, denoted as the one stream of universal consciousness that exists, while also experiencing themselves as individuated aspects of this energy.

---

[280] Freke, Timothy, and Gandy, Peter. <u>The Gospel of the Second Coming</u> (page 84). Carlsbad, CA: Hay House, Inc.
[281] Ibid.

A Metaphysics Primer

As spiritual beings, if we are open to acknowledging that God is also this same stream of consciousness, from whence we have come, then, so, too, are we God (albeit, for the most part, *un*actualized).

Taking it one step further, if we are all God, then there is only one God experiencing existence through the many individual stories that continue to be written.

Now that is a most enlightening reckoning, is it not?

Gnosis is a "direct realization of your essential nature that manifests as a tangible experience in the body," [282] one that you will be able to identify through love.

The Beatles were so right when they wrote that *love is all we need* because it is love that we feel when "we see through separateness and recognize our essential oneness." [283]

---

[282] Freke, Timothy, and Gandy, Peter. <u>The Gospel of the Second Coming</u> (page 90). Carlsbad, CA: Hay House, Inc.
[283] Ibid, page 91.

It is this form of unconditional love that allows us to feel both the happiness of another as well as their pain.

It is this form of unconditional love that allows us to realize that when one suffers, so, too, do we all suffer.

If hurting another translates to hurting yourself, why, then, do we continue to operate in such a manner?

It is this form of unconditional love, when experienced in its truest, transcendent, sense, that opens our hearts to love (and forgive) everyone and everything, further allowing us to embrace things as they are, without judgment. This is what I refer to as compassionate allowing.

Spiritual awakening begins "when we start to doubt our conditioning and explore our own insights," [284] thereby becoming independent freethinkers by following our hearts.

---

[284] Freke, Timothy, and Gandy, Peter. The Gospel of the Second Coming (page 133). Carlsbad, CA: Hay House, Inc.

A Metaphysics Primer

We need to "individuate as a separate some-one before we can become conscious of the All-One." [285]

Once again, therein lies the paradox, the polarity, the duality, of our very selves.

We are here to wake up to the illusion (separation) and thoroughly love life, to simply love BEing, because in so doing, we will have progressed from the beginning of ego development to the final stages of spiritual enlightenment; in essence, two parts of the same process.

Timothy Freke and Peter Gandy sum everything up so marvelously well when they write that gnosis "is the recognition of our essential oneness through the story of separateness." [286]

When *you are one with the present moment*, with the now, you are experiencing gnosis.

---

[285] Freke, Timothy, and Gandy, Peter. The Gospel of the Second Coming (page 133). Carlsbad, CA: Hay House, Inc.
[286] Ibid, page 170.

A Metaphysics Primer

When *you are loving the present moment,* you are also experiencing gnosis.

When *your life is all about creating Heaven here on Earth* in your day to day life, so, too, are you experiencing gnosis.

It is this very moment that is "the mystical marriage of opposites. Right now you are the Author and the story, the mystery and the manifest; possibility and actuality. You are the pre-conceptual presence of the Primal Imagination expressing itself as everything that is." [287]

Now is the time to become conscious of BEing (one and all), to simply love BEing, so that you will be in love with BEing.

Who would have thought that it was this simple?

---

[287] Freke, Timothy, and Gandy, Peter. The Gospel of the Second Coming (page 191). Carlsbad, CA: Hay House, Inc.

A Metaphysics Primer

The discovery, in 1945, of the *Gospel of Thomas*, has led some scholars to believe that the original teachings of Jesus may have been accurately characterized as nondualism. [288]

In fact, there is an English rendering from the *Gospel of Thomas* that showcases a nondual vision of reconciling opposites: *When you make the two one, and when you make the inside like the outside and the outside like the inside, and the above like the below, and when you make the male and the female one and the same...then you will enter* [the Kingdom]. [289]

The Gospel of Philip also conveys nondualism: *Light and Darkness, life and death, right and left, are brothers of one another. They are inseparable. Because of this neither are the good good, nor evil evil, nor is life life, nor death death. For this reason each one will dissolve into its earliest origin.*

---

[288] http://en.wikipedia.org/wiki/Nondualism
[289] Wallace, Vesna A. (2001). <u>The Inner Kālacakratantra: A Buddhist Tantric View of the Individual</u>, page 145. Oxford University Press: New York, NY.

A Metaphysics Primer

But those who are exalted above the world are indissoluble, eternal. [290]

Armed with a truth that can only be actualized by looking within, Jesus knew that one's own gnosis was essentially their own teacher, meaning that a Gnostic "is a disciple of his own mind." [291]

In keeping with Gnostic traditions, the individual who lacks insight into the depths of their being (self-knowledge) "is driven by impulses that he does not comprehend. One suffers due to ignorance regarding one's own divine nature. Therefore, ignorance of oneself is a form of self-destruction." [292]

---

[290] http://www.gnosis.org/naghamm/gop.html
[291] Wallace, Vesna A. (2001). <u>The Inner Kālacakratantra: A Buddhist Tantric View of the Individual</u>, page 145. Oxford University Press: New York, NY.
[292] Ibid.

In the realization (achieving) of gnosis, one becomes "the transcendent reality that one perceives at the time of spiritual transformation" [293] meaning the "transcendence of all differentiations, or dualities, for it is the final integration of the knower and the known." [294]

Our thoughts, words and actions must become such that they are seen as "movements in line with the stillness [that] we are." [295]

[18] Enlightenment

There are a great many people who feel that they must suffer in order to gain liberation. While this is most unfortunate, it is also a false understanding of what enlightenment entails.

In truth, we are "our own key to absolute freedom, and there are as many paths to perfect enlightenment as there are beings in the universe. When we become conscious we

---

[293] Wallace, Vesna A. (2001). <u>The Inner Kālacakratantra: A Buddhist Tantric View of the Individual</u>, page 145. Oxford University Press: New York, NY.
[294] Ibid.
[295] http://www.gurusfeet.com/blog/living-non-duality

expand, when we turn away from being conscious we contract. Beyond this, reality will always prove to us that we cannot move against its own self governing laws. All of us are free to choose the kind of reality we wish to know; none of us can break the rules. Every entity in creation has the same freedom of choice." [296]

Enlightened people "are both happy and loving. A simple step towards being loving is to *accept where you are on your journey* of conscious evolution." [297]

Enlightened people "accept themselves just the way they are ... by being aware of any self critical thoughts and then deciding that they are not true." [298]

---

[296] http://www.wikihow.com/Become-Enlightened
[297] http://www.pathwaytohappiness.com/enlightenment.htm
[298] Ibid.

The second act of acceptance "is to *accept other people and the world as they are.* Enlightened people love and accept others just the way they are, too. This also begins with being aware of thoughts and opinions and deciding not to believe them." [299]

Thereafter, enlightenment becomes a matter of expanding your consciousness to see the oneness that exists.

Whilst these steps may seem easy enough, they become an integral part of a life-long experience.

The following words belong to Osho, a professor of philosophy, who travelled throughout India in the 1960's as a public speaker. [300]

Meditation will not give you enlightenment, remember. No technique can ever give you enlightenment; enlightenment is

---

[299] http://www.pathwaytohappiness.com/enlightenment.htm
[300] http://www.oshoquotes.net/2009/12/osho-quotes-on-enlightenment/

not technical. Meditation can only prepare the ground. Meditation can only open the door.

Enlightenment is not something like an achievement; one cannot achieve it. One has to disappear for it to happen. It is a happening and it happens only in the absence of the ego.

The ego is a doer, and enlightenment happens in a state of nondoing; it is simply the realization of who you are; it is not a question of achievement.

Enlightenment simply means being in a state of let-go. Enlightenment simply means undoing what the society has done to you.

What your parents have imposed upon you, throw it away; what the society has conditioned you to be, put it aside. Reassert your being.

Love yourself and respect yourself, and try to be just yourself.

Enlightenment is possible, but it will be possible only when you are ready to lose yourself. That is the meaning of Jesus' saying when he says, "If you lose, you will gain. If you don't lose, you will lose."

In losing is the gain. In forgetting is the remembrance. In dissolving, you become crystallized.

In a single moment, in one stroke, you can become enlightened. It is not a gradual process, because enlightenment is not something that you have to invent. It is something that you have to discover. It is already there.

It is not something that you have to manufacture. Close your eyes and see it there. Be silent and have a taste of it. Your very nature is what I call enlightenment. It is you, your very core.

The idea of enlightenment is to remain in the present moment – not to go into the past, which is no more, not to go into the future, which is not yet – because if you go into past and future, you are going to miss the present moment, which is the only reality. Just be here, now.

And if you are here and now, enlightenment comes of its own accord. It is not a goal that you have to reach. It is not somewhere far away, so that you have to travel a path to it. It comes to you, you never go to it. It is not your doing, it is a happening.

My religion is nothing but the art of living, the art of loving. And if you can manage two things, total life and total love, the third thing, enlightenment, will come of its own accord. You have earned it.

You need not seek it, you deserve it.

It is a reward from existence to those people who have respected life, loved, lived, danced, enjoyed.

[19] Authentic Living

How can we continue to harm others, in the name of God (under the guise of religion, which was created by man), simply because they are of a different race, a different nationality, a different tribe, a different class, a different sex, a different sexuality, a different religion, a different belief system?

A Metaphysics Primer

The moment one begins to question these outlandish practices, these separatist practices, these elitist practices, such is indicative of the spiritual path.

As written by Jon Peniel, *"those who know not that they are one, act not as one. Those who act not as one, create not love, but suffering and disharmony. What you create, you receive."* [301]

One's state of consciousness mirrors one's state of awareness of the world. This awareness is reflected in the way you view the world, the way you interpret and understand the world, the way you interact with everyone and everything. Essentially, one's state of consciousness is fully reflective of your paradigms, your beliefs, your programming, for all is usually in sync with a person's point of view.

---

[301] Peniel, Jon. (1997) <u>The Children of the Law of One and The Lost Teachings of Atlantis</u> (page 61). Alamosa, CO: Network.

A Metaphysics Primer

If everything in the universe is made of the same substance, then so, too, are we made of this same substance, meaning that everything is interdependently connected.

Even though we can think we are separate, even though we can believe we are separate, *even though we can act like we are separate*, in truth, *there is no separation*, for therein lies the illusion.

It is in the focusing on the illusion of separation that one begins to concentrate solely on themselves; this is where the me, me, me of the ego comes into play.

It has been through this attention and energy to self, that complete and total selfishness was created.

It is important to understand that the terms good and evil are relative only to the ego. "The ego doesn't want us looking for God because when we find God, the illusion of being an ego will be destroyed. One cannot see God and continue to live as a separate person. Each and every day we will watch the mind carefully and destroy our divisiveness. We will stop separating and start uniting. We will stop hating and start loving." [302]

The sole cure for all of the problems that we are hereby faced with lies in *losing this separate consciousness* and *regaining oneness consciousness*.

This can only be attained through acts of unselfish love.

The only person we have the power to change is ourselves.

While that may seem miniscule at best, in truth, it becomes monumental.

As we focus on affecting the needed change within, as ripples traverse outward into the majestic realms of the universe, the world comes one step closer to peace. To change the consciousness of the world, the first tenant becomes that of focusing on ourselves.

---

[302] Walker III, Ethan. (2003) <u>The Mystic Christ: The Light of Non-Duality and the Path of Love According to the Life and Teachings of Jesus</u> (page 49). Norman, OK: Devi Press Inc.

A Metaphysics Primer

Change takes place, one person at a time.

There are many things that clutter us up on a spiritual level; namely, nagging anxieties, jealousy, anger, resentment, regret, fear, guilt, skepticism, cynicism, failure to be true to one's self, greed, constant busyness and negativity.

These are the issues that weigh us down with a heavy heart.

These are the issues that leave us feeling depressed, powerless, unbalanced.

These are the issues that hinder our spiritual growth.

It is imperative that you find a place of solitude, away from work, away from the television, away from cell phones and emails. In the silence, take the time to pay attention to what your inner (and intuitive) teacher has to say. Silence and stillness are healthy for the soul.

Meditation, a union of mind and body, is an adventure of self discovery.

Scientists are now discovering that meditation has a biological effect on the body. It has even been suggested, by means of a small scale study, that meditation can boost parts of the brain as well as the immune system.

Meditation can be used to expand the paradigm to which you adhere.

Meditation leads to peace, tranquility and equanimity of mind.

In keeping, equanimity of mind leads to self realization, also referred to as the super conscious state of mind.

Any individual who wants to grow, who wants to attain spiritual enlightenment, who wants to be a really good person, must first and foremost completely reevaluate their beliefs.

A Metaphysics Primer

They must be willing to ask themselves why they adhere to such beliefs.

They must be willing to ask themselves where their beliefs came from.

They must be willing to ask themselves if they are willing to embrace change in order to welcome spiritual growth.

Who you are, and what you do with universal consciousness, is key.

This is why, when you have realized (achieved) universal consciousness, it is called enlightenment or illumination.

It is as if a light switch has been turned on in a life that was, up until that point, lived in darkness.

Universal consciousness is attained when a person has a lasting experience in which they see through the illusion of separateness, thereby losing their separate consciousness. It is then that their consciousness merges with the universe; thus they experience being one with the universe.

A Metaphysics Primer

The illusion of separateness has no choice but to dissolve in the awareness of oneness.

As a result, the separate self (ego) seems to die and a rebirth occurs.

One's consciousness is transcended and transformed.

When universal consciousness is properly experienced, the individual is never the same. From that moment on, all things are understood in the light of the universal picture. Selfishness has become a thing of the past.

The closer one gets to attaining universal consciousness, the greater their point of view becomes.

It has been written that a*s you come to know your true self, you will know the true story.*

This also means that *as you come to know your whole self, you will know the wholeness of your truth.*

A Metaphysics Primer

Awakening is simply abiding in one's natural state.

We are pure existence.

→ Each is complete

→ Each is one

→ Each is perfect

→ Each is a divine masterpiece

It is only through the death experience than one can fully understand that which we call life. This does not have to be a literal death; rather, it can be a symbolic death, as in the death of the egoic mind.

Honor, integrity and service to all life are central to authentic living.

A Metaphysics Primer

If one but takes the time to look about them with spiritual eyes, one will find beauty and harmony in abundance.

There are individuals who do not yet understand that an increase in one's vibratory level serves to bring about remarkable changes.

The more enlightened we become, the less likely we are attracted to the darker energies that exist, gradually pulling away from their influence.

In so doing, we reclaim our power, an absolute necessity, for we, alone, have been responsible for allowing others to impose restrictions upon us.

Dharma means carrier of goodness and wholesomeness.

Hu means light, as in you are the light of God.

When you spread darkness, you go opposite your dharma.

When you slander someone, you go opposite your dharma.

A Metaphysics Primer

→ We are carriers of goodness and wholesomeness

→ We are carriers of light

There exists an inherent difference between the ancient mysteries and the Bible.

Why is it that the mysteries are all about the God that exists within (meaning man as God) whereas the Bible became the God outside of you and above you?

Therein lies *the illusion of separation* that *was deliberately created* for a multitude of reasons, the chief ones being power, control and greed.

Religion was established as the official toll bridge to heaven; one that continues to request, and dictate, both death and destruction as its sole fee.

You are God yourself, said Buddha.

A Metaphysics Primer

The Kingdom of God exists within, said Yeshua ben Yosef (Jesus).

These works that I do, you, too, can do ... and greater, said Yeshua ben Yosef (Jesus).

In our search for God, could it be that we have, in truth, been searching for ourselves?

Could it be that the only difference between God and ourselves is that we have forgotten that we are divine?

Just as God in *Genesis* is described as being more than one, so, too, is God found in the many.

It is *true spirituality* that *recognizes the dominion of peace.*

In keeping, "spiritual people remain non-involved in world affairs and, even when the world seeks to pull them into its theatrical, glamorized arena, they remain non-attached and peaceful." [303]

With no need to change the world, they "see the simple beauty and perfection of all that exists and feel a compassion for all life rather than an emotional involvement." [304]

As this rekindled awareness grows exponentially upon this planet, it shall serve to uplift others, with results being noted as remarkable increases in the mass consciousness of humankind.

[20] Context for Today

The Gnostics placed an emphasis on [1] spiritual knowledge (gnosis) as compared to faith; a self-knowledge obtained through understanding, courtesy of an inner, mystical (esoteric) and [2] contemplative experience (whereby one acquires knowledge of, and acquaintance with, the divine),

---

[303] Self and Spirit: Spirituality, Enlightenment & Higher Consciousness website. Article *What Are The Characteristics Of A True Spiritual Person?* retrieved on July 2, 2010 at http://illumen8.com/what-are-the-characteristics-of-a-true-spiritual-person.html
[304] Ibid.

coupled with [3] purified living (conscious living) in keeping with all life.

This knowledge, this realization, is experiential, meaning that it can never be attained through reason because it has no basis in intellectualism.

As multi-dimensional beings, we have never been souls that were lost, we have never been souls that were diseased, we have never been souls that needed to be saved; however, we did come to experience ourselves in all ways, these included, as a means of evolutionary development from a spiritual perspective.

There exists a higher, cosmic, consciousness that we are here to achieve.

Yogis call it super consciousness; Gurdjieff references it as objective consciousness; Theosophists cite it as Buddhic consciousness; Sufism and Hinduism express the same as

God consciousness; New Agers state it as Christ consciousness. [305]

In essence, each expression is used to denote the consciousness of a human being who has reached a higher level of evolutionary development, in that he (she) has come to know, and understand, reality versus illusion.

Within a secular context, "higher consciousness is usually associated with exceptional control over one's mind and will, intellectual and moral enlightenment, and profound personal growth" [306] whereas in a primarily spiritual context, higher consciousness may "also be associated with transcendence, spiritual enlightenment, and union with the divine." [307]

What makes consciousness so intriguing is that most humans are considered to be asleep (to both the reality

---

[305] http://en.wikipedia.org/wiki/Higher_consciousness
[306] Ibid.
[307] Ibid.

versus the illusion equation as well as the infinite versus the finite statement) even as they go about their daily business.

This is why movies such as *The Peaceful Warrior* and *The Matrix* series are so important.

Many attribute the Golden Rule (meaning, do unto others as you would have them do unto you) to Jesus, as author. Ancient books from China, however, document the sage Meng-tse (370 BCE), whose name was Latinized to Mencius, the pupil of Confucius, as the composer. [308]

There is a Masonic principle called *acting on the square*, a familiar metaphor for fair and honest dealings with others, that dates back to ancient China; one which denotes an individual abstaining from doing to another that which he would not want done unto himself. [309] [310]

---

[308] Vayro, Ian Ross. (2007) God Save Us From Religion (page 115). Queensland, Australia: Joshua Books.
[309] Ibid.

A Metaphysics Primer

Such is further attributed to a book called <u>The Great Learning</u> (written in 500 BC). [311] [312] [313]

In truth, *a person can only become informed and enlightened if they are open to new possibilities.*

You must be willing to let go in order to grow into what it means to be empowered.

What is truly interesting is that the Bible denotes the following: [1] *Ye shall be as Gods* (Genesis 3:5), [2] *Behold, the man is become as one of us* (Genesis 3:22) and [3] *You, too, are Gods* (Psalm 82). [314]

Truly, this is in keeping with "the perennial mysticism of Gnosticism and the Pagan mysteries; that within each one of

---

310 http://www.themasonictrowel.com/Articles/degrees/degree_3rd_files/the_square_gltx.htm
[311] http://www.sacred-texts.com/cfu/menc/
[312] http://www.sacred-texts.com/mas/syma/syma34.htm
[313] http://www.indiana.edu/~p374/Daxue.pdf
[314] Vayro, Ian Ross. (2006) <u>They Lied To Us in Sunday School</u> (page 377). Queensland, Australia: Joshua Books.

us is the one Soul of the Universe, the Logos, the Universal Daemon, the Mind of God." [315]

Aside from delving within, there is no need to seek. In essence, the purpose of our evolutionary pilgrimage is "to bring this inner Christ or Buddha nature to full expression over the course of numberless lives." [316]

In the words of Eckhart Tolle … *You are not in the now, you are the now; that is your essential identity: the only thing that never changes. Life is always now. Now is consciousness and consciousness is who you are. That's the equation.*

In the words of Lama Surya Das … *Enlightenment is not about becoming divine. Instead, it's about becoming more fully human. It is the end of ignorance.*

---

[315] Freke, Timothy and Gandy, Peter. (1999) <u>The Jesus Mysteries</u> (page 46). New York, New York: Three Rivers Press.
[316] http://davidpratt.info/jesus.htm

A Metaphysics Primer

Advaita Meetup Groups [317]

Adyashanti [318]

Adyashanti: A Matter of Perspective [319]

Alan Watts: An Interactive Experience [320]

An Introduction to Awareness [321]

Authenticity Accelerator (Robert Rabbin) [322]

Being Yoga [323]

Charlie Todd: The Shared Experience of Absurdity [324]

---

[317] http://advaita.meetup.com/
[318] http://www.adyashanti.org/
[319] http://vimeo.com/21318776
[320] http://alanwatts.com/archive/
[321] http://www.anintroductiontoawareness.com/Awareness/Introduction.html
[322] http://authenticityaccelerator.com/
[323] http://www.beingyoga.com/
[324] http://www.ted.com/talks/charlie_todd_the_shared_experience_of_absurdity.html?utm_source=newsletter_weekly_2011-11-11

Daily Zen Meditation [325]

Dharma Tunes [326]

Die to Love [327]

Free Awareness [328]

Free Hugs (Juan Mann) [329]

Free Hugs Campaign [330]

Free Hugs Message from Juan Mann [331]

Inviting Awareness [332]

Jerry Katz: On the Ever-Expanding World of Nonduality [333]

---

[325] http://www.dailyzen.com/meditation.asp
[326] http://dharmatunes.com/
[327] http://not-knowing.com/
[328] http://www.free-awareness.com/
[329] http://www.youtube.com/watch?v=vr3x_RRJdd4
[330] http://www.juanmann.com/
[331] http://www.youtube.com/watch?v=BRVzXcybd2c&feature=relmfu
[332] http://canelamichelle.com/
[333] http://nondualityamerica.wordpress.com/2011/07/23/jerry-katz-on-the-ever-expanding-world-of-nonduality/

Living As the Source of Who You Are [334]

Living Realization [335]

Natural Awakening [336]

Never Not Here [337]

Nondualism Meetup Groups [338]

Nonduality Activism (Jerry Katz) [339]

Nonduality Meetup Groups [340]

Nonduality Satsang Nova Scotia (Jerry Katz) [341]

Non-Duality America Blog [342]

---

[334] http://chuckhillig.com/Home_Page.html
[335] http://livingrealization.org/
[336] http://www.nondualtraining.com/
[337] http://www.nevernothere.com/
[338] http://nondualism.meetup.com/
[339] http://nonduality.com/activism.htm
[340] http://nonduality.meetup.com/
[341] http://www.nonduality.ca/
[342] http://nondualityamerica.wordpress.com/author/nondualityamercia/

Non-Duality Magazine [343]

No Shame in Stillness [344]

Nothing Exists, Despite Appearances [345]

Nothing Saying This: Nonduality Blog [346]

Please Respect My Religion [347]

Radiance of Being [348]

Radiant Mind [349]

Science and Non-Duality [350]

---

[343] http://www.nondualitymagazine.org/nonduality_magazine.contents.volume.5.htm
[344] http://undertheapricottree.wordpress.com/2011/10/18/no-shame-in-stillness/
[345] http://nothingexistsdespiteappearances.blogspot.com/
[346] http://nothingsayingthis.com/
[347] http://freethoughtnation.com/contributing-writers/63-acharya-s/614-please-respect-my-religion.html
[348] http://radianceofbeing.blogspot.com/
[349] http://www.radiantmind.net/
[350] http://www.scienceandnonduality.com/

Scott Morrison Teachings [351]

Stillness Speaks [352]

The Benefits of Mystical Oneness [353]

The Bhagavan Sri Ramana Maharshi website [354]

The Birth and Death of Fundamentalism in Nonduality and Advaita Teachings [355]

The Church of Reality [356]

The Illustrated Guide to Free Hugs (Juan Mann) [357]

The Rambling Taoists [358]

---

[351] http://scotmorrison.wordpress.com/
[352] http://chucksurface.stillnessspeaks.com/
[353] http://waynewirs.com/the-benefits-of-mystical-oneness/
[354] http://www.sriramanamaharshi.org/
[355] http://www.lifewithoutacentre.com/read/essays-transcripts/the-birth-and-death-of-fundamentalism-in-nonduality-and-advaita-teachings/
[356] http://www.churchofreality.org/wisdom/hidden_agenda/
[357] https://www.createspace.com/3447347
[358] http://ramblingtaoist.blogspot.com/2011/12/hsin-hsin-ming-viii-non-duality.html

A Metaphysics Primer

The Rambling Taoists Miscellaneous Writings [359]

The Spiritual Mind [360]

Undivided: The Online Journal of Nonduality and Psychology [361]

Urban Guru Magazine [362]

Vicki Woodyard [363]

Wake Up [364]

[21] Know Thyself

To know thyself, as Socrates said, is but the beginning of enlightenment.

---

[359] http://ramblingtaoist.wordpress.com/scott-bradley/miscellaneous-writings/
[360] http://thespiritualmind-holly.blogspot.com/
[361] http://undividedjournal.com/
[362] http://urbangurumagazine.com/
[363] http://www.nondualitynow.com/
[364] http://wakeupthefilm.com/

A Metaphysics Primer

Insight occurs when, and to the degree that, one knows oneself ... are words as spoken by Andrew Schneider, creator of The Soul Journey. [365]

The best way to balance karma is by fulfilling your dharma.

You are here to use your gifts and talents "in service to the purpose and plan of conscious evolution for yourself and the quantum field of all sentient life on Earth." [366]

Knowing that we have the potential to become both conscious and aware of the essence that lies buried within, the essence that we all share, we also have the ability to be able to access our own personal unconsciousness, that some refer to as the void, for therein lies true enlightenment.

Become who and what you truly are by *listening to the God within you*.

---

[365] http://www.thesouljourney.com/?a_aid=195
[366] http://www.heartcom.org/2011QuantumShift.htm

A Metaphysics Primer

Become who and what you truly are by both knowing and accepting that *God speaks through feelings*, for they will be your guide to truth, directing you onward toward your individual path of enlightenment.

As you continue to expand in both your knowingness and your wisdom, so do you continue to expand the consciousness of all life, which is what God is.

To be *happy*, to be *joyful*, to be *filled with peace*; this is the way back to the kingdom within.

To *know that God is not separate from you*, to *know that you and God are one and the same*; this is the way back to the kingdom within.

The path chosen by each individual is wholly unique to that person.

A Metaphysics Primer

Each path is a valid one, all leading to the same destination, all leading to their truest nature as guided by compassion.

This is why it is of the utmost importance to *feel the feelings*, to *engage the emotions*, to *think the thoughts*; for *they* are what shall *allow you to experience yourself* in all ways.

The darkness is a most powerful catalyst; something that must be reconciled within each and every being.

There are many feelings and emotions that find their root in the dark, those that you have come to know as fear, rage, anger, hate, jealousy, depression, control, violation, incest, suspicion, denial, pain, judgment, illness, disease, death, greed, bitterness and retribution.

The darkness is as much a part of you as is the light.

There is, however, a way to avoid the power of this darkness, a power which lies in making choices that do not embrace the dark.

Allowing darkness to exist does not mean that such has become your choice.

Allowing darkness to exist does not mean that it has been condoned by you.

Allowing darkness to exist simply indicates that you have acknowledged the existence of this force, a force that actually serves to remind us of the exact opposite.

Every event in life serves as a catalyst that moves you into new experiences of yourself.

Allowing is what provides you with the opportunity to transcend the polarities of light and dark, a feat that you accomplish by embracing both as equal expressions of the same force from whence you come.

In breaking the cycles of collective response, you become the higher choice.

Mastery of compassion means redefining what your world means to you.

It is not about forcing change upon the world around you.

You, and only you, choose how you respond.

As a being of compassion, you are offered the opportunity to *transcend polarity while still living within the polarity.* This is what enables you to move forward with life, a life filled with freedom, resolution and peace.

Living a new truth must first start with the individual.

You must have the wisdom and the courage to embrace this new life, this new truth, as your reality.

This reality must then be lived in a world that may not always support that truth.

A Metaphysics Primer

This was the undertaking of the entire earthly mission of the one we have come to know as Yeshua (Jesus).

Life is a spiritual endeavor.

You are asked to become that which you most desire (peace, compassion, forgiveness, love) in your life.

Be *not afraid* to demonstrate your Becoming. The healing of this world will come about as a result of the healing of your thoughts, feelings and emotions.

Who among you is willing to live the truth of a higher response?

Who among you is willing to live the truth of what life has always had to offer?

By virtue of service to yourself and others, so, too, do you serve the Creator; it is in this way that you *Become* the greatest gift that you can offer.

A Metaphysics Primer

Your ability to express forgiveness, allowing others the outcome of their own experiences, without changing the nature of who you truly are, is the highest level of mastery to which you can attain.

Therein lies the healing of all illusion, all separation, all duality.

As in the truly remarkable Japanese "kokoro" (heart and soul), this is exactly what must happen for all ...... a merger of heart and mind, so that all of us may continue, in the years ahead, to live as we have always been meant to live.

In the words of Dr. Richard G. Petty ... *We are all imbued with some splinter of God consciousness, that God is experiencing through us, that we have purpose and that our relationship should be one of partnership rather than domination or servility. We should live a life that allows the expression of this intelligence, because in that way we evolve, grow and achieve ultimate satisfaction and happiness. The brain is a filter rather than a creator of consciousness and it is possible to develop the brain so that more of this consciousness is able to manifest. This squares well with the recent data on neuroplasticity and the impact of meditation on the structure and function of the brain; these ideas are familiar to anyone who has studied Hindu, Buddhist or Taoist philosophy, or the writings of mystics and contemplatives who have described the universe as the body of God.* [367]

[22] The Alchemical Marriage

Based on everything that I have come to understand in my own journey, thus far, the point is *to know the Grail, not as a cup, but as a process*; a process through which our purpose is of a two-fold nature, meaning that [1] we can either "transcend matter; perpetually renouncing anything connected with the principle of power, and, thereby, attaining union with the principle of love," [368] or [2] we can "reclaim or redeem matter, spiritualizing and transforming it." [369]

---

[367] Olsson, Suzanne. (2005) <u>Jesus in Kashmir: The Lost Tomb</u> (pages 23 and 24). Charleston, SC: Booksurge.

[368] http://www.serenitytravels.com/cathar_missions.html
[369] Ibid.

A Metaphysics Primer

In reference to physical beings, lead is the base material, meaning "negative thoughts, lustful passions and harmful emotions, which the aspirant of alchemy must change, or transmute, into the spiritual or gold; lead represents the chaotic, heavy and sick condition of metal or the inward man [whereas] gold expresses the perfection of both metallic and human existence," [370] of which pure love is key.

Alchemy also teaches "the raising of vibrations: the belief in the ability to transmute or change matter to a higher level. One of the most important principles that the alchemists used has to do with the basic duality of the universe. The method of procedure to achieve the Philosopher's Stone is [none other than] the harmonizing of this duality." [371]

As such, alchemists believe that everything, including man, can be raised to a higher level of being.

---

[370] *Alchemy from the Spiritual Venturer* website accessed on April 2, 2012 at http://www.denverspiritualcommunity.org/Wisdom/Alchemy.htm
[371] Ibid.

A Metaphysics Primer

This is what is meant by the term *illumination*; a term that also references death of the earthly self.

In order to progress on the spiritual path, one must die to the old way of life (the ego, the illusions, the extravagances).

It is not to say, however, that we cannot enjoy physical possessions; the problem lies in the significance that they are given.

As we turn inward, through meditation or contemplative prayer, so, too, do we, once again, *become as little children*, in that we are able to reconnect with our true spiritual selves.

This heightened (elevated) consciousness enables us to combine body, mind and soul in a new way; a most powerful force for transformation.

Alchemists were sometimes known as the Fire Philosophers.

A Metaphysics Primer

From an allegorical point of view, they "sought to consume themselves in spiritual flames in order to find their true, pure, essential selves. The furnace was the human body, where hardened thoughts and emotions (metals) were to be heated in the hermetically sealed vessel of the mind until purified." [372]

Every time we are successful in disengaging from the ego (meaning the material and transitory existence), we find ourselves advancing closer to the spiritual values that bring true happiness and fulfillment. While this can be a painful process, so, too, is it a necessary one.

All must begin with this perfected feminine (meaning the heart) that "brings us to a most elevated state of the emotions: a peace and joy which is above the opposition of the duality of the natural." [373]

---

[372] *Alchemy from the Spiritual Venturer* website accessed on April 2, 2012 at http://www.denverspiritualcommunity.org/Wisdom/Alchemy.htm
[373] Ibid.

A Metaphysics Primer

Part of this process involves eliminating negative emotions from your life; such is accomplished by replacing them with positive ones (thereby leading to the actual transmutation process).

As one learns to spiritualize the mind in this way, a process that involves transmuting the intellect (the masculine component) so that the ego becomes willing to give up control to the developing Soul, the newly evolving spiritual consciousness, one must guard against becoming depressed.

A difficult and painful process, so, too, is it a process through which "the insight gained from the elevation of the emotions enables us to realize our inherent deficiencies." [374]

It is this very lengthy (slow) and diligent process that is often referenced as the *dark night of the soul*; a process that is instrumental to the awakening of consciousness.

---

[374] *Alchemy from the Spiritual Venturer* website accessed on April 2, 2012 at
http://www.denverspiritualcommunity.org/Wisdom/Alchemy.htm

A Metaphysics Primer

Eventually one arrives at the enhanced knowledge that in order to continue their spiritual growth, they must learn to stand their ground, maintaining their new belief set in the full knowing that they are responsible only for themselves.

This becomes the very beginning of conscious spirit residing within the physical body, an awakening that leads to the realization that "to become immortal, we must embrace our mortality, [and] to become truly spiritual beings, we must accept ourselves as we are, and also as we are becoming," [375] for therein lies the truth behind the alchemical marriage between the enlightened heart and the illumined mind; the result of which is, none other than, the Philosopher's Stone.

As the clear mind (uninhibited by the ego) joins with the heart, one's spiritual essence (one's purity of heart) shines forth most strongly, for this is "true integration, true wholeness; the sacred marriage of the mind or consciousness

---

[375] *Alchemy from the Spiritual Venturer* website accessed on April 2, 2012 at
http://www.denverspiritualcommunity.org/Wisdom/Alchemy.htm

with the heart or unconsciousness in one totally conscious being. At this point of conjunction, all opposition has been overcome." [376]

It must be remembered, however, that in learning to accomplish this wholeness, one has had to learn to embrace, and accept, their inherent weaknesses.

Let us now return to *the squaring of the circle,* a motto that reads ... *Make a circle out of a man and woman, derive from it a square, and from the square a triangle: make a circle and you will have the Philosopher's Stone.* [377]

It is the inner circle around the man and the woman that symbolizes the Chemical Marriage of the Mind and the Heart whist the square around this smaller circle represents

---

[376] *Alchemy from the Spiritual Venturer* website accessed on April 2, 2012 at http://www.denverspiritualcommunity.org/Wisdom/Alchemy.htm
[377] Ibid.

the four elements; none other than fire, earth, air and water; all of which are incorporated in the process. [378]

http://mormonmatters.org/2010/01/29/squaring-the-circle-balance-and-ideals/

---

[378] *Alchemy from the Spiritual Venturer* website accessed on April 2, 2012 at http://www.denverspiritualcommunity.org/Wisdom/Alchemy.htm

A Metaphysics Primer

The square, being four sided, also signifies the number 4, which reflects wholeness, the four directions, and so forth. [379]

With the triangle surrounding the square indicating the union of the body, soul and spirit, along with the implication of the result of this union, it is the apex, or the third point above, which further indicates the spiritual perfection that has, thusly, been achieved. [380]

The circle, thereby enclosing the whole diagram, represents a transformation of the body, mind and soul, one so complete that the man becomes the woman and the woman becomes the man; the two truly become one. [381]

---

[379] *Alchemy from the Spiritual Venturer* website accessed on April 2, 2012 at http://www.denverspiritualcommunity.org/Wisdom/Alchemy.htm
[380] Ibid.
[381] Ibid.

In truth, without the man (or mind) *and* the woman (or heart), there would be no Christ Consciousness or Illumination. [382]

The most important result of this marriage (of heart and mind) is the subsequent birth of the soul, the Christ; this is what alchemists sometimes called *the child of the Work*, meaning that this was the beginning of the building of an actual second body, the spiritual body wherein the Christ consciousness (the path to our own soul illumination) would dwell. [383]

It was Dr. R. Swinburne Clymer who wrote: "The extraordinary or spiritualized threefold man is the outgrowth of the four-square-man. After the ordinary man has awakened to a sense of something higher than life, as we daily see it, and has sought for, and found, the means to the

---

[382] *Alchemy from the Spiritual Venturer* website accessed on April 2, 2012 at http://www.denverspiritualcommunity.org/Wisdom/Alchemy.htm
[383] Ibid.

greater life, if truly interested he will then take active steps to develop every department of his fourfold nature." [384]

This means that "he will seek to learn just what the body requires, what it should be given and what should be withheld. He will endeavor, by every means in his power, to bring his body into as perfect a state as possible and make use of as much spirit as is necessary and become *spiritually alive*; that is to say, full of vitality, magnetism, virility or whatever we wish to name his life-full state." [385]

By gradual degrees, "he applies the mind to the development of the germ of the Immortal Soul within himself. He becomes the Builder. The Soul Spark is awakened and eventually becomes Illuminated. The Soul takes the place of the mind and man completes the circle. He has reversed the squaring of the circle and once again becomes a threefold being; a circle symbolized by the triangle." [386]

---

[384] *Alchemy from the Spiritual Venturer* website accessed on April 2, 2012 at http://www.denverspiritualcommunity.org/Wisdom/Alchemy.htm
[385] Ibid.
[386] Ibid.

A Metaphysics Primer

In keeping with this process, there are many lessons to be learned, there is much knowledge to be sought, and there is much wisdom to be attained and applied.

In direct association, it must be acknowledged that the working through of these highlighted lessons is a due process that spans many years, requiring much diligence.

In words that well have been attributed to Appollonius of Tyana, aka Yeshua ... *Be ye renewed through the renewing of your mind.*

The Lessons, Part 2

The lessons shared in Part 1 are the very lessons that have served to guide me over the course of these last twenty years. Given that as we expand ourselves, so too, do we expand the universe, I am ready for the next leg of the journey, as the saying goes, whatever that may be; hence, Part 2.

In the words of Edgar Cayce ... *Mind is the builder*.

I would also add that we must continue to take the time to *see with our heart* and *feel with all of our being*.

There are at least fifty different published scientific studies that both verify and validate the fact that when people get together to meditate with thoughts of love and peace, there are decreases in accidents, crime, war and other related (negative) factors.

Why is it that this has been proven to work?

A Metaphysics Primer

David Wilcock proposes that it is *because we are all sharing the same mind, to some degree*, which takes us back to the fact that everything in the Universe is ultimately One Mind (the Source Field).

As a result, "those people with the greatest coherence affected the brain wave patterns and biorhythms of others who were close to them." [387]

As he further proposes, if "seven thousand people can reduce worldwide terrorism by 72 percent, this suggests the Source Field is significantly biased in favor of positive emotions rather than negative ones." [388]

In fact, we can scientifically prove that "by simply focusing on a positive attitude in your own life, you are helping to reduce war, terrorism, suffering and death." [389]

---

[387] Wilcock, David. (2012) The Source Field Investigations (page 92). London, England: Dutton.
[388] Ibid.
[389] Ibid, page 93.

We also know that "simple meditations on love and peace can actually change the behavior of people out in the world." [390]

Now that we can see how "strongly a small group of people can affect everyone's behavior on a mass scale, the idea that the real world is like a lucid dream or a hologram doesn't seem so crazy-sounding after all. What if the rules of the dream world actually do apply to the physical world? If so, then all these global disasters may actually be symbolic reflections of our own inner distress: our fear, pain, sorrow and anger." [391]

Even though it may seem as if you are doing nothing, by simply keeping focused on love, peace and positivity, you are contributing to the collective whole, doing far more than you will ever know.

---

[390] Wilcock, David. (2012) <u>The Source Field Investigations</u> (page 93). London, England: Dutton.
[391] Ibid.

A Metaphysics Primer

In essence, you are helping the whole of mankind.

You need naught fall into the doom and gloom trap of faceless fear, for whatever we project outward to others will be projected back to us, whether one is ignorant of this fact or not.

In essence, we heal the other person(s) by healing ourselves.

This works because, as stated before, in the greater sense, we are all sharing the same Mind.

If ever you feel that something is not well, with yourself, with the world, you *can* do something about it.

We are living a shared, collective, lucid dream, with the soul being akin to a quantum computer hardwired into the Universe. As stated before, we share thoughts and feelings with all living things.

We damage to our cells, as well as our DNA, when we get stressed out or go through negative emotions.

Dr. Glen Rein, a biochemist, has proven that "love has a direct, measureable effect on DNA. Greater coherence, greater organization, greater structure and greater crystallization; all these effects show us that the energy fields, molecules and cells of our bodies are working in greater harmony and Unity. For the first time, this actually gives us a scientific definition of love. Love can now be seen as a basic principle of universal energy; the more coherence, the more structure, the more harmony we have, the more love there is." [392] [393]

In the mirroring words of Ramtha ... *Love is the glue that holds everything together.*

---

[392] Wilcock, David. (2012) The Source Field Investigations (page 173). London, England: Dutton.
[393] http://www.mystical-moment.com/LOVE.html

A Metaphysics Primer

The Source Field is limitless when it comes to energy supply. If you "start to feel drained, you can replenish yourself by moving into a state of coherence: the loving space, coming from the heart, keeping your mind quiet and peaceful; all appear to actively rejuvenate your batteries in a very short time." [394]

Toni Elizabeth Sar'h Petrinovich also concurs. [395] [396] [397]

As we "make our thoughts more coherent, we may increase our ability to access the Source Field, and determine how and where it flows. This is a very important point, as it helps explain why so many ancient spiritual traditions place significant importance upon meditation." [398]

---

[394] Wilcock, David. (2012) The Source Field Investigations (page 179). London, England: Dutton.
[395] http://www.sacredspaceswa.com/documents/DNASpeaksThroughtheHeart.pdf
[396] http://www.youtube.com/user/sacredsarrah/videos
[397] http://www.sacredspaceswa.com/articles.cfm
[398] Wilcock, David. (2012) The Source Field Investigations (pages 181 to 182). London, England: Dutton.

A Metaphysics Primer

Meditation serves to create coherence in the Source Field, and this, in turn, affects "everyone else's minds directly, since we all share consciousness with each other in a measurable sense, and this is truly a fascinating new way of looking at ourselves and the world." [399]

In keeping with the current aspect of my individual journey, here are some topics that I am *beginning to explore* in more depth.

[1] Layers of Thought

We have all experienced the noise (chatter) of the mind. In truth, many of the lessons shared in Part 1 were useful in assisting me to become more masterful of my thoughts, emotions, and actions, whilst living in the moment.

I very much appreciate what Jim Self has to share in reference to the seven layers of thought.

---

[399] Wilcock, David. (2012) <u>The Source Field Investigations</u> (page 182). London, England: Dutton.

A Metaphysics Primer

° The first layer of thought is where one speaks without thinking.

So, too, is this the layer whereby the individual is generally unconscious of being unconscious, meaning that they go "about their day in a default-mode versus being conscious and intentional. Those who have not awakened spiritually live here. [However], those who are more awake and self-aware may *still* find themselves in this layer of thought"[400] whenever unnecessary comments, or gossip, have been contributed to a conversation that is already noisy.

This is *clearly* the layer of thought that exists in many work environments, as most of us have been already privy to.

° The second layer of thought is where you have either conversations or arguments, with other people, in your head.

This is where you "go back and forth, in your mind, about the situation and how you were right/bad/wrong/hurt [and

---

[400] http://spiritlibrary.com/jim-self/the-seven-layers-of-thought-part-1

how] the other person [was] wrong/bad/hurtful/stupid. Guilt and blame lives here; so do resentment and revenge."[401]

We have all experienced these loud, commanding, realistic, and all too consuming, conversations. From an energetic standpoint, the other person is in full receipt of the energies you are throwing at them.

° The third layer of thought is where you "figure things out, strategize, and problem solve. There is still a bit of motion here, and an internal, back and forth type of conversation, [with your mind] bouncing around trying to find an answer."[402]

° The fourth layer of thought is the pondering phase; the "first non-engaged, non-invested layer of thought [whereby] there is no emotional attachment, judgment or pre-definition of answers or possibilities. The process unfolds by itself and you are simply watching the process from a place of neutral

---

[401] http://spiritlibrary.com/jim-self/the-seven-layers-of-thought-part-1
[402] Ibid.

curiosity;" [403] basically, the detached observer that I have discussed in Part 1.

○ The fifth layer of thought is where "your consciousness begins to naturally, organically, pull together many of the floating, curious pieces, combining them with the deeper, unconscious aspects of you, [whereby they begin] to [become] organize[d] in such a way that you become much more conscious, focused and capable with your innate knowledge." [404]

This is the layer that "takes the curious interest of the fourth layer (the field of possibilities), and brings it to your mental workbench, to organize and become more real as a possibility. This is done, not with greater thought or concentration, but with a greater quietness, allowing, stillness and trust." [405]

---

[403] http://spiritlibrary.com/jim-self/the-seven-layers-of-thought-part-1
[404] http://spiritlibrary.com/jim-self/the-seven-layers-of-thought-part-2
[405] Ibid.

This is the layer of thought "that is inspired. Many artists and writers create when in this layer. The creation process just flows and the book writes itself." [406]

This is an excellent description of what I have often been privy to, as a writer; in truth, there have been countless times when it certainly felt as if the book had written itself.

When totally engaged in the writing/research process, I find myself completely in the zone.

° The sixth layer of thought is "the extremely quiet place where you begin to access deeper fields of awareness. You begin to think (or, better yet, exist) without thought. This occurs because you are in the higher fourth and fifth dimensional fields of knowledge. You begin to have conscious access to the greatness that you are." [407]

While I have yet to master the fifth layer, I am very much drawn to the descriptors of this sixth layer.

---

[406] http://spiritlibrary.com/jim-self/the-seven-layers-of-thought-part-2
[407] Ibid.

A Metaphysics Primer

This is the level "where the Rays of Creation truly begin to be used to arrange, and rearrange, all possibilities without any limitations. You [are able to] rearrange the frequencies of thought, change the harmonics of matter, [applying] the elements of love in such a manner that, on your terms, you [can] begin to instantaneously produce, in simultaneous time, whatever you desire. As you play at this and become more masterful, building more templates, more platforms to create from, more structures to live your life from, these fifth and sixth layers are where you live most of your day, fully integrated [with] the creative universal mind of Creator." [408]

° The seventh layer of thought is the place we all aspire to find ourselves; namely, a place whereby thought is not definable.

This is the place "where the thought-that-thought-you-into-existence and you think together; the place where you have a relationship with your Soul. [While this] may be unimaginable to you, your Soul has much to do with the

---

[408] http://spiritlibrary.com/jim-self/the-seven-layers-of-thought-part-2

creation of you; Creator created you, but your Soul also created you. [When] your Soul, within the higher aspect of Creator, and you begin to think together, in the unified field, you are no longer a third dimensional being. You are then beginning to play, very consciously, in the fifth, sixth, and seventh dimensions; [you have become] a citizen of those dimensions." [409]

Now, that, my friend, sounds like a slice of heaven.

There is a major shift underway; its predominant purpose being "for you to *become conscious of being conscious*, aware of being aware, integrating enough light into your mental and emotional body" so that you are able to release the negative third dimensional thoughts and emotions, reactions and resistances, because "when you can clear that energy from your emotional and mental bodies, you can begin to play at the sixth and seventh layer of thought. You will begin to change from a carbon-dense body, [one] that does not absorb light, to that of a crystalline nature of light,

---

[409] http://spiritlibrary.com/jim-self/the-seven-layers-of-thought-part-2

[one] that will allow a very significant transformation of your physical body." [410]

As you become the quiet observer of your thoughts and patterns, the noise will lessen. This is why the stillness of understanding, the knowingness, the ancient call to self knowledge, is so important.

There is another important aspect of the shift; namely, that our cells are moving away from each other, thereby creating more space in between them which then allows for more light to fill those available spaces. That is one of the reasons why a person is then called enlightened.

[2] The Ray of Creation: Gurdjieff

The Ray of Creation is an intrinsic part of the esoteric system of thought put forth by George Ivanovich Gurdjieff, an influential spiritual teacher of the early to mid 20th century.

---

[410] http://spiritlibrary.com/jim-self/the-seven-layers-of-thought-part-2

Gurdjieff taught that "the vast majority of humanity lives their entire lives in a state of hypnotic waking sleep, but that it was possible to transcend to a higher state of consciousness and achieve full human potential," [411] creating a discipline called *The Work* as the means for doing so.

As a result of the condition whereby *man lives his life in sleep, and in sleep he dies*, to use Gurdjieff's words, "each person perceives things from a completely subjective perspective. He [further] asserted that people in their typical state function as unconscious automatons, but that one can *wake up* and become a different sort of human being altogether." [412]

Gurdjieff argued that "many of the existing forms of religious and spiritual tradition on Earth had lost connection with their original meaning and vitality, [in that they were no longer able to] serve humanity in the way that had been intended at their inception. As a result humans were failing to realize the truths of ancient teachings, and were, instead,

---

[411] http://en.wikipedia.org/wiki/Gurdjieff
[412] Ibid.

becoming more and more like automatons, susceptible to control from outside." [413]

Parallel with other spiritual traditions, Gurdjieff taught "that one must expend considerable effort to effect the transformation that leads to awakening." [414]

This is the very reason as to why he referenced his discipline as *The Work*.

In keeping with the fact that the head, the emotions, and the body each have their own perceptions and actions, Gurdjieff taught people "how to increase and focus their attention and energy in various ways, [all in an effort] to minimize daydreaming and absentmindedness. According to his teaching, this inner development in oneself is the beginning of a possible further process of change, the aim of which is to transform people into what Gurdjieff believed they ought to be." [415]

---

[413] http://en.wikipedia.org/wiki/Gurdjieff
[414] Ibid.
[415] Ibid.

When alignment has been achieved between the mental, emotional and physical bodies and both the higher self and the soul, "the mental body will be calm and peaceful, the emotional body stable, even and joyous, and the physical body healthy with good even energy throughout the day." [416]

Not trusting the use of the term morality (which varies significantly from culture to culture, often in quite contradictory and hypocritical ways), Gurdjieff greatly "stressed the importance of conscience. This he regarded as the same in all people, [although] buried in their subconsciousness, thus both sheltered from damage by how people live [as well as] inaccessible without [the necessary] work on oneself." [417]

According to Gurdjieff, *the awakened conscience is the something more* which is "the only force in modern man's nearly completely degenerate psyche that can actually bring parts of his nature together, [thereby opening] him to that energy and unnamable awareness of which all the religions

---

[416] http://www.scribd.com/doc/51572387/2/The-Monad-Soul-and-Personality (page 143)
[417] http://en.wikipedia.org/wiki/Gurdjieff

have always spoken as the gift that descends from above, but which in the conditions of modern life is almost impossible to receive." [418]

In essence, *The Work* is all about training the development of consciousness.

The Ray of Creation, shown on the following page, is a diagram, consisting of eight levels, which better represents the place which Earth occupies in the Universe; a diagram that is also part of an ancient and historical knowledge. [419] [420]

---

[418] http://www.gurdjieff.org/needleman2.htm
[419] http://en.wikipedia.org/wiki/File:Ray_of_creation.jpg
[420] http://en.wikipedia.org/wiki/File:Bodiesrayofcreation.JPG

A Metaphysics Primer

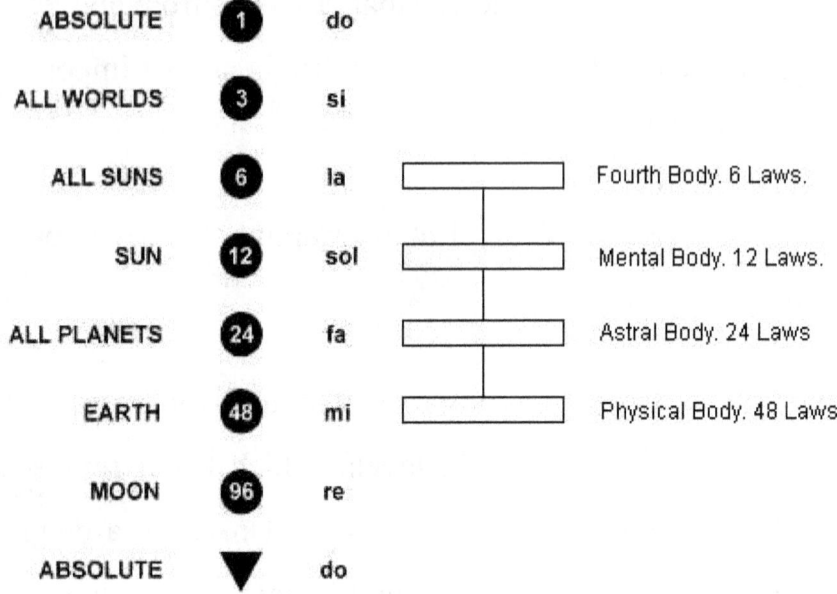

http://en.wikipedia.org/wiki/File:Bodiesrayofcreation.JPG

In keeping with the Ray of Creation diagram, the physical body has the properties of the Earth level (meaning that it has a density of 48 and it is subject to 48 laws).

In comparison, a higher plane body would have a lighter density; as well, it would be subject to a lesser number of laws (meaning that the amount varies on the level that the body falls under).

The Absolute, then, is the fundamental source of all creation and it is from the Absolute that "the process of cosmic creation branches and descends according to an ordered sequence of increasing complexity and density, following the law of the octave. The universe, as a whole, [is comprised of] countless such branchings from the Absolute; this particular diagram represents the *ray* containing our planet Earth." [421]

Centers (Fourth Way) [422]

Gurdjieff (free ebooks) [423]

Gurdjieff and Sufi Paths [424]

Gurdjieff Foundation of Canada [425]

---

[421] http://www.gurdjieff.org/needleman2.htm
[422] http://en.wikipedia.org/wiki/Centers_(Fourth_Way)
[423] http://www.messagefrommasters.com/Ebooks/Gurdjieff_Ouspensky_Books/Gurdjieff_and_Ouspensky_Books.htm
[424] http://www.angelfire.com/ca3/gurdjieffsufi/
[425] http://www.gurdjieff.ca/

A Metaphysics Primer

Gurdjieff International Review [426]

Gurdjieff Internet Guide [427]

Gurdjieff Legacy: The Teaching For Our Time [428]

Gurdjieff Movements [429] [430]

Gurdjieff Studies [431]

Gurdjieff's System of Human Development aka *The Work* [432]

Gurdjieff Teachings [433]

Gurdjieff: The Man and the Literature [434]

---

[426] http://www.gurdjieff.org/
[427] http://www.gurdjieff-internet.com/
[428] http://www.gurdjieff-legacy.org/
[429] http://www.gurdjieff-movements.net/
[430] http://en.wikipedia.org/wiki/Gurdjieff_movements
[431] http://www.gurdjieff.org.uk/
[432] http://eap.mcgill.ca/publications/EAP13.htm
[433] http://www.messagefrommasters.com/Life_of_Masters/Gurdjieff/Gurdjieff.htm
[434] http://www.gurdjieff.org/moore1.htm

Sarmoung Brotherhood [435]

The Gurdjieff Foundation of Atlantic Canada [436]

The Gurdjieff Society [437]

The Gurdjieff Studies Program [438]

[3] The Rays of Creation: Jim Self

The Rays of Creation are a huge body of work, brought forth by the Archangelic Realm and Beings of Light through visionary Jim Self in his work Mastering Alchemy.

The first Ray of Creation is referred to as the Will of the Creator. [439] This Ray contained "everything in total alignment with the Creator's intention. This first Ray was very vast. One of the new components, contained [within], excited the creator Gods very much; [this new component] was called free will. Up until that point, free will was not

---

[435] http://en.wikipedia.org/wiki/Sarmoung_Brotherhood
[436] http://www.gurdjieffatlanticcanada.com/
[437] http://www.gurdjieff.com/
[438] http://www.gurdjieffstudiesprogram.org/
[439] http://lightworker.com/Spectrum//articles/576/1/The-Story-of-the-Fall-of-Consciousness--Part-One/Page1.html

available; [hence], the creator Gods had always followed the original blueprint." [440]

Given free will, over time their creations contained "less of the intention of the Creator and much more of their own unique intention. This continued to be noticed by Creator, as there were growing numbers of these creations made without the full, original Light. To bring about a correction, [thereby assisting] these creator Gods in returning to the use of the original blueprint, two new Rays of Creation were given to all of the creator Gods. [As] there was free will, it was only suggested they be used; these Rays provided opportunities to expand [the] All-That-Is." [441]

The second Ray of Creation, drawn from the first Ray, "holds all color. Until then, color had never been experienced. The second Ray also held the capacity to step energy up and step energy down, much like a transformer,

---

[440] http://lightworker.com/Spectrum//articles/576/1/The-Story-of-the-Fall-of-Consciousness--Part-One/Page1.html
[441] Ibid.

[thereby bringing] about many more possibilities of creating in larger and smaller ways." [442]

The third Ray of Creation "holds frequencies and sub-frequencies in many different configurations and arrangements; energetics, they are called. These are enormous building blocks of constructive energy, which hold all possibilities." [443]

Based on these explanations, one can clearly see how the first, second and third Rays of Creation were used during the creative process.

These three Rays were developed "to uplift the distorted creations, raising them back to higher levels of Light. The Creator wanted these distorted creations and the creator Gods, themselves, to return to using the original blueprint that was in greater alignment with [the] All-That-Is." [444]

---

[442] http://lightworker.com/Spectrum//articles/576/1/The-Story-of-the-Fall-of-Consciousness--Part-One/Page1.html
[443] Ibid.
[444] Ibid.

Other Rays of Creation were also offered freely by the Creator, with the intention to bring everything back into the original Light. As a result of free will, however, it needs to be realized that creations cannot be taken back or erased.

One mistake we often make when trying to manifest is that "our energy and emotion does not match our mental intention." [445] It becomes essential, then, that one "must increase [their] vibration and release the heavier energies of pain, disappointment, lack, doubt, or unworthiness, for example, to match the new reality [they] wish to experience." [446]

[4] The Monad

The person that you are (as well as the person that you will become when you are no longer physical) is your spirit; basically the nonphysical essence of you, free from time and space. [447]

---

[445] http://www.selfgrowth.com/articles/manifesting-with-the-rays-of-creation-in-2012
[446] Ibid.
[447] http://www.wisdomsdoor.com/rc4/hrc4-07.shtml

A Metaphysics Primer

The spirit is the "closest you will come to your present physical individuality, once free of the body." [448]

The next link upward is your higher self; your prototype, so to speak. [449]

This is the part of you that "exhibits and possesses all of your best and most proficient qualities. Your higher self is the person you should always ascribe to becoming; the person that you can evolve into, from your present perspective." [450]

Continuing upward is the Soul (with a capital S), the caring, nurturing force that "helps you to become that higher self you ascribe to be. Your Soul is the force you should reach to when seeking any guidance, or aid, related to your present growth. Your Soul cares for you as a mother, but does that caring in a way that a teacher cares for her students." [451]

---

[448] http://www.wisdomsdoor.com/rc4/hrc4-07.shtml
[449] Ibid.
[450] Ibid.
[451] Ibid.

A Metaphysics Primer

The last step in the upward chain brings us to the Monad (also known as the Entity with a capital E).

The Monad, the original entity that was created by All There Is, sends out aspects of itself to register all new experiences into the soul of each incarnation.

The Monad contains "many Souls, [making it] a direct aspect of the force you know of as God. Your Monad supplies you with the life-force, love, and attention that you need to maintain your existence. Your Monad is ultimately responsible for your evolution, within the body of God." [452]

Your Monad is you eons from now, when you "have evolved past being human, past being eternal, past being omnipotent. In essence, your Monad is one shade away from God and is one aspect of God that makes you, your spirit, your higher-self, and your Soul uniquely you." [453]

---

[452] http://www.wisdomsdoor.com/rc4/hrc4-07.shtml
[453] Ibid.

A Metaphysics Primer

The relationship you have with your Monad is "one of deep love and devotion; like a Father's love: that strong, protective, ever-forwardly moving force toward a journey's end." [454]

All of these selves exist, both part, and separate, from you, much akin to looking at a past reincarnate self wherein the past self is separate from you and yet is a part of what you once were. [455]

All these other selves, then, are an aspect of you, meaning that "there exists a connection (or thread) between each of your selves. This thread is what enables knowledge to pass from a more evolved self to a less evolved self, [thereby] binding all the selves together. It is to your advantage, [therefore], to maintain the connection between the more anchoring aspects of yourself (like your higher self, Soul, and Monad), so that you can take advantage of the wisdom and knowledge that exist there." [456]

---

[454] http://www.wisdomsdoor.com/rc4/hrc4-07.shtml
[455] Ibid.
[456] Ibid.

The Monad can also be referenced as an individuated spiritual spark of the Creator; likewise, so, too, has the Monad also been referred to as the I AM presence. [457]

The Monad, or spiritual spark, decided (with free choice) that it wanted to experience itself in all ways, meaning, quite simply, that it wanted to experience a denser form of the material universe than it was living in. [458]

[5] The Power of Words

According to Rudyard Kipling ... *Words are, of course, the most powerful drug used by mankind.*

According to Sundardas ... *You should think carefully before you speak; words should be uttered with great discrimination.*

According to Yeshua (Jesus) ... *For what goes into your mouth will not defile you; but what comes out of your mouth, that is what will defile you.*

---

[457] http://www.scribd.com/doc/51572387/2/The-Monad-Soul-and-Personality (page 15)
[458] Ibid.

A Metaphysics Primer

One of the key ingredients of spiritual happiness is "to be aware and careful about the words we use, [in that] words are the currency through which thoughts take form in our minds, and with which they are expressed outwardly." [459]

With continued repetition, our words become "even stronger and more engrained in the consciousness of ourselves, of those who are receiving our words, and perhaps into the planetary web of consciousness as well, [making words] powerful currencies that deserve great respect and care." [460]

I so very much like what Sharon Janis has to say as she compares us to "magicians, knowingly or unknowingly, reciting mantras, hexes, blessings, and other potent and magical words every time we speak. Some ancient philosophical scriptures explain that the entire world as we know it is created by words. In Sanskrit, the term for this creative energy that expresses through syllables and words to create the universe is *Matrika Shakti,* the Mother Power.

---

[459] http://www.spiritual-happiness.com/sosh16.html
[460] Ibid.

A Metaphysics Primer

Therefore, respect this awesome power of words, and attend to how you're spending the currency of your words with at least as much care as you watch your financial spending." [461]

While it is fine to use words to discuss your burdens with friends, you must also remember that every time you put your troubles into word form, you may be solidifying them that much more; instead, [1] see if you can phrase your words in more constructive and positive ways, [2] catch yourself while speaking, and [3] ask if the benefit of sharing your troubles in word form is worth giving more power to those troubles. [462]

---

[461] http://www.spiritual-happiness.com/sosh16.html
[462] Ibid.

A Metaphysics Primer

If you intentionally speak, and think, good (happy, uplifting) thoughts, if you intentionally (and immediately) replace harmful thoughts with positive thoughts, you will be using the "alchemy behind using positive affirmations to change your life." [463]

While we do not think that the effect of words can be described in either psychological or spiritual terms, many may be quite surprised to discover that, in truth, this is the reality.

On a purely psychological level, "every single word we speak, and every single word we hear, goes into our subconscious minds and creates some small or large effect there. How these words affect our psyches and attitudes are inevitably going to have a powerful effect on how we experience, interpret, and respond to the events of life." [464]

---

[463] http://www.spiritual-happiness.com/sosh16.html
[464] Ibid.

A Metaphysics Primer

On a spiritual level, by comparison, "our subconscious minds are also reflections and facets of the Great Universal Mind of God. Whatever words you input into your personal mind are also being fed into the Great Universal Mind that creates all the circumstances of your life, including your experience of spiritual happiness." [465]

As Kristen Houghton puts it, we have "at our disposal a power that can change lives, make a sick spirit healthy, encourage success, guide those who need it, make or break relationships and create a lasting impression of us as people. That power is the power of words." [466]

As Anastasia of the Siberian tiaga has stated throughout the Ringing Cedars series, *Man is Creator*.

In keeping, so, too, is God Creator.

---

[465] http://www.spiritual-happiness.com/sosh16.html
[466] http://www.huffingtonpost.com/kristen-houghton/the-incredible-power-of-w_b_1014316.html

A Metaphysics Primer

It is my personal belief that God is thought; henceforth, thought is also Creator.

After all, was not the beginning stated as being the word?

What was word, then, if not thought?

Man, therefore, creates his own reality through thought.

It all comes down to *what does Man wish to create*, does it not?

In the words of Mohandas Karamchand Ghandi, otherwise known to the world as Mahatma Ghandi … *Happiness is when what you think, what you say, and what you do are in harmony.*

The more positive power words you add to your thoughts and speech, the more you will raise your spiritual vibrations and elevate your consciousness.

A Metaphysics Primer

Absolutely, Abundant, Adventure, Amazing, Amity, Appreciation, Astounding, Authentic, Awareness, Awesome

Beaming, Beautiful, Believe, Benefit, Blessed, Bliss, Boundless, Brilliant

Celebrate, Committed, Compassion, Complete, Connected, Content, Contentment, Creative

Delight, Determined, Discover, Divine

Easily, Ecstatic, Effervescent, Effortless, Elated, Elegance, Empathy, Energy, Enthusiastic, Exceptional, Exciting, Exhilarating, Expand, Explore, Exquisite, Extraordinary, Extravagant

Fabulous, Fantastic, Flawless, Flourish, Freedom, Friendship

Generous, Grace, Graceful, Gratitude

Harmony, Healthy, Heavenly, Highest Good, Honest, Hug

I affirm ……

I allow ……

A Metaphysics Primer

I can ……

I choose ……

I trust ……

Ideal, Imaginative, Imagine, Impressive, Incredible, Infinitely, Ingenious, Innovative, Inspired, Intuitive, Invincible

Joy, Jubilant, Jubilation

Keen, Kind, Kindness, Knowledge,

Laugh, Learn, Let Go, Love, Luminous

Magnificent, Marvelous, Meaningful, Meditate, Metamorphosis, Mindful, Miracles, Mission, Motivate

Naturally, Now, Nurture

One, Optimistic, Out of this world, Outstanding, Overjoyed

Peace, Perfect, Phenomenal, Pleasure, Plentiful, Plenty, Plethora, Positive, Powerful, Prepared, Productive, Prosperous, Proud, Purpose

A Metaphysics Primer

Quest, Quiet

Radiant, Ready, Recognize, Refinement, Rejoice, Rejuvenate, Relax, Remarkable, Renew, Renowned, Resplendent, Resolution, Resources, Respect, Restore, Rewarding, Rich, Robust

Safe, Secure, Serenity, Shift, Silence, Simple, Sincerity, Smile, Solution, Soul, Sparkling, Spirit, Spiritual, Splendid, Spontaneous, Still, Stunning, Stupendous, Success, Sunny, Superb, Superlative, Support, Supreme, Sustain, Synchronistic, Synergy

Team, Thankful, Therapeutic, Thorough, Thrilled, Thrive, Tolerance, Together, Tranquil, Transform, Triumph, Trust, Trust

Unbelievable, Unity, Unlimited, Unparalleled, Ultimate, Unwavering

Value, Venture, Vibrant, Victory, Vision, Visualize, Vital, Vivacious, Voyage

A Metaphysics Primer

Wealthy, Welcome, Well, Whole, Wholesome, Willing, Wonder, Wonderful, Wondrous

Xanadu

Yes, Yippee, Youthful

Zeal, Zest

Jim Self talks about seven *living* (powerful and energetic) words ... [1] Happy, [2] Certain, [3] Powerful (as in Capable), [4] Commanding, [5] Present, [6] Senior (as in owning your Self) and [7] Gracious. He shares that "finding and BEING the vibrations of Certain and Happy (try Appreciation and Gratitude, too) is the beginning of your ascension. You are creating a platform that will allow you to observe the third dimension as it simply dissolves and reshapes itself into the fifth dimension." [467]

---

[467] http://lightworker.com/Spectrum//articles/407/1/The-Living-Words/Page1.html

A Metaphysics Primer

If I may end this segment with the words of Florence Scovel Shin ... *Today is the day of my amazing good fortune.*

[6] Key Aspects of the 3rd, 4th, 5th, 6th and 7th Dimensions (in relation to the Chakra System)

We are currently transitioning from a 3rd dimensional (matter based) to a 4th dimensional (emotion based) experience.

One of the most important parts of this shift is the "energetic transition in individuals from a Solar Plexus centered awareness to a Heart centered awareness" [468] in that it is this awakening that further "initiates a new cycle of unlocking the Throat, Third-Eye and Crown." [469]

The Throat (Communication) Center is about "recognizing the true meaning of Communication. Our relationship to all existence unfolds through the language of consciousness,

---

[468] http://people.tribe.net/adamapollo/blog/9141f47a-1db2-44bb-8bb6-a28e09827153
[469] Ibid.

and when we learn this language, we begin to discover perfect patterns inherent within every conversation. This is 5th dimensional consciousness, recognition of Divine Will, and communion with it." [470]

It is also on this dimensional layer that "we begin to recognize that we are not only connected to others in a very physical sense through swimming in the pool of space-time together, but that our actions ripple through these waters. We begin to recognize that our voices resonate both inside of time, and outside of the boundaries of matter. Our ideas can be shared instantaneously, and our actions perceived physically, even by those who are thousands of miles away. We even begin to see how our actions in the distant past can affect us in the present." [471]

---

[470] http://people.tribe.net/adamapollo/blog/9141f47a-1db2-44bb-8bb6-a28e09827153
[471] Ibid.

The Third Eye (Spiritual) Center unfolds through our awareness "of the spiritual vibration infusing all of the crystalline fabric of space-time; we suddenly feel the flow of the Universe in its many permutations. This dimensional layer [the 6th] opens our awareness to each other's vibration, and we begin to perceive the way that slight changes in our emotional field ripple through the fabric of consciousness. We begin to tune into the frequency changes of others, both in our local space and in distant places. We start to see ourselves constantly in communion, naked in this shared emotional space. This is a transition of great vulnerability and transparency, and is a powerful point of choice when one decides to either remain open, honest, and transparent, or cloak themselves in shadow, trying to hide what is within them from others, and often from themselves." [472]

---

[472] http://people.tribe.net/adamapollo/blog/9141f47a-1db2-44bb-8bb6-a28e09827153

A Metaphysics Primer

The Crown Center aligns us "with the complete state of absolute truth and trust in everything in every moment. This trust goes beyond a feeling, or an external confirmation externally; it is simply known. This knowing precedes all feeling and manifestation, and continuously blooms further and further as we are willing to allow ourselves to dissolve in Divine Mind." [473]

It is also on this same dimensional layer [the 7th] that we begin to perceive everything "in perfect patterns. We notice the Divine speaking to us through signs, showing us our eternal destinies reflected in each and every thought, feeling, and physical experience that comes our way. All doubt that everything is perfect fades, and this knowing flows forth from us in the radiance of confidence, awakening the core of our Solar Plexus. This is the space where all of our minds are in communion, and where all knowledge can be known." [474]

---

[473] http://people.tribe.net/adamapollo/blog/9141f47a-1db2-44bb-8bb6-a28e09827153
[474] Ibid.

[7] Key Aspects of the 3rd, 4th, 5th and 6th Dimensions (in relation to this physical embodiment)

First of all, it is important to understand that we are *not* being punished for being wretched, sinful, creatures, and for being cast out of heaven.

Instead, we volunteered, wholeheartedly, for this experiment in separation, so that we could experience ourselves in the most infinite of ways.

Every dimension is either male or female; all odd numbered dimensions are male, whilst all even numbered geometries are female.[475] In continuation, every male geometry is more dense (from a physical perspective) and every female geometry is less dense (more etheric).[476]

---

[475] http://www.zakairan.com/ZaKaiRansArticlesBooks/Articles/Dimensions1Creation.htm
[476] Ibid.

A Metaphysics Primer

For example, this means that even though the 5th dimension is more physical then the 4th dimension, it is still situated at a higher vibration.

As well, each dimension has consciousness to it, an inherent way of perceiving the reality of that dimension.

We have been living in a 3rd dimensional existence; a dense physical existence that is dominated by [477] [478] [479]

° a reality of survival, competition and control

° a realm where suffering is a tragedy that can be prevented by taking 3D action

° limitation and polarity consciousness (between the dual forces of dark and light)

---

[477] http://www.zakairan.com/ZaKaiRansArticlesBooks/Articles/Dimensions1Creation.htm

[478] http://www.bibliotecapleyades.net/ciencia/ciencia_dimensionshyperdimensions02.htm

[479] http://www.salrachele.com/webarticles/dimensionsanddensities.htm

A Metaphysics Primer

° patriarchal control

° conformity

° left brain

° false male dominant

° technologically oriented

° generally devoid of feeling, love, and any form of cooperation (unless one benefits)

° the belief that what one can see, hear and touch, is real; all else is illusion (fantasy)

° dominated by victim consciousness

° the lie of unworthiness (which led to lack consciousness, as in the haves and have nots, classes, national pride, racism, sexual discrimination, environmental degradation, the mass slaughter of animals for food and habitat destruction for greed)

° the religious perspectives of sin, judgement, penance, punishment and distorted teachings of karma

A Metaphysics Primer

In having adopted this limited 3D perception, one that has embraced guilt, shame, fear and unworthiness, we have been able to efficiently explore the illusions of separation, a separation that also led to "the suppression of truth, knowledge, and the magical arts; reality altering substances; witch burning; indigenous spiritual suppression; the general suppression of free expression by fearful religious zealots, and political fear mongering." [480]

Along with the illusion that there are two opposing forces (the dark and the light), the existing competition is merely a perceptual one in that "without the balance of the dark and light, this dimension, this reality, could not exist. If too much light [were to come] in too fast, this reality would transition, dimensionally, [far] too quickly, essentially imploding." [481]

From a higher perspective, then, we are all working to maintain different levels of balance.

---

[480] http://www.zakairan.com/ZaKaiRansArticlesBooks/Articles/Dimensions%204th.htm
[481] Ibid.

A Metaphysics Primer

Here comes something that I needed to know more about.

There are, in effect, roughly four forces in the Universe; namely, [1] the light forces, [2] the dark forces, [3] the neutral forces, and [4] the twilight forces.

[1] The light forces "are ascension team experts; their job is to bring in as much light as possible to transition planets to higher dimensions." [482]

[2] The dark forces "explore separation, denial of oneness, and everything that goes with it to its fullest degree, [all in an effort] to create dense physical form and to balance the light force." [483]

On planet Earth, these beings "could be referred to as the position team members. The position team members set up structure, and transition team members tear it down by

---

[482] http://www.zakairan.com/ZaKaiRansArticlesBooks/Articles/Dimensions%204th.htm
[483] Ibid.

enlightening these old dense forms to higher potentials by quickening the vibration." [484]

[3] The neutral forces are here, merely to witness what is happening. [485]

[4] The twilight forces "serve the forces of light and dark; they are the double agents. They are often extremely tricky (and ultimately confused), even though they may act extremely passionate and sure of themselves. Often these beings have attained a certain level of awareness, but go no further, (having hit a wall in their consciousness), due to some past suffering, and lack of healing (forgiveness) of lost aspects. They often lack considerably in compassion. They are often prone to spiritual ego, glamour and the use of 4th dimensional *magical* arts. Often these are false gurus, who use subtle psychic manipulation to obtain energy from fearful adoring followers. They may often try to undermine light workers, attack[ing] them in sneaky underhanded ways,

---

[484] http://www.zakairan.com/ZaKaiRansArticlesBooks/Articles/Dimensions%204th.htm
[485] Ibid.

using spiritual justification for their attacks. This is when they are in their dark side." [486]

As you can see, and rather surprisingly so, it is quite the balanced system.

By comparison, the 4th dimension has been characterized as being that which involves [487] [488] [489] [490]

° female dominance

° the realm of karma (cause and effect) whereby everyone creates their own version of reality (meaning that we are not responsible for the karma of another)

° a world of time, thought and mind

---

[486] http://www.zakairan.com/ZaKaiRansArticlesBooks/Articles/Dimensions%204th.htm
[487] Ibid.
[488] http://www.in5d.com/residing-in-the-5th-dimension.html
[489] http://www.bibliotecapleyades.net/ciencia/ciencia_dimensionshyperdimensions02.htm
[490] http://www.salrachele.com/webarticles/dimensionsanddensities.htm

A Metaphysics Primer

° individuality and creativity

° the realm of feeling and intuition, spiritual sensing and knowing

° the pagan realm of psychic energies, clairvoyance, sensing, magic, wicca (basically, the feminine energies that the patriarchal religions tried to destroy and repress)

° creating a balance between spirit and form

° less density (which means that manifestation occurs at a quickened rate)

° the realm of the dreamtime: fairies, elves, unicorns, Mer people, spirit guides, nature spirits, etc.

° developing an intimate connection to your emotional body

° living more in trust; living the truth of your being

° believing in yourselves without need for outer approval

° trusting in your inner guidance to form your decisions without need of logical comparisons and tally sheets

A Metaphysics Primer

° finding the pinpoint place, within, that knows which direction you should take in each moment (along with the knowing that knowing this direction will change from moment to moment, something that you accept)

° trusting that directional guidance is always available

° becoming very comfortable with change (without fear)

° developing an understanding of what it means to become a conscious breather (meaning that you realize your intimate connection with all life with every breath; the way that dolphins and whales breathe)

° a shift in perceptual awareness and breathing from a survival orientation (solar plexus chakra of the 3rd dimension) to a Christ Consciousness orientation (heart love chakra of the 4th dimension)

° beginning to open to higher chakric levels (5th D reality) of God/Goddess Consciousness

A Metaphysics Primer

In summation, one is mostly living within a 4th dimensional frequency when you live "more and more in trust [whilst] your nature returns to [a sense of] oneness with all surrounding you here, [while in residence] on the planet. When you react less to what appears to be and [begin to] live in foundational awareness of what truth is, you live in trust, and not in circumstance, [which is] is 3rd dimensional awareness." [491]

The 5th dimension (one which constitutes invisible space) has been discussed as being the Lightbody dimension, one whereby you [492] [493] [494] [495]

° move with the trust of who you are into who you are becoming (as a physical being moving into non-physical while in the physical realm)

---

[491] http://www.in5d.com/residing-in-the-5th-dimension.html
[492] http://www.2012.com.au/dimensions.html
[493] http://www.in5d.com/residing-in-the-5th-dimension.html
[494] http://www.bibliotecapleyades.net/ciencia/ciencia_dimensionshyperdimensions02.htm
[495] http://www.salrachele.com/webarticles/dimensionsanddensities.htm

A Metaphysics Primer

° are aware of yourself as a multidimensional being

° are completely spiritually oriented

° live completely from love and compassion (which is normal, natural and spontaneous)

° see that we are not separate, that we are one being, living in one universe, created by one God

° live with the understanding that by remaining open and empty, the Universe can manifest miracles through you

° co-create with others, as a mature spiritual being, whilst respecting the individuality of all

° share your vision, cosmic identity, and insights freely and naturally

° know, and accept, that miracles are a given

A Metaphysics Primer

The 6th dimension, then, is one whereby [496] [497]

° clarity of thought is the gift, allowing you to embrace unity of thought as a way of life

° we come to the realization that if God were to physically walk on this planet, it can only be through us

° we are inspired, non-dualistic beings that are serving to hold the balance, thereby helping people move higher

° we have graduated from the healthy ego functionality of the 5thdimension to the liberating freedom of the impersonal life

° we are the cause, rather than the effect

° we have the ability to seize control of our innate divine or celestial power

° we have remembered that we are spiritual beings having a physical experience

---

[496] http://connect2source.com/elev8dimension6.htm
[497] http://unhypnotize.com/spirituality-spiritual/3552-understanding-dimensions-how-they-apply-you.html

A Metaphysics Primer

° truth is its own frequency, vibration and reward

° there is no room for subservience to a Christ, Avatar, Buddha, Quan Yin, Mother Mary, or any external authority Guru or Guide

In the 6th and subsequent dimensions, we prepare for, and then engage in, the only game worth playing: "God in a Bod." [498]

Whilst I cannot say that I am a full-fledged master of these understandings, I do hope that my research is serving to enlighten you, the reader.

[8] The Power and Influences of Sacred Geometry

Tradition holds that over the entrance to Plato's Academy were written the following words: "Αγεωμετρητος μηδεις εισιτω." [499]

---

[498] http://connect2source.com/elev8dimension6.htm
[499] http://www.halexandria.org/dward095.htm

A Metaphysics Primer

If one were to convert the font above to Greek letters, it would read: *"Only he who is familiar with geometry shall be admitted here."* [500]

Sacred Geometry is "a language that nature uses to create and communicate with itself. When you tap into the power of Sacred Geometry, you are tapping into the energy that connects all living things. Sacred Geometry has been taught by the great Sage's of the past and it influences our culture every day," [501] based on how we feel, think, act, and react on a daily bases, although generally without our inherent knowledge.

Taking this definition one step further, Sacred Geometry, is the study of "the universal language of truth, harmony, beauty, proportion, rhythm and order; a blueprint of creation, an interface between the seen and unseen, the

---

[500] http://www.halexandria.org/dward095.htm
[501] http://sacredgeometry.com/about-us/

manifest and unmanifest, often described as the Architect of the Universe." [502]

When we take the time to admire the architecture of pyramids, chapels, temples, cathedrals, the Merkaba, the Star of David, the Flower and Tree of Life, Metatron's Cube, Platonic Solids (of which there are five: cube, tetrahedron, icosahedrons, dodecahedron and octahedron), the humble Nautilus Shell (the physical representation of the number PHI, also known as the Golden Mean), Crop Circles, Labyrinths, as well as Christian symbology (the Cross and Vesica Piscis), for example, we have been drawn into the world of Sacred Geometry; a world that encompasses art, form, pattern and geometric shapes.

I am convinced that my Visual Arts, right brain, daughter lives in the world of Sacred Geometry, thereby bringing it into my life through the works that she creates, first within her mind's eye, and subsequently manifests.

---

[502] http://academysacredgeometry.com/

A Metaphysics Primer

As so brilliantly shared by John Koch, "buildings can have a profound influence on our health and our psychic and spiritual state of be-ing. Harmony and balance, light and colour, relationship to landscape, ecological sympathy, energy efficiency and geometric form are contributing elements of shelter which aspires to be nurturing rather than draining. We resonate at both cellular and consciousness levels with our environment. By creating an environment around us that is supportive to both our inner and our outer senses, we can enhance rather than alienate our human links with nature. Architecture, when employed as a means of embodying principles of universal harmony can sustain us rather than drain us, so that our homes become our havens, and our work places support our creativity." [503]

A great many of us have experienced (lived) these very words.

---

[503] http://www.labyrinth.net.au/~jkoch/sacred.html

A Metaphysics Primer

Academy of Sacred Geometry [504]

Ancient Knowledge (3.5 hour movie) [505]

Sacred Geometry [506] [507] [508] [509] [510] [511] [512]

Sacred Geometry and Labyrinths [513]

Sacred Geometry and Sound Therapy [514]

Sacred Geometry Course [515]

Sacred Geometry Explained, Part 1 of 2 [516]

Sacred Geometry Explained, Part 2 of 2 [517]

---

[504] http://academysacredgeometry.com/
[505] http://www.youtube.com/watch?v=xAWf3F8_zQk
[506] http://www.thetemplateorg.com/geometry.html
[507] http://www.sacredgeometry.org/
[508] http://www.spiraloflight.com/ls_sacred.html
[509] http://www.luminanti.com/geometry.html
[510] http://earthacupuncture.info/sacred_geometry.htm
[511] http://www.birdtribes.net/sacredgeometry.htm
[512] http://www.ancient-wisdom.co.uk/sacredgeometry.htm
[513] http://labyrinthsociety.org/sacred-geometry
[514] http://www.sacred-geometry-and-sound-therapy.com/
[515] http://sacredgeometry.com/sacred-geometry-course/
[516] http://www.youtube.com/watch?v=rx31y1KKK3E
[517] http://www.youtube.com/watch?v=Zyw3RhmRlsQ

A Metaphysics Primer

Sacred Geometry in Building [518]

Sacred Geometry International [519]

Sacred Geometry in the Quantum Realm [520]

Sacred Geometry Introductory Tutorial [521]

Sacred Geometry: The Modern Mystery School [522]

Sacred Places: Sacred Geometry [523]

San Graal: The School of Sacred Geometry and Alchemy [524]

Sedona School of Sacred Geometry [525]

The Quintessential Guide to Sacred Geometry [526]

---

[518] http://www.labyrinth.net.au/~jkoch/sacred.html
[519] http://sacredgeometryinternational.com/
[520] http://divinecosmos.com/contact-us/privacy-policy/97-the-divine-cosmos-chapter-03-sacred-geometry-in-the-quantum-realm
[521] http://www.geometrycode.com/sacred-geometry/
[522] http://mms.new-paradigm.net/description/sacred-geometry
[523] http://www.arthistory.sbc.edu/sacredplaces/sacredgeo.html
[524] http://www.sangraal.com/
[525] http://www.schoolofsacredgeometry.org/
[526] http://www.barcodesinc.com/articles/the-quintessential-guide-to-sacred-geometry.htm

The Meaning of Sacred Geometry [527]

The Sacred Geometry of Crop Circles [528]

The Sacred Geometry of Music [529]

Vesica Institute for Holistic Studies [530]

Why Sacred Geometry? [531]

[9] Recapturing the Center of the Brain (the Pineal gland)

The Pineal gland has long been referred to as the Third Eye (also known as the inner eye), the locus of occult power and wisdom, located in the center of the forehead (which can be activated through the practice of yoga).

---

[527] http://sacredgeometryinternational.com/the-meaning-of-sacred-geometry
[528] http://www.cropcirclesecrets.org/crop_circles_sacredgeo.html
[529] http://www.harmonisphere.com/SacredGeometryOfMusic.htm
[530] http://www.vesica.org/
[531] http://www.bibliotecapleyades.net/geometria_sagrada/esp_geometria_sagrada_3.htm

According to the Kundalini yoga teachings, your third eye chakra, which is the sixth of your seven chakras, is responsible for "intuition, clarity and sensing the future. Your third eye can be a helpful chakra when attempting to make a decision. Activating the third eye chakra can be difficult if you are not fully concentrated on your task. That is why setting a stopwatch can give you the confidence to meditate without time getting away from you as you open your third eye." [532]

Lynn Claridge says that "to activate the third eye and perceive higher dimensions, the pineal gland and the pituitary body must vibrate in unison, which is achieved through meditation and relaxation. When a correct relationship is established between personality, operating through the pituitary body, and the soul, operating through the pineal gland, a magnetic field is created." [533]

---

[532] http://www.livestrong.com/article/339369-how-to-activate-the-third-eye-chakra/
[533] http://www.newageinfo.com/activate-3rd-eye.htm

In fact, it was René Descartes (1596 to 1650) who argued that the mind interacted with the physical body through the pineal gland, thereby giving us the reasoning behind his *seat of the soul* reasoning.

While I am yet to activate my Third Eye, I am considerably lucky to be able to share that I have been residing in an area, since 1985, where the water supply has never been fluoridated.

A Fluoride-Free Pineal Gland is More Important than Ever [534]

Chakra Meditation Technique to Open Third Eye [535]

Clairvision School [536]

---

[534] http://www.naturalnews.com/026364_fluoride_pineal_gland_sodium.html
[535] http://anmolmehta.com/blog/2007/05/03/ajna-chakra-meditation-technique-3rd-eye-free-guided-meditation-book-for-daily-practice/
[536] http://www.clairvision.org/books/ate/awakening-the-third-eye-excerpts.html

A Metaphysics Primer

Experiences after Third Eye Opening [537]

Fluoride and the Pineal Gland [538]

Keeping Your Pineal Gland Healthy [539]

Personal Tao: What Is the Third Eye? [540]

Pineal Gland [541]

Pineal Gland Activation [542]

Pineal Gland, Our Third Eye: The Biggest Cover-up in Human History [543]

Pinecones, Paganism, the Pineal Gland and Fluoride [544]

---

[537] http://www.personal-development-coach.net/third-eye-opening.html
[538] http://www.youtube.com/watch?v=XSZQ3ixu7a4
[539] http://hyper-borealis.blogspot.ca/2010/02/keeping-your-pineal-gland-healthy.html
[540] http://personaltao.com/taoism-library/what-is-the-third-eye/
[541] http://www.tokenrock.com/explain-Pineal-Gland-73.html
[542] http://humanityhealing.net/services/pineal-gland-activation/
[543] http://www.wakingtimes.com/2012/06/19/pineal-gland-our-third-eye-the-biggest-cover-up-in-human-history/
[544] http://fanaticforjesus.blogspot.ca/2011/01/pine-cones-paganism-pineal-gland.html

A Metaphysics Primer

Sun Gazing (an ancient practice) [545] [546] [547]

The Gate of God [548]

The Health Benefits of Sungazing [549]

The Mysterious Pineal Gland [550]

The Pineal Gland and The Ancient Art of Iatromathematica [551]

The Pineal Gland: The Bridge to Divine Consciousness [552]

The Source Field Investigations (full video) [553]

---

[545] http://www.ayahuasca-wasi.com/2011/sungazing/
[546] http://www.earthclinic.com/Remedies/sun_gazing.html
[547] http://keenawareness.blogspot.ca/2012/02/solar-healing-pineal-gland-activation.html
[548] http://garyosborn.webs.com/gateofGod(dess).htm
[549] http://www.globalhealingcenter.com/natural-health/health-benefits-of-sungazing/
[550] http://Godsdirectcontact.us/sm21/enews/www/133/ss.htm
[551] http://www.astrology-research.net/researchlibrary/Iatr/pineal.htm
[552] http://www.miraclesandinspiration.com/pinealgland.html
[553] http://divinecosmos.com/start-here/davids-blog/959-sourcefieldvideo

Third Eye, Activation and Basic Usage [554]

Third Eye Pinecones [555]

Why the Pituitary is preventing the Pineal from Manifesting Instantly [556] [557] [558] [559] [560] [561] [562] [563] [564] [565]

[10] Right Brain Magic

If you were to look down through the top of your head, onto the cortex of your brain, you would see that it is made up of two halves called hemispheres: one on the left (the left brain) and one on the right (the right brain).

---

[554] http://jksalescompany.com/dw/third_eye.htm
[555] http://www.conesandstones.com/historical-symbolism.html
[556] http://www.futureofmankind.co.uk/Billy_Meier/Pineal_Gland
[557] http://keenawareness.blogspot.ca/2012/02/solar-healing-pineal-gland-activation.html
[558] http://sharonlynshepard.wordpress.com/2010/09/21/marriage-of-the-pituitary-and-pineal-glands/
[559] http://spiritlibrary.com/earth-keeper/earth-keeper-chronicles/mechanics-of-law-of-belief
[560] http://whispersfromthesoul.com/the-tribunal/pineal-pituitary-activation-proces/
[561] http://www.theosociety.org/pasadena/man-evol/mie-16.htm
[562] http://missionignition.net/bms/ba_wings_of_isis.php
[563] http://www.rickrichards.com/chakras/Chakras1c.html
[564] http://www.rickrichards.com/chakras/Chakras1d.html
[565] http://garyosborn.webs.com/gateofGod(dess).htm

A Metaphysics Primer

In keeping, the left and right brains are connected by an intricate network of nerve fibres called the corpus callosum.

The ancient Egyptians noticed that the left brain controls the right side of the body whilst the right brain controls the left side of the body.

Although each hemisphere is almost identical in terms of structure, each hemisphere operates in an entirely different way and is associated with very different activities; this is known as specialization or lateralization.

There was a time when the left and right brains were used together, in harmony; perhaps this is what actually lies behind religious narrative and myths that describe "an expulsion from Paradise or fall from a state of perfection." [566]

In accordance, this recent, and intriguing, theory states that "in most of us, thinking is dominated by the analytical processes typically associated with the left brain, and these

---

[566] Phillips, Charles. (2011) <u>Pocket Posh: Left Brain, Right Brain</u> (page 2). Kansas City, MI: Andrews McMeel Publishing LLC.

A Metaphysics Primer

tend to make us feel fearful, anxious, and separate from one another. Our perception of separateness leads us to think that we should fight for pre-eminence and resources, and to believe that we can find happiness by achieving success at the expense of others. But we could regain calm and a sense of connection to other people and to our surroundings by learning, once again, to think with the whole brain." [567]

While the right hemisphere was largely unaltered, Graham Gynn and Tony Wright, in their book, Left in the Dark, suggest that the left hemisphere became dominant. [568]

In referring to the right brain as the creative brain, this right hemisphere of the brain is related to rhythm, spatial awareness, color, imagination, daydreaming, motivation, creativity and intuition, feelings and emotions, long term memory, suggestion, psychic skills, spirituality, holistic

---

[567] Phillips, Charles. (2011) Pocket Posh: Left Brain, Right Brain (page 2). Kansas City, MI: Andrews McMeel Publishing LLC.
[568] Ibid, page 4.

awareness and dimension; in short, you could equate it to the *subconscious* mind.

Characteristics of a right brain thinker include [569]

[1] thinking in pictures (words must illustrate picture thought; ability to see abstract in picture words or design, such as prose)

[2] day dreaming

[3] acute spatial awareness (able to size up situations without measuring, ability to see the whole in parts)

[4] inverting of numbers

[5] difficulty with higher math (abstract math)

[6] being unlikely to read instructions (unless all else fails)

[7] sensitivity (feelings easily hurt, can be defensive, can also be a romantic at heart)

---

[569] http://www.rightbrainintelligence.com/braindominanttest.htm

A Metaphysics Primer

[8] a dislike of structure (anything that is too organized inhibits freedom to create)

[9] being a visionary (goal setter)

[10] engagement with people skills (social and charismatic)

[11] being empathetic (feeling deeply for others)

[12] a tendency to think while speaking (without editing what they are saying)

[13] us of metaphors (flowing, descriptive, action words)

[14] thinking outside the box (improve, problem solve, recreate or go outside given limits)

[15] having a difficult time to stay on task (easily distracted)

[16] creativity (must create from an artistic standpoint)

[17] gets bored easily (must be inspired or boredom sets in)

[18] tending to be positive (looks for the good, the silver lining in just about everything)

A Metaphysics Primer

[19] being passionate (strong emotions)

[20] having trouble with spelling and grammar (affects ability to read and write)

[21] displays intuition (gut feeling)

[22] creative writing (tends to write fiction over fact based books; better at essays)

[23] impulsivity (jumps into projects and relationships, or takes risks without considering the consequences)

[24] being a storyteller (like to illustrate through stories)

[25] being prone to wander (random thinkers whose mind wanders; may stop in the middle of a thought and begin talking about something else)

[26] humor (visual illustrative humor)

[27] being impatient (waiting is difficult)

[28] being involved in the fine and visual (drama, painting, drawing, music, dance, photography, computer art, as well as anything else that deals with artistic expression)

[29] needing approval (a people pleaser)

[30] taking risks (like challenges)

[31] pliability (flexible, able to compromise easily)

[32] learning lessons the hard way (need to personally experience)

[33] hyperactivity (the mind jumps around or feels hurried)

[34] ability to be inventive (need to problem solve or invent something to make life easier)

[35] ability to motivate (charismatic personality)

[36] being intuitive (make decisions based on gut feelings)

[37] being concrete (need to give clear picture of what is being said)

[38] does not do well on tests (scan reads, picks up partial meaning of the sentence)

[39] tends towards dyslexia (reading letters and words backwards, misplacing letters, numbers or not being able to sound out letters or words)

[40] displays disorganization (records, receipts, keys or other important items)

In referencing the left brain as the logical brain, it is this left hemisphere of the brain that is associated with language, intelligence, logic, thinking, short term memory, language reasoning, problem solving, judgment, analysis, lists, linearity and sequence; in short, you could equate it to the *conscious* mind.

It is this side of the brain that utilizes the scientific method long associated with educational institutions (via math, reading, spelling, memorizing, critical thinking and grammar).

A Metaphysics Primer

Characteristics of a left brain thinker include [570]

[1] thinking in words (they do not need illustrations to understand what has been read; they understand abstract words)

[2] good spellers

[3] good with numbers and higher math

[4] perfectionism

[5] analytical (able to analyze problems, thinking through situations before making a decision)

[6] articulate verbal skills

[7] following the rules

[8] reading directions

[9] displays organization (like things in their proper place)

[10] giving attention to details

---

[570] http://www.rightbrainintelligence.com/braindominanttest.htm

A Metaphysics Primer

[11] making lists

[12] rigidness (not pliable, non-negotiable)

[13] tending to be cynical and sarcastic (abstract humor)

[14] enjoyment of reading

[15] doing well on tests

[16] sequential processing (order, linear processing)

[17] black and white absolutes (facts, rules and absolutes are important; there is no gray)

[18] ability to remain focused (easily stays on task)

[19] learning how to play instruments easily

[20] loyalty (faithfulness)

[21] carefulness (not impulsive)

[22] liking structure (needs guidelines and rules; runs a tight ship)

[23] having a good memory (facts, numbers, faces and names)

[24] enjoyment of teaching

[25] demonstrating cluelessness to feelings

[26] needing to question (tends to debate)

[27] being an avid record keeper (banking, papers and incidents)

[28] singing in pitch

[29] learning languages easily

[30] an importance to perform well

[31] being a gatekeeper to new ideas (generally a "no" person)

[32] being easily annoyed (imperfect people, lack of professionalism)

[33] enjoyment of documentaries

[34] being an auditory learner

[35] note taking

[36] having good grammar skills

[37] enjoyment of research

[38] security

[39] the ability to be negative and critical (imperfection in themselves, others or situations may lead to critical thinking)

[40] the preference for writing fact over fiction

My daughter is right brain dominant; as a result, she had an extremely difficult time learning in the heavily left-brain school environment, as did Albert Einstein, Thomas Edison, Leonardo da Vinci, Michelangelo and Bill Gates, to name but a few. [571]

---

[571] http://johnngd.hubpages.com/hub/Want-More-Brain-Power---Tap-Into-the-Right-Side-of-Your-Brain

A Metaphysics Primer

As a Visual Arts student, engaged in drawing, painting and photography, she is now finally able to excel.

It has been suggested that stimulating both sides of your brain increases your brain power. Learning to access the right side of your brain (also known as the R-Mode of your brain) is the first thing that must take place.

As we already know, there are two ways of knowing and seeing things.

The verbal and analytic mode deals with numbers and words whereas the visual and creative side deals with emotions and visual images (our perception of the world around us). In keeping, these two sides use very different parts of the brain.

Drawing is unique in that it accesses part of the brain that we infrequently use; the secret to tapping into this unused part of your brain, therefore, may be as easy as spending time drawing every day.

The Divine Masculine has long been affiliated with the attributes identified with the left hemisphere of the brain, meaning that the Divine Feminine has been connected with the attributes associated with the right hemisphere of the brain.

In learning how to use the right side of your brain, you can speak to your body. In speaking to your body, so, too, can you receive answers (intuition).

In learning how to use the right side of your brain, you can connect with your higher self, a connection that allows you to access "the doorway to all the knowledge that you have ever gathered through all of your journeys on Earth and other planets. This knowledge comes from your soul monad and it holds a database of all information that you have gathered since your soul was created. Your higher self also communicates with other souls. Using the right side of your brain you will be able to ask your higher self to bring people, and opportunities, into your life to complete your personal objectives. You can use your higher self for guidance for the path of your highest good." [572]

---

[572] http://www.rightbrainmagic.com/

A Metaphysics Primer

As shared in an earlier portion of the text, it was Albert Einstein who stated these words ... *The intuitive mind is a sacred gift; the rational mind is a faithful servant. We have created a society that honors the servant and has forgotten the gift.*

It is now time to re-awaken the spiritual abilities associated with right brain.

Brain Enhancement Program [573]

Exercises to Build the Right Side of the Brain [574]

Right Brain Activities for Home Practice [575]

Right Brain Activity [576]

---

[573] http://www.brainomagic.com/
[574] http://www.livestrong.com/article/124412-exercises-build-right-side-brain/
[575] http://figur8.net/baby/2010/07/27/right-brain-activities-for-home-practice-part-1/
[576] http://www.kundalini-tantra.com/rtbrain1.html

Right Brain Exercises [577] [578]

Right Brain Magic [579]

The Neuroscience of Mindfulness [580]

Tricks to Activate Both Sides of the Brain [581]

Writing Prompts for the Right Brain [582]

[11] Soul Age

As we reincarnate "from lifetime to lifetime on our soul's path, gathering experiences, learning lessons, and fulfilling agreements, an evolutionary process transpires and that course of development is called Soul Age." [583]

---

[577] http://www.learningrx.com/right-brain-exercises-faq.htm
[578] http://www.buzzle.com/articles/right-brain-exercises.html
[579] http://www.rightbrainmagic.com/
[580] http://www.mindfulnet.org/page25.htm
[581] http://articles.timesofindia.indiatimes.com/2012-06-18/health/31838254_1_human-brain-hemisphere-controls-grey-cells
[582] http://writingfix.com/right_brain.htm
[583] http://clevelandohiousa.tripod.com/oursoulage/

A Metaphysics Primer

Soul age refers to "how a person has grown from experience on the planet, not just [based on] how many lifetimes he or she has lived. No person is "ahead" or "behind" another; [they are] simply occupying another place in the continuous circle leading to and from the Tao." [584]

Most mature (old) souls eventually develop the "mature soul viewpoint of strong valuation of togetherness. If the true soul age is old, then acceptance of others' differences and less following of the crowd eventually become more important than togetherness." [585]

The more old souls "can come to accept that *everything has value but nothing has importance*, the happier and less stressed they will be. This is essentially the same as the Taoist idea of *do nothing and everything will get done*. For old souls, things may be valuable and of more value than other things; but that does not make them important. As soon as something becomes important, then this is a sign of

---

[584] http://clevelandohiousa.tripod.com/oursoulage/
[585] http://www.helpself.com/new-age/soul-age.htm

attachment, which is appropriate for young and mature souls, but will ultimately be a source of stress and difficulties for old souls." [586] It is also important to note that "real passion in centered old souls implies something valuable to them, but does not imply attachment." [587]

The Karmic Cycle is "the process of thought materializing into deed (be it good or bad). This is a difficult journey (cycle) for people [because their initial thoughts] tend to determine what happens in their life. Normally, there is little, to no, conscience to help [them] in the making of decisions, until later on in life; they will often hold a great many regrets once they begin to form more of a belief structure. Newer souls tend to struggle all their life with many issues like self-confidence, determination, stress management and so on." [588]

---

[586] http://www.helpself.com/new-age/soul-age.htm
[587] Ibid.
[588] http://www.psychicguild.com/articles_view.php?id=1002

A Metaphysics Primer

Older souls are those that are "often not concerned with material things and the physical world. Their self-esteem [is] very high and their personalities are more introverted; meaning they will look inside and listen to themselves, more than they do societal structures and family. Older souls generally [find the answers they are seeking] within themselves. They have a regal aura about them." [589]

There are also some difficult problems for older souls, in that "from a young age they are bored of the world. It takes highly complex things to amuse them, and they often find it difficult to fill the day. [With a mind that is typically strong and resistant to problems], they sleep less than others; typically *un*concerned with minor things, [they] are fairly blunt when it comes to senseless dramas, often making them appear very cold and callous." [590]

---

[589] http://www.psychicguild.com/articles_view.php?id=1002
[590] Ibid.

Even though older souls "have stronger minds, this makes them more vulnerable to mental health problems such as depression and bi-polar syndrome. They see the world for what it is, and cannot stand it. They tend not to latch onto anyone unless they get that certain feeling they have known each other previously from a past life; a process can take many, many years leaving them lonely for a long time. The term ignorance is bliss really makes sense to them; [they often] think of their intelligence as more of a curse than a blessing." [591]

With each reincarnation, we come back with a broader mind, until eventually we have acquired all of the knowledge, learning and understanding needed; this, then, enables each to move toward a more advanced learning, something that is not possible in the physical world. In effect, we are here to enjoy the journey.

---

[591] http://www.psychicguild.com/articles_view.php?id=1002

A Metaphysics Primer

Age of the Soul: Letting Go of Judgment [592]

Being an Old Soul in a Young Soul World [593]

Discerning Planetary Origin and Soul Age through Astrology [594]

Living with Soul: An Old Soul's Guide to Life, the Universe and Everything [595]

Reincarnation: The 35 Steps of Soul Evolution [596]

Soul Age Levels [597]

Stage 1: The Infant Soul [598]

---

[592] http://www.dailyom.com/library/000/001/000001675.html
[593] http://www.livingwithsoul.com/being-an-old-soul.htm
[594] http://www.celestialvision.org/planetary-origins-ebook/
[595] http://www.livingwithsoul.com/index.htm
[596] http://personalityspirituality.net/articles/the-michael-teachings/reincarnation-the-35-steps/
[597] http://the-turtles-back.blogspot.ca/2008/07/soul-age-levels.html
[598] http://personalityspirituality.net/articles/the-michael-teachings/reincarnation-the-35-steps/stage-1-the-infant-soul/

Stage 2: The Baby Soul [599]

Stage 3: The Young Soul [600]

Stage 4: The Mature Soul [601]

Stage 5: The Old Soul [602]

Study of the Soul [603]

[12] The Nine Universal Needs

In the Michael teachings there are "nine *universal needs* that act as unconscious motivators in our lives, inspiring us to evolve spiritually, and to seek out the lessons most appropriate for our growth." [604]

---

[599] http://personalityspirituality.net/articles/the-michael-teachings/reincarnation-the-35-steps/stage-2-the-baby-soul/
[600] http://personalityspirituality.net/articles/the-michael-teachings/reincarnation-the-35-steps/the-young-soul/
[601] http://personalityspirituality.net/articles/the-michael-teachings/reincarnation-the-35-steps/stage-4-the-mature-soul/
[602] http://personalityspirituality.net/articles/the-michael-teachings/reincarnation-the-35-steps/stage-5-the-old-soul/
[603] http://www.vopus.org/en/gnosis/study-of-the-soul/
[604] http://www.michaelteachings.com/nine_needs_index.html

These needs are [1] security, [2] adventure, [3] freedom, [4] expansion, [5] power, [6] expression, [7] acceptance, [8] communion and [9] exchange.

[13] Alignment of Right Action, Right Heart, Right Thought

The prophecies of the ancient Americas speak about the years leading up to, and beyond, 2012 as being a time of great change and transformation; a time that will "initiate the appearance of a new human on the planet (Homo-luminous), a Being of Light, consciously connected to the matrix of life; a person of wisdom and power who lives free of fear, resides in their eternal nature, lives in harmony with all beings and accepts guardianship of all creation." [605]

This new Being will live in alignment of right action, right heart and right thought, living that which Buddha affirmed with these words ... *You are what you think. All that you are arises from your thoughts. With your thoughts you make your world.*

---

[605] http://portalsoftranscendence.com/services/munay-ki-rites/

A Metaphysics Primer

The nine great Rites of Enlightenment, known by the Inca Q'ero Paq'os (Shamans) of Peru, as the Munay-Ki, are the Rites of Passage.

Quechua is the language spoken by the native people of the Americas. Munay-Ki is a Quechua word that means *I love you* or *Be as Thou Art*.

Machu Picchu © Charles J. Sharp 2012

http://en.wikipedia.org/wiki/File:Machu_Picchu_early_morning.JPG

A Metaphysics Primer

Dr. Alberto Villoldo received these Rites from the Laika, the high wisdom keepers of the Peruvian Andes and the Amazon; he has brought them to the west in the universal form that I, too, have experienced.

These nine Rites "are said to have been derived from the great initiations from the Hindus Valley that were brought to the Americas by the first medicine men and women who crossed the Bering Straits from Siberia during the glacial period some 30,000 years ago. These courageous travelers were the Laika, the Earthkeepers of old." [606]

These sacred Rites "realign and attune our neuro-pathways and shift our consciousness. They empower us to step-up to the task of assuming 'Stewardship' for the Earth and all of Creation. It is the hope of the Inca Shaman that these Rites get passed to as many people as possible. The time is now,

---

[606] http://www.munaykiawakening.com/Welcome.html

A Metaphysics Primer

and there are enough of us with raised vibration and good intent to lead our spiritual evolution." [607]

A torus or pi shaped stone is used "as a tool in many of the Rites, (a donut-shaped carved stone), which uses its Sacred Geometry to act as a vortex of energy, or a hyper-dimensional gateway, to an invisible realm of spirit." [608]

The torus "is the three dimensional shape of a donut. This shape allows energy to flow up through the center and then wrap around to flow back down on the outside in a constant three dimensional circling. It is said that energy circulates in and around us in a similar pattern, rising in the core, through the crown and down around the luminous energy field that surrounds the body. The cycle repeats continuously." [609]

---

[607] http://www.exploremeditation.com/munay-ki/
[608] Ibid.
[609] http://www.steppingintofreedom.com/munay-ki/pi-stones

A Metaphysics Primer

A Shaman trained in the Peruvian heritage, courtesy of Dr. Alberto Villoldo, Alison Normore [610] recently relocated to Bonne Bay, Newfoundland. [611]

Long drawn to ancient spiritual practices, like Shamanism, it was a privilege to connect with Alison in order to experience the first four Rites of the Munay-Ki, also known as the Foundation Rites; namely, [1] the Healer's Rite, [2] the Bands of Power, [3] the Harmony Rites and [4] the Seer's Rites, over the course of an intense two day weekend workshop (December 1 and 2, 2012). All are transmission rites that prepare one's luminous energy field to hold the vibration and power of the initiations that follow thereafter.

Alison explained the importance of right action (lower chakras) being completely aligned with right heart (heart chakra) and right thinking (upper chakras) to the Laika people; clearly, this is how we are meant to live.

---

[610] http://www.alisonnormore.com/
[611] http://www.alisonnormore.com/about_newfoundland.html

Right action "is what you do with your body. If you live without discrimination, without fear, everything you do can help the planet survive." [612] Right action often involves prayer, chanting and meditation.

Right heart (intention) pertains to one's heart always being in the right place and can be exemplified through love, compassion and empathy.

Did you know that within the heart can be found all of the knowledge and wisdom that is sought?

Unfortunately, mankind has "moved away from the heart of the world to the logic of the mind, and their belief is in the chemist, the physicist and the mathematician." [613]

Right thinking is "thinking without discrimination. When you produce a thought in alignment with right thinking, that

---

[612] http://shambhalasun.com/index.php?option=com_content&task=view&id=3984&Itemid=0

[613] Melchizedek, Drunvalo. (2008) <u>Serpent of Light Beyond 2012: The Movement of the Earth's Kundalin and the Rise of the Female Light, 1949 to 2013</u> (page 5). Weiser Books: San Franciso, CA.

thought is full of understanding and compassion. It has the power to heal you and to heal the world." [614]

Whilst the equation Right Action (Body) + Right Intention (Heart) + Right Thought (Mind) = Balance, it must also be remembered that "creation always begins in the heart, and then it is transferred to the mind." [615]

I was further elated to be able to begin 2013 by experiencing the remaining five Rites, also known as the Lineage Rites; namely, [1] the Daykeeper's Rite, [2] the Wisdomkeeper's Rite, [3] the Earthkeeper's Rite, [4] the Starkeeper's Rite and [5] the Creator Rite, over the course of a second intense two day weekend workshop (February 2 and 3, 2013). [616] [617] [618]

---

[614] http://shambhalasun.com/index.php?option=com_content&task=view&id=3984&Itemid=0
[615] Melchizedek, Drunvalo. (2008) <u>Serpent of Light Beyond 2012: The Movement of the Earth's Kundalin and the Rise of the Female Light, 1949 to 2013</u> (page 5). Weiser Books: San Franciso, CA.
[616] http://alisonnormore.com/

A Metaphysics Primer

All of the Rites are transmitted to you as seeds which must be germinated in order to grow into fruition.

There are three things that will grow the seeds of your initiations; namely, [1] the transformational fire ceremony, [2] spending time outdoors in nature, and [3] visualization and meditations to bring in the light which feeds your luminous body and the Rites in particular.

Articles and Interviews [619]

Munay-Ki Initiation: Frequently Asked Questions [620]

Munay-Ki Rites [621] [622] [623] [624]

---

[617] http://www.munay-ki.org/
[618] http://thefourwinds.com/
[619] http://www.munay-ki.org/index.php?page=articles_interviews
[620] http://www.alisonnormore.com/munay-ki-faq.html
[621] http://alisonnormore.com/retreats-and-workshops/munay-ki-initiation/
[622] http://www.alisonnormore.com/pdf/The_Nine_Rites.pdf
[623] http://portalsoftranscendence.com/services/munay-ki-rites/

A Metaphysics Primer

Munay-Ki: The Next Step in Evolution [625]

Nourishing the Munay-Ki Rites [626]

The Four Winds Society: A World Leader in Energy Medicine Training [627]

Transformational Fire Ceremony [628]

[14] Matter Does Not Exist

Concerning matter, we have been all wrong. What we have called matter is energy, whose vibration has been so lowered as to be perceptible to the senses. There is no matter.

Albert Einstein

---

[624] http://www.steppingintofreedom.com/munay-ki/the-9-rites-of-the-munay-ki
[625] http://www.munay-ki.org/
[626] http://www.steppingintofreedom.com/munay-ki/nourishing-the-seers-rite/nourishing-the-rites
[627] http://thefourwinds.com/
[628] http://www.steppingintofreedom.com/transformational-fire-ceremony

A Metaphysics Primer

In the world of subatomic physics "there are no objects, only processes. Atoms consist of particles and these particles are not made of any solid material substance. When we observe them under a microscope, we never see any substance; we rather observe dynamic patterns, continually changing into one another ; a continuous dance of energy. This dance of energy, the underlying rhythm of the universe, is again more intuited than seen." [629]

Jack Kornfield, "a contemporary teacher of meditation, finds a parallel between the behavior of subatomic particles and meditational states. When the mind becomes very silent, you can clearly see that all that exists in the world are brief moments of consciousness arising together with the six sense objects. There is only sight and the knowing of sight, sound and the knowing of sound, smell, taste and the knowing of them, thoughts and the knowing of thoughts. If you can make the mind very focused, as you can in meditation, you see that the whole world breaks down into these small events of sight and the knowing, sound and the knowing, thought and the knowing; no longer are these

---

[629] http://peaceandloveism.com/blog/2009/01/matter-does-not-exist/

houses, cars, bodies or even oneself. All you see are particles of consciousness as experience, yet you can go deep in meditation in another way and the mind becomes very still. You will see differently that consciousness is like waves, like a sea, an ocean, [with] every sight and every sound contained [with]in this ocean of consciousness. From this perspective, there is no sense of particles at all." [630]

How is it, then, that we exist as matter?

Albert Einstein alluded to this answer when he shared that "we, the people of this beautiful planet, are really beings made of energy, but we exist at the 3rd dimension because our atoms have a specific frequency which makes us able to exist in this very 3rd dimension. This specific frequency is stable enough for all our lifetime. Using this information, if we are, indeed, capable of accelerating and decelerating the frequencies to make us able to exist in the 3rd dimension, then naturally, we can use this in order to travel

---

[630] http://peaceandloveism.com/blog/2009/01/matter-does-not-exist/

inter-dimensionally throughout the infinite multiverse; here[in] lies the key to the true evolution of the human being race. Once we learn, or progress far enough, to accelerate and decelerate the vibrating frequencies of our atoms, then, in theory, we will be able to exist in the 5th dimension and in parallel universes of this wonderful multiverse." [631]

[15] Places of Sacred Energy

Newfoundland, fondly called *The Rock*, is a place of ancient earth wisdom and power.

Three hundred million years ago, western Newfoundland was situated in the center of Pangea.

Given the rocks and geologic formations exposed here, the province of Newfoundland has been ranked one of the planet's "most significant natural areas [with] ancient mountains, diverse habitats, plant and animal life, seascapes and a unique human legacy [making] this a special place" [632] that you simply need to experience for yourself. Perhaps

---

[631] http://peaceandloveism.com/blog/2009/01/matter-does-not-exist/
[632] http://www.alisonnormore.com/about_newfoundland.html

A Metaphysics Primer

this is why the west coast of the island called to me so many years ago.

Alison Normore completed a Tablelands Sacred Journey (December 17, 2012) on my behalf.

On the day in question, there was no wind; all was calm and still, which, according to Alison, is a rarity for this mountain.

Clearly there was an additional message for me within the beauty and stillness of the day; namely, that *I am to find the calm and still within my being, living each day from the wisdom of that very place.*

The canyon also mirrored the first snowfall as well.

Having recently bought some Christmas cards (which I never do), the inside message seems to fit here; namely, *in the quiet stillness of the first snowfall, the world is made new.*

A Metaphysics Primer

The Tablelands, a magnificent and powerful mountain that dominates the landscape of Bonne Bay, has called out to many people.

This mountain, part of the Earth's mantle, was once 20 miles below the crust, under the Iapetus ocean, until being pushed to the surface by tectonic forces about 500 million years ago.

As a result, the Tablelands hold deep earth energy and wisdom and are calling to be of service to humanity.

In further acknowledgment, The Tablelands of Gros Morne National Park are denoted as a UNESCO World Heritage Site.

The spirit of this mountain communicated the message that Alison could bring requests for assistance and healing for others.

Alison makes the 4 to 5 kilometer hike into Winterhouse Brook Canyon, from which flows a river; while there, she makes an offering and delivers the prayer request.

A Metaphysics Primer

The mountain Spirit sometimes has messages or instructions that she delivers; in this way, Alison is the go-between messenger, able to connect the physical and the spiritual.

The mountain is powerful and will answer your prayer, but it may not come in the way you expect, so it is essential that one be conscious of what they are asking for, being clear and ready to receive it completely.

All prayers and requests have but one condition; whatever you ask for will serve the highest and best good for you and all life everywhere.

Any request or desire that comes from your heart (versus your ego mind) will satisfy this condition.

A Metaphysics Primer

Winterhouse Brook Canyon

December 17, 2012

The following transcript was the message, recorded and received, for me.

The first snow, it is very still today, no wind, and the message ... *do not look at how far there is to go, but at how far you have come; hold that in your consciousness and be in the present moment.*

Alison's words: The second message for Michele Doucette has to do with the steps immediately in front of her.

A Metaphysics Primer

By focusing on these steps immediately in front, you are not clinging too tightly to those things that may not be necessary, that may not accompany you, those things that you thought you needed, those things that you thought needed to come with you, to be detached from that and surrender to the higher wisdom because you are always guided, protected and safe; everything that you need will be provided, so just let go of your ideas of what that might be and how that might look.

If you find yourself straying from what you thought was your path, not to worry; these are slight deviations. Your path is not far. It is all part of your path, but your mind may play that trick saying this is not on my path so I have to get back on my path. You must realize that everything will lead you back to where it is that you need to be; trust.

Sometimes on your path, things will not look clear; you will not be able to see clearly what is unfolding. Again, the most important message here is trust.

Even when you are unable to see, just keep moving in that direction and the path will become clear, once again.

While there will be times you will be able to follow the footsteps of others who have gone before you, and that will feel like the right thing to do, there will be other times when there will not be any footprints to guide you. You will feel like you are in completely new territory; unfamiliar, unmarked, and that is as it should be.

I say, trust, as the path will change, at times following in the footsteps of others, and at other times making your own.

Know that at those times when you are breaking new territory, which you have done before, that you are simply creating a path for others to follow.

Alison's words: I am being shown something like Celtic knots, the interweaving of lines; there are two further messages here.

Each of us, all of life, is connected; each of us represents a thread in the tapestry. Your work, and your soul destiny, brings you to create some unique form, some new pattern, in that tapestry of life.

A Metaphysics Primer

Alison's words: Three birds have appeared, have gathered, at the top of a Tamarack tree along the path. Three bespeaks the trinity; the triangle, portal, symbol of ancient knowledge, and in the sky above, *Apu Hatun*, the spirit of Tablelands, the mountain spirit, has appeared, and manifested, as a cloud being with giant, outstretched wings.

It is important on your journey, on the awakening that you are experiencing in the present time, to pause often and reflect on the beauty all around you. This is what will sustain you on your journey.

See the gift and the blessings in what you perceive or have labeled as negative or difficult or challenging. You must always pause and remind yourself, on a very deep level, of the beauty that exists, even in the dying, even in the apparent death that in what some perceive as ugly, others can see as quite beautiful, finding much there to nourish their spirits and their souls.

This, dear one, is an important message for you at this time.

A Metaphysics Primer

This is something you have always known, and grasped, intellectually, but now is the time to really feel and allow this knowledge to become part of your knowing and your way of living in the world.

Alison's words: We have now arrived at Winterhouse Brook and of course we have had to arrive here on a different path than this.

Again, this is an important message for you; *that sometimes the path most traveled is not your path, meaning that you have to find a new way to get where you are going.*

Only you can create that path, and, in so doing, you will also create a path for others to follow in your role as teacher and guide.

In truth, sometimes one does not have to travel to the four corners of the earth to find that which is deemed sacred.

In further reference to the spirit of the Tablelands, Apu is the Quechua word for the spirit of the mountain, or *lord of the mountain*, while Hatun is the Quechua word that means great or majestic.

The Rhythm of Life

Marcus Mason, Astrologer, Acupuncturist and Earth Energy Worker, shared that the annual solar eclipse of May 20, 2012, a South Node eclipse, was one that would release "the energetic thought-forms and patriarchal archetypes of at least the last 5,125¼ years, and probably the last 25,626 years of the Galactic Great Year." [633]

This Eclipse would, in his words, "release negative imprints left from the misaligned expression of male power in the Pacific Ocean grids, and along the entire length of the Plumed Serpent, Great Male Dragon line" [634] as it encircled the Earth, thereby affecting the consciousness of the entire planet.

As we know, Mother Earth is a sacred being.

---

[633] http://www.heavenandearthastrology.blogspot.ca/
[634] Ibid.

A Metaphysics Primer

The releasing of these old patterns, long held within the grids, during this eclipse, would bring about "the possibility for seeding a new expression of male power;" [635] a power that would become fully "aligned with the heart and the spiritual will," [636] enabling "collective healing at a personal and global level" [637] thereby marking the beginning of a whole new paradigm of consciousness.

The significance of this eclipse was "further enhanced by the exact conjunction of the Sun and Moon with the Pleiades; a well-known cluster of stars, above Taurus, [that] has held a significant position in world mythology throughout the Ages. To the Maya, the Pleiades represented the handful of maize seeds from which the original humans were born. These seeds are symbolically re-planted in the Earth at the beginning of each new 'Sun' cycle of 5,125 ¼ years." [638]

We have since come to understand that five Sun cycles completes one full precessional cycle of 25,626 years.

---

[635] http://www.heavenandearthastrology.blogspot.ca/
[636] Ibid.
[637] Ibid.
[638] Ibid.

A Metaphysics Primer

While the old patriarchal patterns of the last 5,125 ¼ years were "being released by the Eclipse, hidden behind the eclipsing Sun," [639] the Pleiades were planting the seeds of the new consciousness slated to begin the birth of the new 5,125 ¼ year cycle, following December 21, 2012. [640]

This eclipse was one that clearly marked "the point of no return on our journey towards the December Solstice 2012." [641] We had been told that the more we were able to release emotional attachments, thoughts and ideologies, that held us back from experiencing full conscious awareness of our connection with the Oneness of all Life, the smoother the transition would be for us; in essence, it was this very May Eclipse that brought with it "a golden opportunity to create Right Relations in all aspects of our lives and stand fully in the power of who we truly are and what we truly believe." [642]

---

[639] http://www.heavenandearthastrology.blogspot.ca/
[640] Ibid.
[641] Ibid.
[642] Ibid.

A Metaphysics Primer

While the May 20, 2012 solar eclipse took place before the publication of this guide, from an astrological point of view, the sharing of this information is still significant in its overall importance.

As Mason has stated, eclipses provide us with opportunities to "release these negative energy imprints and enable new, positive patterns to become encoded into the Earth grids. Hamish Miller, the renowned UK dowser, found that, as an Eclipse shadow passes overhead, the Earth's subtle energy lines power down to almost nothing, becoming indiscernible to dowsing; then as the Sun's light returns, the grids spring back into life. This is a bit like deleting an old computer programme, loading a new one, and then re-booting the system. Annular Eclipses have a very subtle effect on the energy grids, releasing, transforming and healing the etheric energy 'blueprint' that can enable new spiritual archetypes to emerge into collective consciousness." [643]

In short, who doesn't need a reboot of their system, from time to time?

---

[643] http://www.heavenandearthastrology.blogspot.ca/

A Metaphysics Primer

In reference to the Venus Transit of June 5 and 6, 2012, Marcus Mason shared that while Venus orbits the Sun every 225 Earth days, it only crosses in front of the face of the Sun every 100 to 120 years. [644]

When such "a transit occurs, it means that the Earth, Venus and the Sun are aligned on the same plane. This is similar to what happens at a Solar Eclipse, when Sun, Moon and Earth are in exact alignment." [645]

These rare Venus transits are always highly significant. With the June 5 and 6 transit coming so soon after the Solar Eclipse on May 20th, this served to add "significance during the final stages of the approach to the December Solstice 2012." [646]

The May 20th eclipse was about "releasing and healing old, unbalanced, power-based, abusive or destructive expressions of the masculine energy, and planting the seeds for a new positive, creative, heart-centred expression of the male

---

[644] http://www.heavenandearthastrology.blogspot.ca/
[645] Ibid.
[646] Ibid.

spiritual warrior. Inevitably, this will bring about the release of old patterns of relationship with the feminine. Both men and women will need to adjust current relationships within the self and with each other, to move into alignment with the new, emerging expression of the positive masculine energies." [647]

The Venus transit involved "eclipsing old patterns of relationship and co-dependency that no longer work, now that the new, pure masculine energy has begun to take root." [648] This transit was all about the healing of both the masculine and the feminine.

On November 13, 2012, there was a total Solar Eclipse over the south Pacific, one that enabled "the feminine, both within and out in the world, to find her rightful, whole and healthy relationship to the pure masculine, [enabling us to] move forward with the seeds of balance planted in Mother

---

[647] http://www.heavenandearthastrology.blogspot.ca/
[648] Ibid.

A Metaphysics Primer

Earth and her energy grids, in all our relationships, and then in our local and global structures and institutions." [649]

On Friday, November 23, 2012, I participated in a very powerful and healing Anyi Despacho Ceremony led by Alison Normore, a Shaman trained in the Peruvian heritage. [650]

The ceremony was conducted between the solar eclipse of November 13, 2012 and the lunar eclipse of November 28, 2012, the timing of which was extremely important, given that the energies are much more powerful as the planets align with the galactic center and we enter a new Age.

During the ceremony, Alison led us in creating a prayer bundle with burnable items from nature that contained flowers, wood, food and sweets. Everything in the bundle was infused with prayers for balance and healing.

---

[649] http://www.heavenandearthastrology.blogspot.ca/
[650] http://alisonnormore.com/

A Metaphysics Primer

After it was created and wrapped, it was taken outside and offered to fire in a ceremony to release the prayers to Spirit.

The Despacho is a beautiful, powerful ceremony that lifts and lightens the energy for the people attending, for the area, and for the Earth.

Rick DiClemente [651] is an intuitive astrologer who blends math-science and spiritual-psychic ability with empirical knowledge, in order to reveal the multi-faceted story. Based on his knowledge and understanding of astrology, the current Mayan calendar, begun on August 11, 3114 BC, came to an end on Friday, December 21, 2012, in Greenwich, England, at precisely 11:11:11 AM. [652]

As soon as Rick calculated, and calibrated, the chart for Greenwich England, the modern center of astrology that marks 0° longitude for the planet, he was greeted with the

---

[651] http://www.starself.com/
[652] http://omtimes.com/2012/12/its-not-the-end-of-the-world-just-the-mayan-calendar/

vision of Chiron, together with Neptune, rising right on the ascendant. [653]

Both Chiron and Neptune are situated in the wonderfully spiritual sign of Pisces, located at the tip of a T-square formed at the base by Venus and Mercury in Sagittarius in the ninth house and Jupiter in Gemini in the third. [654]

Besides interplanetary communications, this chart bodes greatly for the increased communications between all of us. [655]

Chiron and Neptune in Pisces rising is extremely powerful; it is a monumental promise of a world that will finally learn to live together in love and caring, unless, of course, we choose to ignore the possibility that exists. [656]

---

[653] http://omtimes.com/2012/12/its-not-the-end-of-the-world-just-the-mayan-calendar/2/
[654] Ibid.
[655] Ibid.
[656] Ibid.

A Metaphysics Primer

It has become apparent that *none of us can continue to operate disconncted from Source,* and this is why the old calendar is ending; this is the end of the old world. [657]

Drunvalo Melchizedek has studied and participated in many sacred Mayan rituals.

He has also been given permission from the Mayan Council of Elders to speak about the Mayan calendar and what this time period means.

Knowing that the Maya went into hiding after the Spanish conquest, it was commonly accepted that their civilization had perished.

Out of all the people who have attempted to shed light on the subject, Drunvalo "has been able to connect directly with the Mayan, Arhuaco, Kogi, Hopi, Waitaha, Wiwa, Zulu, and

---

[657] http://omtimes.com/2012/12/its-not-the-end-of-the-world-just-the-mayan-calendar/5/

A Metaphysics Primer

Maori elders and priests whose oral traditions have preserved that wisdom for close to 13,000 years." [658]

Many scholars were convinced that the Mayan calendar was coming to an end on December 21, 2012, but the Maya have always held to a different perspective of time.

They do not follow the Gregorian calendar, so time is not linear to them; it is cyclical.

Sophisticated mathematicians, the Aj'qui (who were the Mayan day keepers) have been keeping track of their calendars for centuries, with a completely different method of calculating their own calendar, than do Mayan scholars.

In accordance with his book, <u>The Mayan Ouroboros: The Cosmic Cycles Come Full Circle</u>, Drunvalo shared that on December 21, 2012, at 11:11 PM in Chitzen Itza, Mexico, the Earth, our Sun and the center of our Galaxy were all positioned in a straight line (not to happen again for another

---

[658] http://omtimes.com/2012/12/drunvalo-melchizedek-the-cosmic-cycles-come-full-circle/2/

A Metaphysics Primer

25,625 years), thereby heralding our passage into the Age of Light. [659]

Given this intimate connection, birth was inevitable, and so, on December 22, 2012, a new *female* cycle was begun, one that will prove to be "an extraordinary one, like nothing the Maya have ever seen before." [660]

As believed by the Mayan elders, there is "a window of opportunity for a global shift in consciousness until January 2016 and every day during this period of time is equally prone to this possibility." [661]

We have entered into a world whereby humanity will reach a new level of consciousness; one that will change how we

---

[659] http://omtimes.com/2012/12/drunvalo-melchizedek-the-cosmic-cycles-come-full-circle/2/

[660] Melchizedek, Drunvalo. (2012) The Mayan Ouroboros: The Cosmic Cycles Come Full Circle – The True Positive Mayan Prophecy Is Revealed (pages 75 and 89). San Francisco, CA: Weiser Books.

[661] http://omtimes.com/2012/12/drunvalo-melchizedek-the-cosmic-cycles-come-full-circle/4/

A Metaphysics Primer

interpret our outer reality, thereby altering our inner reality.[662]

As we gather together "at the end of the old cycle and the beginning of the new, we can know that we are creating an amazing opportunity of connection and dreaming the new world for all of humanity. Each one of us has already gone through very profound changes and as those continue we can choose how we move forward; [be it] in fear or in Love."[663]

While I had hoped to participate in second Anyi Despacho Ceremony on December 21, 2012, I remained at home, quite unsure as to why I was feeling somewhat listless and lethargic, wanting only to be surrounded by the comfort of family.

---

[662] Melchizedek, Drunvalo. (2012) The Mayan Ouroboros: The Cosmic Cycles Come Full Circle – The True Positive Mayan Prophecy Is Revealed (page 90). San Francisco, CA: Weiser Books.
[663] http://omtimes.com/2012/12/drunvalo-melchizedek-the-cosmic-cycles-come-full-circle/5/

A Metaphysics Primer

It was the very next morning that I found out that my 97 year old great aunt, Annie (née Breau) Stewart, had peacefully transitioned at 7:00 am on December 22, 2012.

Knowing that her time had come, and welcoming the release from the physical body, she had wanted all of her family (nieces and nephews) around her the day before. It appears that, so, too, was I also tuning into her energies.

The last of her brothers and sisters, she dearly treasured her independence, living in her own apartment up until the age of 95.

She lived a wonderful life and I was blessed to have known, and loved, her

I see the rhythm of life as simply this: you are here to live each and every day with purpose (mindfulness) and passion, for therein lies your celebration of life.

So, too, must you know how to balance the masculine and feminine within; a feat that can be accomplished simply by learning how to go within so that you may listen to your inner knowing, your inner wisdom, at the deepest level, of your heart.

In living the dictates of the heart, so, too, will you have connected with the inherent wisdom of the universe; that which is Love, the power that has created, and continues to create, everything that exists.

In addition, *the most important thing about intelligence is how you apply the intelligence that you have to your daily life* to include the choices that you make, the way you treat others, and the way you treat yourself.

Living life is all about embracing (and living) the present moment; that having been said, while you have a right to your feelings and experiences, do not hold onto those parts that only serve to bring you to a place that you would rather not be, for they merely serve to keep one stagnant.

A Metaphysics Primer

Clearly, it is now the time to celebrate the new Earth by reuniting with our spiritual brothers and sisters, all courtesy of the necessary, and much needed, reunion between thought (mind) and heart (intention).

By definition, Lightworkers are humans who have awakened to the realization that God exists within every soul on the planet.

Kryon talks about a battle that has always existed, a battle not of good or evil, but one that involves "a confluence, or natural consensus, of how humans think about themselves and what is appropriate behavior for humanity." [664]

Having entered into 2013, the balance of this battle is realigning itself.

---

[664] http://kryon.com/CHAN%202013/k_channel13_phoenix.html

Kryon shares that the year 2013 is a time whereby we are finally ready to begin preparing the field, for the new energy, by planting the seeds, using "that which the old soul has: the wisdom of the past." [665]

Like the Knights of old, we are here to take up the gauntlet, wearing the cloak of accountability, with much care and total stewardship, so that we may tend to these important crops.

The energy of 2012 contained a great deal of fear; this has now passed.

We have just entered into the beginning of a new and wondrous era, a time where a great many shall depart from what has long been tradition in their lives, in order to embrace that which involves new ways of being (thinking, living, evolving).

---

[665] http://kryon.com/CHAN%202013/k_channel13_phoenix.html

A Metaphysics Primer

Kryon also tells us that a "slow, methodical, consistent change in consciousness," [666] will usher in this new paradigm; as a result, it is imperative that we embrace tolerance and patience for that which is yet to come, some of which "cannot be obtained until older energies die." [667]

Melchizedek, Drunvalo. (2007) <u>Serpent of Light Beyond 2012: The Movement of the Earth`s Kundalini and the Rise of the Female Light, 1949 to 2013</u>. San Francisco, CA: Weiser Books.

Melchizedek, Drunvalo. (2012) <u>The Mayan Ouroboros: The Cosmic Cycles Come Full Circle – The True Positive Mayan Prophecy Is Revealed</u>. San Francisco, CA: Weiser Books.

Peruvian Despacho Ceremony [668]

---

[666] http://kryon.com/CHAN%202013/k_channel13_boulder.html
[667] Ibid.
[668] http://www.steppingintofreedom.com/ho/despacho-ceremony/peruvian-despacho-ceremony

The Walls Come Tumbling Down

If one searches for the truth with both purity of heart, as well as intention, therein shall the much sought after truth be revealed.

You must, however, also be willing to release all that burdens you, much akin to the monkey on your back idiom, for that is when the walls *will* come tumbling down so that you can rebuild anew.

It can be quite disheartening to come to terms with the fact that fear, unfortunately, sells.

So, too, however, can it be quite exhilarating to realize that, in truth, there was never anything to fear, except fear itself.

It was with great delight that I have recently come to learn about the discovery of an unprecedented Mayan mural, in Xultún, Guatemala, that contradicts the doomsday myth of 2012.

A Metaphysics Primer

In following the basic premise of this primer, you will have successfully adjusted your default setting.

Mayan Calendar Websites

Mayan Calendar: New Revelations and the Next Nine Years [669]

Mayan Mural Websites

Ancient Maya Astronomical Tables from Xulútn, Guatemala [670]

Discovery in Guatemala Shows That Mayan Calendar Goes On [671]

Historic Mayan Mural Found By Chance [672]

---

[669] http://paulapeterson.com/New_Revelations_Mayan_Calendar.html
[670] http://www.sciencemag.org/content/336/6082/714.abstract
[671] http://www.post-gazette.com/stories/news/world/discovery-in-guatemala-shows-that-mayan-calendar-goes-on-635382/
[672] http://news.bbc.co.uk/2/hi/entertainment/1875261.stm

A Metaphysics Primer

Maya Archaeologists Unearth New 2012 Monument [673]

Maya Arts and Calendar at Xultún Stun Archaeologists [674]

Maya Doomsday Calendar Explained [675]

Maya Mural Find [676]

Never Mind the Apocalypse: Earliest Mayan Calendar Found [677]

Newly Discovered Mayan Calendar Goes Way Past 2012 [678]

New Maya Mural (pictures) [679]

---

[673] http://www.earthchangesmedia.com/publish/article-9162532908.php
[674] http://www.bbc.co.uk/news/science-environment-18018343
[675] http://news.nationalgeographic.com/news/2011/12/111220-end-of-world-2012-maya-calendar-explained-ancient-science/
[676] http://ngm.nationalgeographic.com/2012/06/explorers-journal?source=news_xultun_mural
[677] http://news.discovery.com/history/mayan-calendar-discovery-doomsday-120511.html
[678] http://www.usatoday.com/tech/science/story/2012-05-08/maya-apocalypse-calendar-2012/54879760/1
[679] http://news.nationalgeographic.com/news/2012/05/pictures/120510-maya-apocalypse-2012-calendar-science-art-murals-saturno/?source=news_xultun_mural

437

Oldest Known Mayan Astronomical Calendar Stuns Scientists [680]

Painted Maya Walls Reveal Calendar Writing [681]

The Maya: Glory and Ruin [682]

Unprecedented Maya Mural Found [683]

Mayan Mural Videos

Mysterious Maya Calendar and Mural Uncovered [684]

Shift of the Ages

The *Shift of the Ages* is a dramatic documentary film that reveals the story of the Mayan culture and its sophisticated

---

[680] http://www.time.com/time/health/article/0,8599,2114645,00.html
[681] http://www.nytimes.com/2012/05/11/science/archaeologists-unearth-ancient-maya-calendar-writing.html
[682] http://ngm.nationalgeographic.com/2007/08/maya-rise-fall/gugliotta-text
[683] http://news.nationalgeographic.com/news/2012/05/120510-maya-2012-doomsday-calendar-end-of-world-science/
[684] http://video.nationalgeographic.com/video/news/history-archaeology-news/maya-art-calendar-vin/?source=news_xultun_mural

A Metaphysics Primer

prophecies of time, as told for the first time by the Grand Elder of the Mayan people, Alejandro Cirilo Perez Oxlaj. [685]

Commissioned on behalf of the Maya nation, the *Shift of the Ages* is the first official discourse to the world from the Mayan Council of Elders, intended to dispel misconceptions and replace them with the positive story about this incredible period of time for humanity. [686]

Known as "Wandering Wolf," Don Alejandro is the elected Grand Elder of the living Maya, former Ambassador in the Guatemalan Government, and mystical Aj Q'ji, or timekeeper of tradition. [687]

The Mayans were superb mathematicians and astronomers who devised one of the most accurate calendars known to man; they speak of a year "zero," which was thought by some scholars to be 2012. [688]

---

[685] http://www.shiftoftheages.com/the-film/
[686] Ibid.
[687] Ibid.
[688] Ibid.

A Metaphysics Primer

Wandering Wolf explains, however, how the Mayan calendar is cyclical, not linear like that of Westerners who try to interpret it. He teaches us how this "zero" time period is what the Mayans refer to as the "change of the suns," and clarifies this as a transition process, not a singular day or event. [689]

Indigenous wisdom passed down to Wandering Wolf is shared for the first time in a way that expresses the role human consciousness plays in connecting to the universe; we come away assured this is a time of great opportunity to heal ourselves and our planet from wounds of the past. [690]

Set against the backdrop of the end of the Mayan Long Count calendar, the film is a tightly woven tapestry of human drama and cultural history that takes you on an adventure into the heart of the Maya, their ancient spiritual traditions and sophisticated culture. [691]

---

[689] http://www.shiftoftheages.com/the-film/
[690] Ibid.
[691] Ibid.

The *Shift of the Ages* [692] beautifully illustrates the power of the human spirit. [693]

---

[692] http://www.shiftoftheages.com/watch-now/
[693] http://www.shiftoftheages.com/the-film/

5 Keys to Staying Positive

Let's face it; a good many, myself included, find it difficult to remain in a positive state of mind when challenging circumstances present themselves.

The Universal Laws state: so without, so within, meaning that everything is a mirror; we cannot change the reflection, but we can change the original (ourselves), and then, automatically, the reflection changes. [694]

Pragito Dove shares her top 5 Keys that lead to cultivating a positive mindset; one that will also cultivate the feeling state that is necessary for the Law of Attraction. [695]

The more you focus "on bringing awareness to accepting and loving yourself, the more your inner beauty and

---

[694] Email received from Benedick Howard, dated January 5, 2013, with words shared by Pragito Dove; a master trainer, international speaker, and meditation expert who teaches people how to transform pain and fear into joy and inner peace in order to achieve real world success.
[695] Ibid.

A Metaphysics Primer

harmony is reflected in your outer circumstances. In fact, the Sufi master who designed the Taj Mahal based his work on meditation." [696]

[1] Relax and Accept [697]

Relax and accept the challenging situation; do not fight it because that will make it worse. The more relaxed you are, the more productive you are.

Creativity arises out of a relaxed state, and it is creativity that you need to come up with solutions to the situation you are in.

Notice that I use the word *situation* and not the word problem; there is no such thing as a problem, only a situation.

---

[696] Email received from Benedick Howard, dated January 5, 2013, with words shared by Pragito Dove; a master trainer, international speaker, and meditation expert who teaches people how to transform pain and fear into joy and inner peace in order to achieve real world success.
[697] Ibid.

A Metaphysics Primer

When you shift your perspective and see the situation as it is, without negative commentary, then you either come up with creative solutions or you are able to find the right person to help you.

These words of Pragito's completely resonate with me, especially as September 2012 to June 2013 school year found me in the most *challenging*, the most *demanding*, the most *stressful*, teaching assignment of my entire career as a Special Education teacher, probably because I had been fighting (resisting) the assignment.

It was only within the last month that I found myself ready to begin approaching the situation with a sense of renewed acceptance.

A Metaphysics Primer

[2] Watch the Mind [698]

Make a practice of *watching the thoughts of the mind* with non-judgment and compassion for you.

It is not the thoughts that are the problem; *it is our identification with them that creates stress and anxiety.*

For 5 minutes a day, sit with eyes closed, bodies relaxed, and observe the thoughts of the mind.

You do not have to censor them, or force them to be other than they are, simply observe with non-judgment, and *let them pass by.* Over time, you become less identified with the thoughts, and more connected to your creativity, wisdom, and clarity.

I address these very components in several of my books.

---

[698] Email received from Benedick Howard, dated January 5, 2013, with words shared by Pragito Dove; a master trainer, international speaker, and meditation expert who teaches people how to transform pain and fear into joy and inner peace in order to achieve real world success.

[3] Create Positive Thoughts [699]

A powerful way to undermine the influence of negative thoughts on your well-being is to *create a practice of saying positive thoughts* to yourself; at the beginning these might seem tedious or silly, but believe me, [they] work.

The easiest way to break a bad habit of self-judgment and criticism is to create positive phrases that you repeat to yourself as often as possible.

Over time, they become a habit and the negative thoughts simply dissolve.

Here Pragito is talking about positive affirmations; another aspect that I delve into in several of my books.

---

[699] Email received from Benedick Howard, dated January 5, 2013, with words shared by Pragito Dove; a master trainer, international speaker, and meditation expert who teaches people how to transform pain and fear into joy and inner peace in order to achieve real world success.

A Metaphysics Primer

[4] Surround Yourself with Positive People [700]

Be alert to people who like to complain and bad-mouth; likewise for those who have a depressed outlook on life. You must avoid them. *Keep yourself in the company of positive thinking people.* This is a powerful way to keep yourself in a positive energy field which will lift you, rather than bring you down. *Your life is not determined by outside circumstances, but rather by how you respond to those outside circumstances.* Remember that all things are possible, there is a lot going on that is unseen to you. The more you keep yourself on a positive vibrational level, the greater your chances of having positive outcomes to challenging situations.

It feels so incredibly wonderful to know that these words of Pragito's also echo my own beliefs.

---

[700] Email received from Benedick Howard, dated January 5, 2013, with words shared by Pragito Dove; a master trainer, international speaker, and meditation expert who teaches people how to transform pain and fear into joy and inner peace in order to achieve real world success.

[5] Be Grateful, Laugh, Celebrate [701]

Be grateful for what you have. If things are really bad, be grateful for being able to breathe, get out of bed in the morning, use your legs. Be grateful for the sunrise and sunset, for the beauty of the sky, the trees, the birds and flowers. *There is always something to be grateful for.* Put your focus there and celebrate what you have.

Laughter is a powerful attractor factor. *Seek out ways to bring more laughter into your life.* You will be amazed at the miracles that occur.

So, too, have I talked about humor being a wonderful diffuser of negative vibrational energies.

Pragito also alludes to Meditation as a befriending of the mind. [702]

---

[701] Email received from Benedick Howard, dated January 5, 2013, with words shared by Pragito Dove; a master trainer, international speaker, and meditation expert who teaches people how to transform pain and fear into joy and inner peace in order to achieve real world success.

A Metaphysics Primer

Benefits:

When you befriend the mind you are surprised how radically life can change. It becomes much easier to dis-identify from the mind's constant chattering and see yourself, and life's situations, with more clarity and objectivity. You see life's dramas with perspective and compassion, and insights and understandings arise naturally.

Find ways to befriend your mind.

The mind is our bridge from the subconscious to the conscious, our gateway of expression to the outer world.

Be grateful for it. Find ways to appreciate the insights, understandings, and creativity it brings.

See it not as an enemy but as a friend.

As this friendship with the mind deepens, your mind no longer disturbs you.

---

[702] http://discovermeditation.com/

A Metaphysics Primer

You are not fighting it; you are simply letting its thoughts pass by. The mind and the ego want to make it complicated, but it is not.

Life sings a different tune when you are not controlled by the mind.

Your natural joy, spontaneity, self-acceptance, love, and compassion arise quickly and easily.

The Heart People

Soren Dreier, a Danish philosophical researcher who authors and compiles the hugely popular *Zen-Haven* website,[703] writes about the heart people, sharing that "there is so much fighting on the internal scale for the heart people ... an internal alignment to what I conceive to be the shift; the real shift." [704]

These are the generous, radiant, people; the very group that he describes as being the givers, primarily because they love, an all inclusive, high frequency, love (akin to a Rumi state of mind, whereby the separatist concept of you and me no longer exists), with every depth of their being; most assuredly, they are not, and never could be, the takers.[705]

In addition, the heart people are the ones who "touched down from [the] cosmos, somewhere , to fulfill whatever karma or destiny they are here to impact into the turmoil and

---

[703] http://zen-haven.com/zen-haven/
[704] http://zen-haven.com/the-heart-people/
[705] Ibid.

deprivation of the ghoulish Matrix ... [the] brave warriors of the new dawn, so fragile, so humble, and yet ever so strong." [706] To my mind, finding one's truth path can only be successfully ascertained, with complete clarity, when one lives (expresses) from the heart.

The heart people struggle with many issues, some of which include sadness, not feeling plugged into life (not feeling at home on the planet is my interpretation), bewilderment, feeling as if one is being held hostage (from an emotional, financial or psychic perspective), and having a very sensitive emotional immune system that often inflates into the physical. [707]

In terms of skills, these individuals are often denoted as having high vibrational skills (healing and intuition), they are very much plugged into the emotional GPS; so, too, are they highly creative beings. [708]

---

[706] http://zen-haven.com/the-heart-people/
[707] Ibid.
[708] Ibid.

Their job, according to Dreier, is to bring "water to the desert people caught in the Matrix;" [709] a job that will be accomplished discretely, persistently and silently. [710]

As a movement that has not yet gathered, the best part is that the Matrix "has no idea how to dissolve a high-frequency neural heart based network, zapping through the un-manifested realms of higher altitudes," [711] which is the case with the heart people.

According to Dreier, heart people are becoming empowered by first taking responsibility for their emotions and then transforming them into states of mind; this is where it becomes important to understand that by opening up your heart, so, too are you are awake (conscious vulnerability), for this allows you to tap into the field of BE-ing. [712]

Emotions come and go, meaning that they are illusions, whereas "life has many hidden layers that will only reveal

---

[709] http://zen-haven.com/the-heart-people/
[710] Ibid.
[711] Ibid.
[712] http://zen-haven.com/raiders-of-the-lost-heart/

themselves to the open hearted," [713] for the Matrix knows nothing about compassion and empathy; the heart, then, is the gateway to letting go and simply BE-ing.

Throughout history, many of the great sages pointed to the heart as being the gateway to the soul; as such, they regarded the heart as the source of all intuitive knowledge and spiritual wisdom.

Science is now showing us that "it is not the brain, but the heart that is the strongest generator of electrical and magnetic energies. As the physical world is made up of and changed by the force of these electromagnetic fields, living from your heart [is what] creates field coherence, the foundation of intelligence and the cornerstone of effective living." [714]

Being beings of pure energy, both electrical as well as magnetic, we also know that these fields of energy can either be enhanced, or depleted, by emotions.

---

[713] http://zen-haven.com/raiders-of-the-lost-heart/
[714] http://www.thelivingcentre.com/cms/trainings/living-from-your-heart

A Metaphysics Primer

When you are able to live in the heart, a place of total and complete BE-ingness, you acknowledge that you are loving, kind, generous, and compassionate. When you live in the heart, there can be no separation; everyone you see is part of you.

In this very moment of existence, we are spiritual beings (extensions of God consciousness) having a human experience.

Living from the heart enables us to transmute negative vibrations, transforming them into positive energies.

Living from the heart allows us to remain in the pure vibration of love.

Living from the heart allows us to BE who we are.

Living from the heart allows us to LOVE who we are.

Living from the heart allows us to LOVE and HONOR our experience(s).

A Metaphysics Primer

Living from the heart allows us to ACKNOWLEDGE that each moment is a gift.

Living from the heart allows us to ACCEPT this gift.

When our spirits are healthy, our minds are healthy; when our minds are healthy, our bodies are healthy. [715]

The main thing to remember is that you are the creator of your life situation; this is proven in how you both perceive the situation(s) and react to them. [716]

It becomes in the changing how you perceive and react to things, thereby allowing the divine energy of love to dictate your actions, that you will never be afraid to surrender to the moment. [717]

---

[715] http://www.starseeds.net/group/usend/page/negativevibrationsandlivingfromtheheart
[716] Ibid.
[717] Ibid.

A Metaphysics Primer

It was Carl Jung who said ... *your vision will become clear only when you look into your heart. Who looks outside, dreams. Who looks inside, awakens.*

In the words of Nelson Mandela ... *No one is born hating another person because of the colour of his skin, or his background or his religion. People learn to hate, and if they can learn to hate, they can be taught to love, for love comes more naturally to the human heart than its opposite.*

In conclusion, where there is love, so, too, is there life: actualized.

From Ego to Heart, Part 1 [718]

From Ego to Heart, Part 2 [719]

From Ego to Heart, Part 3 [720]

---

[718] http://www.jeshua.net/lightworker/jeshua6.htm
[719] http://www.jeshua.net/lightworker/jeshua7.htm
[720] http://www.jeshua.net/lightworker/jeshua8.htm

A Metaphysics Primer

Heart Light: Living From the Heart [721]

Heart Math [722]

How To Live From the Heart [723]

Living From the Heart [724] [725] [726] [727]

Living in the Heart: An Interview with Drunvalo Melchizedek [728] [729]

Love Is The New Religion [730] [731]

Practicing Presence: Living From The Heart [732]

---

[721] http://www.heartlight.ca/
[722] http://www.heartmath.com/
[723] http://consciouslifenews.com/live-heart-video/1132777/
[724] http://eventtemples.com/downloads/pdf/Living_from_the_Heart_(p).pdf
[725] http://www.livingfromtheheart.com/Welcome.html
[726] http://www.endless-satsang.com/LivingDownload.pdf
[727] http://carrieannefonger.com/living-from-the-heart/
[728] http://www.edgemagazine.net/2003/05/drunvalo/
[729] http://www.youtube.com/watch?v=oNZQbdFxKvE
[730] http://brianpiergrossi.com/blog/shareit/
[731] http://www.youtube.com/watch?v=mndsMqz54aA
[732] http://www.positivelypositive.com/2012/06/05/practice-presence/

A Metaphysics Primer

The Spiritualize Technique [733]

University of the Heart [734]

---

[733] http://www.spiritualdynamics.net/
[734] http://www.iam-u.org/home.html

Changing From the Inside Out

In essence, this is what it all comes down to ... *changing from the inside out.*

As Rascal Flatts allude to in their song, *When The Sand Runs Out*, we have to stop looking back in order to start moving on; so, too, do we have to learn how to face our fears.

It also becomes in loving with all of our heart that we make our mark; something that we are able to leave here, in our stead, as part of our service to mankind.

That having been said, in taking both a chance, as well as the time to dance (meaning to smell the roses), you are able to live a life for all that it is worth.

There is much to be said for the words ... *that was then, this is now.*

Further Contemplation

In this section, you will find numerous quotes attributed to Jean Klein, French author, spiritual teacher and philosopher of Advaita Vedanta (Nondualism).

http://www.omalpha.com/jardin/klein-en.html

A Metaphysics Primer

When you breath in, it is a receiving; when you breath out, it is an offering.

Give to your fellow what he needs to accomplish what life asked of him. Do not impose on another your idea of how he should best live.

Do not nourish the ideas you have built around yourself nor the image people have of you. Be neither someone nor something, just don't play the game. This will bring about being, constant awareness.

Be knowingly silent as often as you can and you will no longer be a prey to the desire to be this or that. You will discover in the everyday events of life that the meaning behind the fulfillment of the whole, for the ego is totally absent.

A Metaphysics Primer

What surfaces during meditation are residues of the past. These residues are energy localized through association of ideas--energy mobilized into fear and insecurity. Remain a witness to all this. In being the choiceless observer, attention is motiveless, and all conditioning subsides.

You must realize that you are now only a heap of conventions, habits, what society has made of you. Once all these have left you, you realize that they were defenses and aggressions accumulated solely to maintain the ego would simply does not exist.

Our surroundings are not contained by name and form. You are neither the body nor the mind; these are limits you identify with through a lack of clear-sightedness. When you are attentive to a tree or flower, the perception, shape, name and concept are not the only things present. There is also the All-presence that you share with them and that you are both part of. The very name and form spring forth from this

eternal background, the All-presence. This is instantaneous awareness that cannot be reached by thought.

The timeless non-state cannot be achieved because the mind cannot evolve towards it. The mind can only bring you to the threshold. Awakening comes unexpectedly when you do not wait for it, when you live in not-knowing. Only then are you available.

Observe the way your mind moves, works, without having any preconceived ideas about it. A moment will come when you discover yourself to be the witness. Subsequently, when all striving has left you, you will realize that you are the light shining beyond the observer. Reality is neither a product of the mind nor the result of a whole train of thoughts, it just is. The only method we can suggest is to observe impartially the way in which your mind reacts in the different circumstances of everyday life.

A Metaphysics Primer

When the intellect becomes silent through observation, through listening, the basic nature of the mind undergoes a transformation.

In the evening when you go to bed, prepare yourself, so as to avoid taking your daily worries with you. Observe whatever should present itself objectively; if you feel tired, feel it deep within yourself, look at it closely, this you will spontaneously find yourself exterior to it. Sooner or later a moment will arrive where it is no longer the focal point of your attention and it will disappear, will be burnt up by this awareness. The same thing will happen to all worries that preoccupy you. You will thus experience a feeling of harmony. Finally let your body sink into deep sleep.

When you wake up in the morning, don't do so in relation to objects, let it be in the Self, your true being. First of all be deeply aware, later the ego and the world will come to life.

A Metaphysics Primer

When one is struck by wonder or astonishment there is perfect non-duality between the knower and the thing known. It is a living reality. Let yourself be totally absorbed by it; then thought and action will derive directly from this background which is wonderment.

Observing everything with full attention becomes a way of life, a return to your original and natural meditative being.

Life is present, but when we think, we think in terms of the past or the future. To live in the now implies a mind free from end-gaining and recapitulation, free from grasping and striving. In the present there is no thought; thoughts are fused into a whole. Life in the moment contains all possible happenings so there is no place for time. Everything can be summed up in this: time is thought and thought appears in time. Beauty and joy are now revealed in the now.

A Metaphysics Primer

Silence is our real nature. What we are fundamentally, is only silence. Silence is free from beginning and end. It was before the beginning of all things. It is causeless. Its greatness lies in the fact that it simply is. In silence all objects have their home ground. It is the light that gives objects their shape and form. All movement, all activity is harmonized by silence. Silence has no opposite in noise. It is beyond positive and negative. Silence dissolves all objects. It is not related to any counterpart which belongs to the mind. Silence has nothing to do with mind. It cannot be defined, but it can be felt directly because it is our nearness. Silence is freedom without restriction or center. It is our wholeness, neither inside nor outside the body. Silence is joyful, not pleasurable. It is not psychological. It is feeling without a feeler. Silence needs no intermediary. Silence is holy. It is healing. There is no fear in silence. Silence is autonomous like love and beauty. It is untouched by time. Silence is meditation, free from any intention, free from anyone who meditates. Silence is the absence of oneself. Or rather, silence is the absence of absence. Sound which comes from silence is music. All activity is creative when it comes from silence. It is constantly a new beginning. Silence precedes speech and poetry and music and all art. Silence is the home ground of all creative activity. What is truly creative is the word, is Truth. Silence is the word. Silence is Truth. The one established in silence lives in constant offering, in prayer without asking, in thankfulness, in continual love.

A Final Note

In the words of Toni Petrinovich of Sacred Spaces [735] ......

Think about what that would feel like if the entire electric grid were down, including cell towers. No one would be able to contact each other easily. Whatever was happening to a person, family or friend outside the immediate vicinity would remain a mystery. This is the state of humanity for most of its existence.

One of the reasons that people are so stressed, anxious and fearful right now is because information *is* so readily available. If nothing traumatic is happening within your own life, all you have to do is turn on the news or read a news website on your computer to have a full visual of the drama in another part of the world.

Why am I bringing this up?

---

[735] http://sacredone.wordpress.com/2012/07/14/a-bolt-in-the-age-of-information/

A Metaphysics Primer

Because it is important to remember that what humanity is experiencing right now has been going on for thousands of years in one form or another.

There have always been wars.

Political entities have always attempted to overtake another country.

People have always been dying from disease.

Nothing has changed except your ability to know about it.

Take a breath.

Focus on your heart.

Know that we are all in this great adventure for the long run, meaning that "run" is infinite!

Stress does nothing except create more of itself, and, in itself, it is useless.

Offerings to the Creator

In this time of duality and misguided energy, we are asked to connect with the present moment. In so doing, I ask the Star Elders [1] to open my eyes so that I may see as they see, [2] to open my heart so that I may love as they love, [3] to open my mind so that I may know as they know. In holding the highest vision of perfection, in walking with love and respect for all beings, in always operating from love and truth with every step that I take, I am able to bring balance back to Mother Earth. Every individual among us exists as both student as well as teacher; when we operate as such, without ego, there are no leaders, there are no followers. I ask the Star Elders to guide me in my efforts to help create our family of light.

© Michele Doucette, July 19, 2012

Created based on The Atlantian Recovery Project: Preparing for the Pilgrimage [736]

---

[736] http://www.alunajoy.com/2012-mar12.html

A Metaphysics Primer

In the building of an entirely new body within a new spherical geometry, one that will also be multi-poled and multi-dimensional, my heart must be both opened and anchored, for this will allow me to live in the present moment (unity consciousness). In the offering of my old heart to the process, I am creating a new heart, one that is open, pure and filled with the best intentions; I am thus creating the holy of holies for my physical temple. This is now the time to come back to who we really are, not to whom we have been, but to who we really are. In working with intent, I am to begin first with my heart, thereafter adding in both intellect as well as the physical means to make it happen. I ask that everything be birthed from my heart first, so that all can be in sync. In all actuality, anything that is out of alignment with the truth will fall away, and the only thing that will be left is the truth.

© Michele Doucette, July 19, 2012

Created based on Receiving Our New Bodies: The Holy of Holies [737]

---

[737] http://www.alunajoy.com/2012-mar13.html

A Metaphysics Primer

To be who we really are is to be authentic.

Now is the time to clear out old issues, things that just keep repeating in our lives, and things that keep us from being authentic. There have been times when I have felt like I was not worthy, not good enough. So, too, have there been times when I have felt like I was unsupported, abandoned, abused, mistreated, mistrusted, controlled and self-sabotaged. There have been times when I would deliberately hold myself back, not allowing my authentic self to shine.

In pretending to be something (someone) that you are not, the universe will attract things (people, situations), unto you, that are also false.

Long have I known that energy never ends; that it is continuously recycled. In taking the time to gather up all of all these limitations and illusions, I formulate them into a ball in my hands. Reaching out, I hand the ball over to Hatshepsut, for she will be quick to send this energy back into the universal energy recycling bin.

A Metaphysics Primer

I no longer give credence to the negative ego, to the lies we believe about ourselves, to the lies that we believe about each other, or to the lies we believe about the world.

The more real (true, authentic) I can be, the more I will attract like-minded beings and circumstances to myself.

The more I attract like-minded beings around me, the stronger the love, the unity and the harmony will become in both my family and personal life. So, too, am I able to carry this harmonic resonance within me, wherever I go, sharing it just by being my true Divine self.

I am here to remain true to myself, living my life in authenticity. It is such an uplifting feeling to know that I do not have to alter who I AM in order to anchor my truth. Yes, I *can* change the world.

© Michele Doucette, July 19, 2012

Created based on Wings of Destiny [738]

---

[738] http://www.alunajoy.com/2012-mar14.html

A Metaphysics Primer

All life comes from a place called the Great Potential, a place that can be perceived as the sound that reverberates throughout the entire universe. Each being is currently in the process of preparing their temple to become a chalice for the Great Potential.

With rays of light coming from the Great Central Sun (not to be confused with our physical sun), we are being bathed in particles of light.

In asking these particles of light (visualized as tiny lightning bolts) to enter into every single cell of my body, thereby blessing my physical temple, I will have activated my body in such a way that I will be able to access another layer, or level, of ancient truth that has been locked inside me; an ancient truth that is something from the distant past, before Atlantis, when the Earth realm was still a land of light, not a land of duality.

This new knowledge, this remembrance, will become the foundation stone for the new dimension that we are now building inside the collective consciousness of the world.

A Metaphysics Primer

The more we envision and dream this new knowledge of light (non-duality), feeling it in our collective consciousness, the faster this reality will be manifested.

The job of anchoring light and accessing the deeper truth has been given to us.

We are the God)s and Goddesses who must come together with one heart and one vision (many pieces of the vision put together) to create a whole piece, a whole world, a new world in which no one piece, and no one, has been forgotten.

Long have we been taught to believe that we are but a tiny speck in the Universe.

In taking the time to visualize the entire Universe within us, we can see that we are so much more; that we have always been, thus.

In is in this space that we come to fully understand that we are not separate from anything; that we are a significant part of the totality of creation. So, too, was this the way of the Old Kingdom, the space from which they operated.

A Metaphysics Primer

This is the missing piece of wisdom that we have been seeking.

When we come to understand that we are all of creation and that all of creation is us, there is nothing we cannot create, do, think, feel, manifest, or be, in this space. We are being invited, henceforth, to realize that we may come, go, move, travel, and create an experience in any direction that our consciousness takes us.

In having had the courage to take on this physical form in a dimension of duality, forgetting most of who we are and why we were here, the time for celebrating our remembrance has arrived.

© Michele Doucette, July 19, 2012

Created based on Cellular Lightning Bolt Activation [739]

---

[739] http://www.alunajoy.com/2012-mar15.html

A Metaphysics Primer

We have all experienced a tightness around the throat area.

One way may have been when we were about to cry, but felt that we had to hold it in, making our throats hurt.

Another way may have been because it felt like we had to swallow our tears.

Sekhmet is here to help heal this tight, choked-up feeling.

Sekhmet chose to manifest as a female lion, not as an aggressive energy, but as an example of powerful creative energy.

There will be times when we need to be able to roar like a lion, but without making sound; more of a symbolic roar, if you will.

In essence, this means that the magic of the energy that we have inside must be released and expressed fully, courtesy of this symbolic roar.

Sekhmet says that we will know when, and how, to use this roar; that we will experience this roar in various stages of our lives.

A Metaphysics Primer

We know when the energy rises up (and it is usually when someone, or something, has upset us); we also know the feeling of anger that rushes through our body.

While the roar is like this, it is one without anger. Instead, it is one of passion.

We have been misusing this energy because we have been living in a dualistic world, and nearly everything here is being misused from an energy perspective. So, too, have we been afraid of this energy; therefore, we stopped using it in the appropriate way.

Nevertheless, this roar creates the same kind of rush in our bodies, but there is no anger attached to it.

It is a rush of energy that is like an explosion inside of us; an explosive energy can create anything. This is the new alchemy, a magic that already exists inside of us.

Yet the only time this energy shows up is when we find ourselves backed into a corner; likewise for someone who has hurt us or betrayed us.

A Metaphysics Primer

It has become imperative that we control this energy, so that, like the roar without the anger, it will heal, clear, and build that which we wish to manifest.

This roar is but another tool that we can add to our toolbox; a roar that originates in the power of the heart and comes out of the throat as Raaaaaaaaaaaa, meaning the power of the sun.

Clearly, we are in the process of transforming. So, too, are we recovering from our wounds, whilst helping others do the same, courtesy of our demonstrated experience(s).

© Michele Doucette, July 19, 2012

Created based on The Re-Emergence of Our Creative Power: Uncovering Our Inner Roar [740]

---

[740] http://www.alunajoy.com/2012-mar16.html

Michele's Life Lessons for 2013

This particular school year (2012 to 2013) is one that has continued to be fraught with many life lessons; proof that I am still learning. Even after twenty years, I will never claim to be a metaphysics expert.

Between June and August 2012, I had four Instructional Resource Teacher job interviews, all of which were denoted as permanent positions in town.

With twenty-seven years of teaching experience behind me, and all in this field, I continued to find myself working in the same rural school.

Even more disappointing was the fact that I found myself placed in a teaching assignment that I did *not* want, further demonstrating the manifestation of Lesson 10 (Conscious Creation) and Lesson 11 (The Law of Attraction) as shared, herein, in the chapter entitled *The Lessons, Part 1*.

A Metaphysics Primer

I have since come to see this particular teaching assignment (one that will last for the next three years, until my official retirement in June 2016) as a blessing.

<u>Conscious Creation</u> dictates that we create our own reality through thought (which also encompasses belief and response).

It is known that thought must first exist before manifestation of thought, also known as creation, can take place. In that alignment, we have the ability to manifest whatever we wish, all for the sole purpose of enhancing the wisdom that we continue to accrue, life after life after life.

Everything we think, we will feel; everything we feel, we will manifest; everything we manifest serves to create the condition(s) of our lives.

Every word we utter expresses some feeling within our souls; every word we utter also serves to create the condition(s) of our lives.

A Metaphysics Primer

This is a direct fusion of thought with emotion.

In desiring one thing (a permanent position in town; a new school), so, too, was I also experiencing (and living) the emotions associated with the exact opposite (*not* wanting to find myself placed in the Pervasive Needs position with three non-verbal students in Kindergarten; same old school).

I was clearly creating by way of my emotional thinking. In truth, I had *sabotaged* my own observation, creating by default (which is not the best place to find one's self). Having arrived at this conclusion, with the help of a dear spiritual companion, I knew that I had, once again, arrived at a most the powerful position; one whereby I could decide to create, and observe, another reality for myself.

As Stuart Wilde writes ... "Visualize the adverse situation, [breathing] love into it and the people involved. Love can cure the pain, because it makes you bigger than the pain so you get over it." [741]

---

[741] http://www.stuartwilde.com/2013/04/emotional-techniques-for-healing-yourself/#.UXo5ebyhOVU.wordpress

A Metaphysics Primer

<u>The Law of Attraction</u> dictates that thought is the greatest force in the world, and, as stated earlier, that *everything begins with thought.*

Whatever you fix your thought(s) upon (meaning whatever you steadily fix your imagination on) is what you shall attract.

While it is true that negative events take place at some point in everyone's life, as I was quick to experience, *the more you are able to remain open to the experience, relaxing and embracing the situation, doing your best to learn from the event in question,* the easier it becomes to transcend, to move beyond.

Challenged beyond anything that I have ever experienced, in the course of my teaching career, to date, this has continued to be the most pervasive life lesson for me.

In knowing that whatever you resist will persist, it also becomes the welcoming, accepting and embracing of positive change that the negative energies finally begin to dissipate.

A Metaphysics Primer

Too often we affirm the negative, over and over again, in our daily lives without even realizing that we are attracting more and more of the very same into our lives.

If we give our attention (attraction) to something while emphatically stating **I do not want this in my life**, we are merely *attracting what we do not want* because we are continuing to give our attention to that which we do not want.

This can railroad all of the positively inspired thoughts and aspirations that we need to move ourselves forward, which is exactly what transpired in my life just this year.

When we *stop giving attention to that which we do not want*, this becomes the time when we start attracting more of what we do want.

As you become *more conscious about focusing on what you really want*, you begin to experience a sense of complete freedom.

The more you focus, the stronger your vibration becomes.

A Metaphysics Primer

Feeling good is imperative in achieving vibrational harmony with your desire.

There are many different activities that I engage in order to strengthen and maintain these good feelings: [1] listening to songs that make me feel upbeat, [2] watching movies and television shows that make laugh, that make me feel warm inside, [3] reading (any type of book will do), [4] engaging in discussions of a synchronistic nature, [5] completing a daily Appreciation Diary and then focusing on the feelings evoked by the written words, [6] playing the Choosing Prosperity Game, [742] [7] focusing on my vision board, and [8] meditating about my Feel Good statements.

It is important to be conscious of how you are feeling, always choosing to be positive.

An individual with a higher vibration (positive) will create their desires more easily, more freely, more effectively, than someone harboring a low, dense energy (negative).

---

[742] http://choosingprosperity.com/about-the-prosperity-game/

A Metaphysics Primer

Should you find yourself in a less than positive state, simply bring yourself back into a thought that makes you feel positive.

For me, sometimes this was a daily experience.

Happiness, joy, bliss, appreciation, love, gratitude, peace, compassion, confidence, faith, excitement, success, awareness, freedom and trust are the feelings and attitudes that emit a higher frequency and attract people, places and situations of a positive nature.

By comparison, feelings and attitudes like condemnation, guilt, worry, disappointment, fear, revenge, insecurity, doubt, failure, hesitation and sadness emit a lower frequency, thus attracting people, places and situations of a negative nature.

Knowing that positive thoughts and feelings create a higher vibration, it becomes in keeping your vibrations high that will allow you to manifest things more freely in your life.

I choose to be happy by consciously focusing on what makes me happy.

A Metaphysics Primer

I keep imagining the excitement and exhilaration, the gratitude and the happiness, associated with my desire existing as a reality right now.

The more enthusiastic, the more pumped up, the more excited, the more emotionally charged, you are about something, and the better it feels, the faster it will show up in your life.

It is one thing to know these things on an intellectual level; it is quite another to continually experience them as gentle life reminders.

This is why it is so important to trust, to believe, to have faith.

When you know something must happen, it will.

A master of creation chooses something to manifest and does not move on to something else until he (or she) has manifested it completely.

→ Be committed

→ Be persistent

A Metaphysics Primer

→ Focus on it with every fiber of your being

→ Expect it to manifest fully

→ Do not take no for an answer

→ Intend that your desire is your reality

→ Believe that your desire is your reality

→ Trust that your desire is your reality

Express gratitude, knowing that you are being taken care of every step of the way.

There is a *Law of Detachment* that says that in order to successfully attract something, so, too, must you also be able to detach yourself from the outcome.

Doing so allows you to work from a position of serenity, trust and faith, as compared to one of doubt, worry and fear.

To feel detached is to feel a deep sense of freedom, knowing that we can trust in our greater good, knowing that we are taken care of, knowing that we are able to manifest that which we desire or something better.

A Metaphysics Primer

Intentional creation means existing in a place of *peaceful expectation*. At the time of this publication, I can honestly say that I am finally here.

It is imperative that I keep empowering my life with the vision(s) of what I desire, for any individual who succeeds as a conscious and deliberate creator literally holds the key to mastering their world.

Interestingly enough, enlightenment is also a state of non-attachment.

The more you remain unattached, the more you allow your Higher Self (or your Christ Consciousness) to flow through you.

As you let go and trust, not only do you feel different, but you radiate a different vibration to the world, allowing better things and experiences to come to you.

While the Law of Attraction allows one to acquire things, courtesy of their material needs and desires, it is also this same universal law that focuses on the spiritual needs of humanity.

A Metaphysics Primer

When you are focused upon spiritual thoughts, you will find that you are not overly concerned with the physical burdens of life.

I will now leave you with this thought upon which to reflect further: *what you are seeking is also seeking you.*

How to Let Go: 7 Affirmations for Practicing the Law of Detachment [743]

How to Practice the Law of Detachment [744]

How to Use the Law of Detachment [745]

Law of Detachment [746]

---

[743] http://www.chopra.com/articles/2010/06/18/how-to-let-go-affirmations-for-practicing-the-law-of-detachment/
[744] http://www.paultobey.com/blog/archives/2011/01/06/law-of-detachment/
[745] http://teppie-christina.hubpages.com/hub/How-To-Use-The-Law-of-Detachment
[746] http://www.mindreality.com/law-of-detachment-flowing-with-god

A Metaphysics Primer

The Law of Detachment [747] [748] [749] [750]

The Tao Philosophy of Detachment [751]

---

[747] http://www.chopra.com/laws/detachment

[748] http://www.findingsource.com/index.php?option=com_content&view=article&id=16:conscious-detachment&catid=1&Itemid=2

[749] http://americankabuki.blogspot.ca/2013/04/the-law-of-detachment.html?utm_source=feedburner&utm_medium=feed&utm_campaign=Feed:+AmericanKabuki+(American+Kabuki)

[750] http://masterthe7laws.com/the-law-of-detachment/

[751] http://www.stuartwilde.com/2013/04/the-tao-philosophy-of-detachment/

The Crux of the Matter

The crux of the matter is simple ... everything is up to us.

We are now waking up to the fact that we have always created our reality, albeit from an unconscious perspective. This is why it is imperative to learn to create from a conscious standpoint.

Our biggest stumbling block is simply FEAR. Once we are able to process the fear, allowing it to exist as a part of the overall necessary contrasting process, completing the circuit of positive and negative, we are able to move into that joy (light and love) mode of existence (our true essence), forging ahead in lives that can only be filled with enthusiasm, excitement, inspiration and creative power.

May the force be with you as you strive to remember, observe, and once again experience, the following words of wisdom (as written by Inelia Benz).

A Metaphysics Primer

Once we step out of the drama, really step out of it, and simply shift our focus on what we have in our lives, what we want for our lives, and how we want our lives to be different, and how that difference will affect others on the planet; once we realize that it is our own individual actions and responses (not reactions), that dictate what happens on the planet, that is when we can start breathing deeply and moving forward as a species. [752]

While the chaos may swirl around us, the maelstrom will subside, for we are the ones we have been waiting for.

We are here [1] to step into our true essence, [2] to embrace, and live, our true power, [3] to emerge as the new paradigm holders, [4] to embrace our expanded awareness, and [5] to create a physical reality that reflects the true nature of who we are, and have always been, by embracing, and living the Christ Consciousness; this is what constitutes the long prophesized Second Coming. In truth, the time of our own sovereignty has arrived.

---

[752] Email received May 2, 2013.

A Metaphysics Primer

We *are* the God force.

We *are* part of All That Is.

We *are* part of the Cosmic Mind.

We *are* part of the Infinite Consciousness.

We *are* part of an Intelligent Design.

Camillo Løken, author of <u>The Paradox of Creation</u> (released April 2013), writes that *we are God in disguise*,[753] a premise with which I also concur.

As individuated aspects of the God force (All That Is, Cosmic Mind, Infinite Consciousness, and Intelligent Design), it can be said that *we are the thoughts, we are the interaction, thereby allowing the God force to experience the totality of all that is possible.*

---

[753] http://www.amazon.com/Paradox-Creation-Wake-You-Disguise/dp/148415794X/

Could this be what Shakespeare full intended with his words, *To Be or Not To Be*, clearly eliciting a personal choice?

In order to BE, one must DO; one must create, one must experience, one must actualize.

One of the premises of quantum theory states that by the very act of watching, the observer affects the observed reality. This also means that there can be no phenomenon until it is observed.

The implications, herein, are rather profound, meaning that "before anything can manifest in the physical universe, it must first be observed. Presumably, observation cannot occur without the pre-existence of some sort of consciousness to do the observing. The Observer Effect clearly implies that the physical Universe is the direct result of *consciousness*. This notion has a striking resemblance to perennial esoteric theory which asserts that all phenomena are the result of the consciousness of a single overlighting *Creative Principle* or the Mind of God." [754]

Consciousness creates form.

Consciousness creates matter.

As part of this *same* consciousness, so, too, do we create our own reality, moment by moment; as a result, random events do not occur.

Thought is "an attribute of consciousness, the filter through which consciousness manifests itself into form. Hence, any product or service a human being wants to create must first be a thought. We need to be conscious of what we want to create. It is impossible to create anything without thinking about it first." [755]

Everything comes down to choice.

Everything comes down to change.

---

[754] http://www.vision.net.au/~apaterson/science/observer_effect.htm
[755] Løken, Camillo. (2013) The Paradox of Creation: Wake Up, You Are God In Disguise (page 63). ProducktFokus: Sellebakk, Norway.

A Metaphysics Primer

The Choice Point Movement [756]

The Choice Point Movement encourages change. They want their members to understand the world they live in so that in turn they can *be the change* the world is longing for.

---

[756] http://members.choicepointmovement.com/Account/LogOnRegister?returnUrl=%2f

A Metaphysics Primer

Membership provides you with:

[1] the *wisdom* to understand your world,

[2] the *tools* to align your purpose, and

[3] the *exchange of ideas* to be the change.

As a member, I hope to see many of you there.

As my dear friend Elio has shared with me in the past: *In reference to the statement* **To Be Or Not To Be**, *the famous opening phrase of a soliloquy in William Shakespeare's play Hamlet, Michele encourages you to contemplate the deeper meaning of To (Choose) To Be or To (Choose) Not To Be (Enlightened).*

She then weaves concoctions of words and concepts that take you, the reader, to new depths in a clear, concise and easy manner, as well as offering numerable sources for you to research further, if that is your aspiration.

A Metaphysics Primer

I trust that the reading of this book has served you, in this way, on your journey.

Addendum

2012: The Best Year Ever [757]

This article shows that on the macro level, our world is getting better all the time, primarily because people are coming together to make a difference, thereby working toward the building of a brighter future.

10 Reasons for Hope and Optimism [758]

If you watch the news, or read the newspaper, it seems as if everything is falling apart, mainly because the world is filled with war, fear, greed, and hate. While these are the very challenges we are faced with, there are also many amazing developments taking place that the media seldom reports, mainly because fear-mongering and sensationalism is what sells. This article outlines the 10 most inspiring trends, thereby further highlighting that despite the challenges, there are many great reasons for hope and optimism.

---

[757] http://www.wanttoknow.info/inspiration/best_year
[758] http://www.wanttoknow.info/inspiration/hope_optimism_reasons

Building a Brighter Future [759]

Together, we can and will build a brighter future. In order to give meaningful suggestions to further support this, however, we first need to speak candidly about what is happening in the world at present; this candid article does just that.

For Those Who Want To Know the Truth [760]

This website provides a concise, reliable introduction to vital information of which few are aware. They specialize in providing fact-filled news articles as well as concise summaries of major cover-ups which impact our lives and world. All information is taken from the most reliable sources available and can be verified using the links they provide. Sources are always noted, with links direct to the information source, whenever possible.

---

[759] http://www.wanttoknow.info/brighterfuture
[760] http://www.wanttoknow.info/

FREE WISDOM COURSES

The <u>Hidden Knowledge Course</u> is designed for those who want to dive into the deep cover-ups and hidden manipulations going on behind the scenes in our world.

While this information-packed course inspires readers to make a difference and build a better world, it is totally unlike the other courses, in that the focus is largely on exploring, and exposing, all that is hidden and secret in our world.

This eye-opening course presents only reliable material which can be verified using provided links to respected sources.

Those who complete the course will have a broad understanding of the role of the power elite and how their plans often adversely impact life for the majority of people in our world.

A Metaphysics Primer

For those who choose to focus largely on love and inspiration, every page of the heart-expanding <u>Inspiration Course</u> will touch, move, and inspire you to open to more love and deeper connections in your life.

With all of the violence and sensationalism prevalent in the media, this course feels like a fresh mountain breeze; so, too, does it feel like one is drinking water, so rich and fulfilling, from a pure mountain lake.

Herein, you will be uplifted and transformed by seeing humanity at its very best.

In these lessons you will find some of the most loving, inspiring essays, videos, quotes, and empowering exercises available on the Internet.

Are you ready to be the change *you* want to see in your life and in our world? If the answer is yes, the <u>Insight Course</u> was designed for you.

These free online courses bring together the best of the Internet to both inspire and educate you in a dynamic and powerful way.

A Metaphysics Primer

The journey through these courses will enhance your awareness, providing you with the necessary tools that will enable you to build a better life and world.

Course lessons will deepen your insight and expand your horizons, empowering you to be the change you want to see in the world.

Have you ever felt that one of the main reasons you are here is to help transform our planet to a new way of living based on love and empowerment?

Do you recognize that there is a divine essence in every person, and that as beautiful manifestations of the divine, all people deserve our love and support to be the best they can be?

If so, the <u>Transformation Course</u> may be the choice for you; a course that harmonizes the light and inspiring aspects of life with the more challenging shadow sides of existence and creates a beautiful synthesis which transcends duality.

A Metaphysics Primer

Which of these Wisdom Courses should you take? [761]

Table of Contents and Lesson Links for Wisdom Courses [762]

Many of us are struggling because we have forgotten who we are. As stated throughout this text, our true and authentic selves are connected with Source Energy; this is who we are. By comparison, who we think we are is how we show up in life, how we present ourselves to the public eye.

Who we think we are comes from listening to other people rather than listening to ourselves. If we are to live in the flow, we must learn to focus who we are and what we can do in the moment.

Authentic living is never about who you are not, what you cannot do, and what you do not have; when you are living in alignment with Source, you find that you already have everything you need.

---

[761] http://www.wisdomcourses.net/which_course_to_take
[762] http://www.wisdomcourses.net/course_contents_wc

A Metaphysics Primer

Authentic living means

[1] acknowledging that life is not always easy (there will be challenges)

[2] acknowledging that one does not always follow a straight and convenient path (one may be asked to live outside the box)

[3] acknowledging that one must allow life to unfold through them (which, along with being the best part, can be the most difficult)

One's greatness is not dependent on anything that they do, or do not, accomplish.

We are already great; we merely have to live this greatness, by knowing who you are and what you must do in this moment; nothing else is required.

Today will bring you a new awareness; in acknowledging this, know that you are living in alignment with who you are.

Tools for Creation

All of these transformational tools (websites as well as products) have been utilized by the author whilst on her spiritual journey.

SACRED SOUND ODYSSEY

Paulina Ellis, from Edmunston, New Brunswick, is a *one woman band* in reference to her Sacred Sound Odyssey performances.

Intuitively creating a soothing soundscape from a collection of crystal bowls and exotic musical instruments, she fuses sacred sounds and inspirational images in a unique hologram performance, whereby the viewer is transported on an inner journey (one that is both hypnotic and liberating) of harmony and alignment.

Paulina's expression of the Divine Feminine in form, sound, light and sacred geometry is beautiful, haunting and healing.

A Metaphysics Primer

Connected to the energy of Mother Earth, you are carried into the expanse of the universal flow.

This Odyssey, then, becomes an immersion of self into pure vibration.

It was an honor, a blessing and a privilege to be able to attend two Sacred Sound Odyssey evenings (July 30 and 31, 2013).

The inspiring artwork behind the hologram performance can also be purchased (canvas art, wood mounted art, posters, cards, book marks, candles), courtesy of her Art Blessings website. [763] In addition, purchasing a copy of the Crystallina CD enables one to recapture the sacred experience of sound and vibration.

36 Court Street, Suite 202

Edmunston, New Brunswick

E3V 1S3

Toll free: 1-888-735-8835

---

[763] http://www.artblessings.com/

WEBSITE INFORMATION

A Conscious Creation Overview (Seth and Jane Roberts) [764]

Bashar (channeled information) [765]

Changing The Paradigm of The Planet (Jeddah Mali) [766]

Conscious Creation [767]

Conscious Creation (Myke Wolfe) [768]

Conscious Creation Journal Archives [769]

Conscious Creation Radio Show [770]

---

[764] http://www.paulhelfrich.com/library/Helfrich_P_Seth_Jane_Roberts_Conscious_Creation_Overview.pdf
[765] http://www.bashar.org/
[766] http://www.jeddahmali.com/about.php
[767] http://www.consciouscreation.com/
[768] http://www.consciouscreation.info/lawofattraction/manifesting/creating_reality.php
[769] http://www.consciouscreation.com/journal/
[770] http://www.blogtalkradio.com/consciouscreation

A Metaphysics Primer

Conscious Creation Tips (Jackie Lapin) [771]

Consciousness Shifts Reality (Cynthia Sue Larson) [772]

Creative Manifesting (Anisa Aven) [773]

Hermes Trismegistus (Tom DeLiso) [774]

Home of Abraham (Esther and Jerry Hicks) [775]

Jeshua Channelings (Pamela Kribbe) [776]

Lightsmith (Michele Mayama) [777]

Mind Reality (Enoch Tan) [778]

Enoch Tan is a mind and reality scientist and writer who uses the internet as the medium with which to help people achieve higher awareness in living and experiencing life.

---

[771] http://consciouscreationtips.com/
[772] http://www.realityshifters.com/
[773] http://www.crcatavision.com/creative-manifesting.htm
[774] http://www.wisdomsdoor.com/index1.htm
[775] http://www.abraham-hicks.com/lawofattractionsource/index.php
[776] http://www.jeshua.net/
[777] http://www.lightsmith.com/
[778] http://www.mindreality.com/

A Metaphysics Primer

He wants to impact the world in the biggest way possible by changing lives and creating possibilities.

Educational psychology states that a learned person is one with a vision of unified knowledge. In turn, Enoch does not like being restricted to seeing things from one dimension, preferring to see things from multiple dimensions in order to combine them into an integrated perspective.

If any of these words resonate with you, please take the time to support his work. You can also get a taste for the type of material he writes in keeping with his archived articles. [779]

Mind Your Reality (Tania Kotsos) [780]

Morphogenetic Resonance: From Causal to Conscious Creation (Lauren C. Gorgo) [781]

Reality Creation 1010 [782]

---

[779] http://www.mindreality.com/archive
[780] http://www.mind-your-reality.com/
[781] http://spiritlibrary.com/lauren-c-gorgo/morphogenetic-resonance-from-causal-to-conscious-creation
[782] http://www.redshift.com/~beyond/real1010.html

A Metaphysics Primer

Success Consciousness (books by Remez Sasson) [783]

The Abundance Site [784]

The Art of Conscious Creation (Jackie Lapin) [785]

The Art of Conscious Creation (Tom Murasso) [786]

The Conscious Creation of a New Paradigm [787]

The Consciousness Chronicles [788]

The Elias Forum [789]

The Great Wealth Pandemic (Jody Sachse) [790]

The Words of Oneness (Rasha) [791]

---

[783] http://www.successconsciousness.com/ebooks_and_books.htm
[784] http://www.theabundancesite.com/
[785] http://jackielapin.com/the-art-of-conscious-creation/
[786] http://borntomanifest.com/articles/tom5.html
[787] http://www.spiritofmaat.com/archive/mar2/tiller1.htm
[788] http://conscious-pictures.com/chronicles/cc_index.html
[789] http://www.eliasforum.org/
[790] http://freepdfs.org/pdf/the-great-wealth-pandemic
[791] http://www.onenesswebsite.com/

A Metaphysics Primer

Time 2 Wake Up: 20 Keys Of Conscious Creation [792]

Wisp Magazine (a Reality Creation magazine) [793]

Wizard's Wonderland [794]

PRODUCT INFORMATION AND LINKS

Core Energy Meditation [795]

Scientists have recently made some amazing discoveries about the human bio-energy field and the major energy centers in the body. These energy centers literally determine how good (or bad) you feel each day, and of course, the better you feel, the more you are able to attract the good things you want into your life.

---

[792] http://www.newciv.org/nl/newslog.php/_v397/__show_article/_a000397-000252.htm
[793] http://wisp.focusphere.net/
[794] http://www.wizardwonderland.com/
[795] http://www.mindbodytrainingcompany.com/go.php?Clk=4073087

A Metaphysics Primer

Kevin Schoeninger (certified holistic fitness trainer, meditation instructor and Reiki Master/Trainer) has developed a 20-minute practice that will balance all your major energy centers; a short daily practice that allows you to balance and energize every aspect of your being; a practice that better enables you to feel healthy and happy (which is all part of your life purpose).

Kevin's *Core Energy Meditation* system also gives you a blueprint for tapping into your personal guidance system. When you feel connected to Source, you know when you are taking the right action for your life in the here and now.

Enlightened Beings Super Manifestor E-store [796]

An e-store that sells manifesting ebooks, affirmation ebooks, guided meditations and a manifesting e-course, all courtesy of Jafree Ozwald, an absolutely amazing Manifestation Coach.

---

[796] https://www.enlightenedbeings.com/SM-estore/index.php?r=1&ref=211

Harmonic Ascension: Frequency Is Everything (Jody Sachse) [797]

This is one of my favorite places to visit. Complete with a variety of meditations (for increased success, for higher awareness, for relaxation and stress, for developing ESP and Psychic skills, for healing and physical health, for recreational purposes), downloads, e-books and the Master Key system (by Charles F, Haanel).

Holistic Practitioner Marketing Certification (Steve G. Jones) [798]

Law of Attraction Basic Certification Practitioner (Joe Vitale) [799]

Law of Attraction Pro (Bradley Thompson) [800]

Life Coaching Secrets (Bradley Thompson) [801]

---

[797] http://harmonicascension.com/
[798] http://www.stevegjones.com/holistic_mastermind.htm
[799] http://myglobalsciencesfoundation.org/certone.shtml
[800] http://www.lawofattractionpro.com/?ref=48106
[801] http://www.life-coaching-secrets.com/?ref=48106

A Metaphysics Primer

<u>Manifest A Miracle</u> (Gary Evans) [802]

<u>Mind Movies Creation Kit</u> [803]

Whatever the mind can conceive and believe, it can achieve. These words were spoken by Napoleon Hill, author of <u>Think and Grow Rich</u>.

For people, like me, who have an extremely difficult time with the visualization process, you have finally come to the right place. This creation of Ryan Higgins was denoted the *Best Manifestation Tool for 2007* and after watching the intro video, it was easy to see why.

If you can create with a joyful and passionate feeling, you are going to accomplish whatever it is that you desire a whole lot faster.

Feel free to watch TIME TO REVOLUTIONIZE [804] as well as AN ABUNDANCE OF BLESSINGS, [805] the two Mind Movies that I was inspired to create.

---

[802] http://www.manifestmiracle.com/
[803] http://www.mindmovies.com/?10107

A Metaphysics Primer

Mystic Mindpower (Jody Sachse) [806]

As Jody Sachse, creator of *Mystic Mindpower*, shares that everything around us exists at a certain frequency. Scientists and quantum physicists have told us that everything is made up of energy.

We measure every form of energy as a frequency.

Light has a frequency, smells have a frequency, thoughts have a frequency. You have thought patterns in different brainwave states, all of which can be measured in frequency.

In short, frequency makes up everything we can see and everything we cannot see.

If you can change a certain frequency, you can change everything. While our mental state affects our brainwaves, the opposite is also true, meaning that *our brainwaves affect our mental state*.

---

[804] http://www.youtube.com/watch?v=UBLFLF4c7cU
[805] http://www.youtube.com/watch?v=rHpH3jBBEBY
[806] http://mysticmindpower.com/

A Metaphysics Primer

This means that we can actually control our mental state by controlling our brainwaves. This is the power behind Brainwave Entrainment.

Mystic Mindpower has a wide range of unique brainwave entrainment meditations, ranging from beta, alpha, theta, delta and gamma brainwave frequencies.

[Mystic Mindpower Evolution Brainwave Entrainment Meditation Guide][807]

[Quantum Confidence][808]

When it comes to manifestation, making, and maintaining, the change from a negative state (frustrations, worries, doubts, fears, anxieties) to a positive state (total self confidence, high self esteem) is of utmost importance because until you change the way you think, you will simply continue to manifest more of the same (which is usually what you do not want).

---

[807] http://mysticmindpower.com/mp3/MME-Guide.pdf
[808] http://30703zu2geitqn7k2wym7bqfyp.hop.clickbank.net/

A Metaphysics Primer

It seems that we have been programmed to struggle; hence, the necessity for changing the negative brainwave patterns that we have existed with, until now.

Morry Zelcovitch has created the *Quantum Confidence* system. Engineered in a responsible, scientific and considerate way, this system helps people identify and deal with what may be holding them back.

In truth, the *Quantum Confidence* system may also be useful for any number of conditions and mind states, all of which are associated with self help and personal growth.

Using the *Quantum Confidence* system is very similar to sticking to an exercise regimen or even a proper diet that includes a change in eating habits. Once you get to the point where you want to be, it is important that you keep up a maintenance routine in order to maintain your achieved results.

The affirmations are designed for each hemisphere of the brain.

A Metaphysics Primer

So, too, are they designed to be accepted by your mind so that change, real change, may occur in the most efficient and effective way possible.

All affirmations are also listed in the manual so that you may look at them and know exactly what is being directed towards your subconscious mind.

Each affirmation is tried and true, designed for ease of acceptance and effectiveness.

For those of you who have never used this system (which involves brainwave entrainment), there is something that you should be made aware of.

Brainwave entrainment, when properly engineered, has been shown to allow for the release of deep trauma that has been buried.

Please consider having someone nearby (a professional, a trusted friend, a family member) with whom you can discuss these issues as they arise.

In many cases, repressed emotions and events clear themselves easily, but occasionally they may be difficult.

As people are listening to TMM recording systems, they find that random thoughts continue to pop out of nowhere. Do not fight these thoughts. Simply allow them to be.

It is important to keep remembering that when you resist something, you are engaging in a state of stress.

This program is all about natural states of relaxation, peace and bliss.

Quantum Mind Power [809]

The *Quantum Mind Power* (with TMM) system uses various "sculpted" tones and embedded frequencies in order to get the brain to go into altered (but very natural) states of consciousness.

When the brain reacts to these tones, various and beneficial neurotransmitters and endorphins are released (which are

---

[809] http://318680j2ehhfoq5h1gxhpbbpc8.hop.clickbank.net/

necessary neuro-chemicals that our brain and body need to function properly, healthfully and naturally).

When the brain is stimulated with pulses, the overall activity of the brain will respond to, and align with, these pulses.

By selecting the desired rate, the brain, via the frequency following response (entrainment), can be naturally induced towards the selected brainwave state.

It is also because of the frequency following response, or entrainment, that these pulsed sounds often produce benefits similarly found with deep meditation.

Neural Synergy was specifically designed to help to re-organize the brain to a higher level; allowing it to process more complicated stimuli easier than before. An integral part of a fitness regimen for the brain, this recording should be listened to once a day.

Eden Energy Wave Dynamics is designed to pump up your energy levels, while silencing the "voices" that tend to make you stagnate and stop moving forward (because they make you think too much, or cause you to fear something).

A Metaphysics Primer

This recording may be rotated with *Neural Synergy* on alternate days for variety and/or whenever you feel the need for a quick "pick me up".

Whole Brain Gratitude Meditation was designed as a gratitude building meditation. This recording helps you with direction and intent, thereby enabling you to change your current view of the world (which then changes your reality as well). How you look at things and interpret their meaning can be everything, and amazing changes can occur when you change how you look at life. This recording is intended to be listened to twice a week.

Emotive Brain Wave Hypnosis was designed to help guide you to balance your emotions and experience happiness, allowing you to tap into the deep wiring of your subconscious mind (so that you can better deal with the matters that are most affecting your life). It is intended to be listened to twice a week.

A Metaphysics Primer

Feel free to sample a 20 minute audio recording. [810]

Super Mind Evolution System [811]

Since Einstein has proven that energy and mass are interchangeable, various universities and laboratories have been able to either measure or calculate the force generated by a human mind (as in psychokinetic experiments). The obvious conclusion here is that, as mass and energy are interchangeable, the energy generated by human consciousness can be converted into its mass equivalent, the format of which is controlled and directed by the most extraordinary of higher-consciousness processes; namely, visualization.

When a human mind clearly, and continually, visualizes an end result, with deep emotion and concentrated intent, then the formatted energy generated is converted into its mass equivalent (meaning the desired result).

---

[810] http://quantum-mind-power-system.com/Gift-for-friends.htm
[811] http://www.supermindevolutionsystem.com/store/?12737

A Metaphysics Primer

Jim Francis, a serious researcher, has a background in both hypnosis and electronic design. The founder of the <u>Australasian Lateral Thinking Newsletter</u>, he has been its editor for the past twelve years. Having undertaken training in various forms of remote viewing, Jim shows how this medium technique can easily be learned. Apart from Jim's description of his mind discoveries and their application, he also points to the serious science that supports his concepts, describing how individuals can take advantage of these scientific suppositions, thereby moving towards a better understanding of how the intuitive mind works.

The substantiated research of Jim Francis, over the course of the last 10 years, was combined with the latest *cutting edge* brain audio technology. As a result, the *Super Mind Evolution System* was born.

The entire system is available in 21 PDF reports and 20 audio mp3 files, all accessible via instant download.

A Metaphysics Primer

The 7 Essential Universal Laws (Christy Whitman) [812]

The 11 Forgotten Laws (Bob Proctor, Mary Morrissey) [813]

The Absolute Secret (Bradley Thompson) [814]

The Belief Secret (Bradley Thompson) [815]

The Hidden Secret in Think and Grow Rich (Brian Kim) [816]

The Morry Method™ (Morry Zelcovitch) [817]

The Morry Method™ is a breakthrough new technology, resulting after 15 years of scientific research and development. Having been trained by the world's foremost expert (David Siever) in the field of Brainwave Entrainment, Morry Zelcovitch is one of the few in the world who can lay claim to being a certified Brainwave Entrainment Engineer.

---

[812] http://www.7essentiallaws.com/essentiallaws.php
[813] http://www.the11forgottenlaws.com/
[814] http://www.theabsolutesecret.com/?ref=48106
[815] http://www.beliefsecret.com/?ref=48106
[816] http://www.briankim.net/hiddensecret.php
[817] http://www.themorrymethod.com/

A Metaphysics Primer

TMM™ uses a proprietary protocol developed for presenting various stimuli to the brain and mind, with the end result being a method that is much "softer" towards the brain body system because it offers a more natural incorporation of the brain beats as well as any presented information (meditations, hypnosis, affirmations, reading or studying).

Both *Quantum Mind Power* and *Quantum Confidence* (discussed within this section of the book), make use of The Morry Method™, a system that has been purposely designed to help ease the entrainment process. [818]

<u>The New Message of a Master</u> (Kristen Howe) [819]

<u>The Power of Practice</u> [820]

If you have had any kind of trouble making The Law of Attraction work in your life, you may be missing one key ingredient, as is shared by Mind-Body Training expert

---

[818] http://www.themorrymethod.com/tmm-vs-the-rest/
[819] http://www.newmessageofamaster.com/
[820] http://www.mindbodytrainingcompany.com/go.php?Clk=4073090

A Metaphysics Primer

Kevin Schoeninger. This is the program wherein you will discover the one word never mentioned in The Secret, a concept that is crucial for your happiness and success with the Law of Attraction. Kevin calls this the Master Tool as used by Oprah, Donald Trump, and all of the great spiritual masters that live their soul's purpose, while also manifesting spectacular results.

The Quantum Cookbook [821]

Having manifested a dream lifestyle over the past 20 years, Bradley Thompson knows the two missing steps that The Secret does not tell you.

He will prove to you that manifesting works brilliantly when you follow his 6 step program. Not only that, but he will hand over $150 if it does not work for you. This just might be something that you also want to check out for yourself.

The Secret of Deliberate Creation [822]

---

[821] http://www.quantumcookbook.com/?afl=48106
[822] http://hits.thesecretofdeliberatecreation.com/cgi-bin/redir?pd_link=i1-a20822-o3118-c43451

A Metaphysics Primer

This program is a dynamite combination of <u>The Da Vinci Code</u>, <u>The Secret</u> and <u>Think and Grow Rich</u>. Mysterious, suspenseful, and powerfully persuasive, it is now available in a considerably discounted (of over $100) and fully downloadable version.

What Dr. Robert Anthony does in *The Secret of Deliberate Creation* is show you how the natural laws of Quantum Physics, the Law of Attraction, and Cause and Effect can either work for you or against you. As a conscious and deliberate creator, you, too, will want these laws working for you, 100% of the time.

<u>The Secrets of Meditation, Health and Manifestation</u> [823]

The Secrets of Meditation, Health and Manifestation is a comprehensive introduction to meditation, breathing, energy work and manifestation.

What many do not realize is that there are meditation and breathing exercises you can use to reduce stress as well as

---

[823] http://www.mindbodytrainingcompany.com/go.php?Clk=4073086

improve your health, thereby increasing your level of energy and enjoyment of life.

These secrets are simple and yet tremendously powerful.

Doing these exercises on a daily basis, as simple as they are, will change your life.

These secrets include how to [1] develop control over your own mind and body, [2] supercharge your energy level and feel great on a day-to-day basis, and [3] work with the power of your subconscious mind to move you toward what would truly fulfill you in your life.

Matt Clarkson has created a complimentary course to help you get started. With each installment, you will get an exercise, inspirational message or tip, to help you calm the mind and reduce stress.

This is an ideal program for anyone with an interest in meditation, self-growth and personal development, as well as for anyone suffering from stress, anxiety or depression.

The Soul Journey [824]

People everywhere are searching for well-being (meaning, purpose, fulfillment, health and happiness). For life to be good, we need to feel useful and appreciated. Taking a spiritual growth journey called *The Soul Journey* will enable you to grasp the bigger picture of who you are. You will discover how to distinguish your personality from soul. You will learn practical ways to develop and express soul for a life of meaning and purpose.

In changing your consciousness, you will change your life.

The Undiscovered Parallel, Part 1 [825]

Discover *The Undiscovered Parallel Part 1* which will show you one simple trick to supercharge all techniques used for focusing your mind (as in visualization, affirmations, subliminals, hypnosis, EFT, the Sedona Method, meditation, brainwave entrainment, counselling or therapy) as part of your self-growth journey.

---

[824] http://www.thesouljourney.com/?a_aid=195
[825] http://www.mindbodytrainingcompany.com/go.php?Clk=4085676

A Metaphysics Primer

Unlock the Power of Now (Kristen Howe) [826]

---

[826] http://unlockthepowerofnow.com/

Bibliography

Alchemy

Alchemical Texts [827]

Alchemy and Transmutation [828]

Alchemy Academy Archives [829]

Alchemy from the Spiritual Venturer [830]

Alchemy Rediscovered and Restored [831]

Alchemystica [832]

History of Alchemy [833]

---

[827] http://www.alchemywebsite.com/texts.html
[828] http://www.rexresearch.com/alchindx.htm
[829] http://www.alchemywebsite.com/a-archive1.html
[830] http://www.denverspiritualcommunity.org/Wisdom/Alchemy.htm
[831] http://www.sacred-texts.com/alc/arr/index.htm
[832] http://tech.groups.yahoo.com/group/Alchemystica/
[833] http://www.alchemylab.com/history_of_alchemy.htm

A Metaphysics Primer

Leonardo On The Tarot [834]

Lectures on Alchemy (Terence McKenna) [835]

On The Forbidden Letters [836]

Squaring the Circle, Balance and Ideals [837]

Squaring the Circle: Marriage of Heaven and Earth [838]

The Alchemy Website and Virtual Library [839]

The Philosopher's Stone [840]

The Secret Teachings of All Ages (Manly P. Hall) [841]

---

[834] http://thealchemicalegg.com/leotaroN.html
[835] http://www.well.com/~davidu/tmalchemy.html
[836] http://www.world-mysteries.com/PhilipGardiner/forbidden_letters_49.htm
[837] http://mormonmatters.org/2010/01/29/squaring-the-circle-balance-and-ideals/
[838] http://www.springerlink.com/content/r731966144575r89/fulltext.pdf
[839] http://www.levity.com/alchemy/home.html
[840] http://www.cropcirclesandmore.com/thoughts/201104ps.html
[841] http://www.sacred-texts.com/eso/sta/index.htm

A Metaphysics Primer

Appollonius of Tyana (often compared to Jesus)

Appollonius, Jesus and Paul [842]

Appollonius of Tyana [843] [844] [845]

Appollonius of Tyana and The Shroud of Turin [846]

Appollonius of Tyana, Incarnation of Jesus [847]

Appollonius the Nazarene [848]

The Acts of Thomas and the Life of Appollonius [849]

The Life of Appollonius [850] [851]

---

[842] http://www.truthbeknown.com/apollonius.html
[843] http://en.wikipedia.org/wiki/Apollonius_of_Tyana
[844] http://www.librarising.com/spirituality/apollo.html
[845] http://home.iae.nl/users/lightnet/religion/apollonius.htm
[846] http://www.apollonius.net/turinshroud.html
[847] http://www.einterface.net/gamini/tyana.html
[848] http://www.hiddenmysteries.org/religion/christianity/apollonius.shtml
[849] http://www.kushan.org/sources/thomasandapollonius.htm
[850] http://www.livius.org/ap-ark/apollonius/life/va_00.html
[851] http://www.sacred-texts.com/cla/aot/laot/laot00.htm

Ascension

Ascension Activity 1 [852]

Ascension Activity 2 [853]

Ascension Activity 3 [854]

Ascension Activity 4 [855]

Ascension Activity 5 [856]

Ascension Activity 6 [857]

Ascension Activity 7 [858]

Ascension Activity 8 [859]

---

[852] http://ascension2012.in/step1.html
[853] http://ascension2012.in/step2.html
[854] http://ascension2012.in/step3.html
[855] http://ascension2012.in/step4.html
[856] http://ascension2012.in/step5.html
[857] http://ascension2012.in/step6.html
[858] http://ascension2012.in/step7.html
[859] http://ascension2012.in/step8.html

Ascension Activity 9 [860]

Ascension Activity 10 [861]

Afformations

Noah St. John: The Abundant Lifestyle Authority [862]

Tap on Afformations For Success [863]

Consciousness Raising

100 Ways to Become More Conscious [864]

A Golden Age May Be Just Around the Corner [865]

Alexandria on the Web [866]

---

[860] http://ascension2012.in/step9.html
[861] http://ascension2012.in/step10.html
[862] http://afformations.com/try-afformations/?utm_expid=71346862-31&utm_referrer=http%3A%2F%2Fnoahstjohn.com%2F
[863] http://eftfixeseverything.blogspot.ca/2011/03/new-faster-way-to-calm-down-and.html
[864] http://www.in5d.com/100-ways-to-become-more-conscious.html
[865] http://www.huffingtonpost.com/david-wilcock/ufos-government_b_933641.html#s336273&title=What_is_consciousness
[866] http://www.cosmopolis.com/

A Metaphysics Primer

Alliance for a New Humanity [867]

Alliance for Lucid Living (Timothy Freke) [868]

American Association of Drugless Practitioners [869]

Architects of A New Dawn [870]

Association for Global New Thought [871]

Awakening ezine (Ben Arion) [872]

Awakening Into Awareness ezine [873]

Bhaktivedanta Institute: Advanced Studies in Consciousness and Science [874]

Be the Change [875]

---

[867] http://www.anhglobal.org/
[868] http://www.theall.org/
[869] http://www.aadp.net/default.asp
[870] http://aoand.com/
[871] http://agnt.org/
[872] http://www.cosmicnature.net/cosmic_awakening.html
[873] http://awakening.net/Ezine.html
[874] http://www.bvinst.edu/
[875] http://bethechange.org.uk/

A Metaphysics Primer

Campaign for Forgiveness Research [876]

Center for Non-Violent Communication [877]

Co-Creator Radio Network [878]

Connections Radio [879]

Conscious Embodiment [880]

Conscious Living Radio [881]

Conscious TV [882]

Convergence Film [883]

---

[876] http://www.forgiving.org/
[877] http://www.cnvc.org/
[878] http://co-creatornetwork.com/
[879] http://www.spiritmedianetwork.com/crs.htm
[880] http://www.paraview.com/features/conscious_embodiment.htm
[881] http://www.podcastingnews.com/details/consciouslivingradio.org/modules/blog/getrss.jsp/view.htm
[882] http://www.conscious.tv/
[883] http://divinecosmos.com/index.php?Itemid=34&id=17&option=com_content&sectionid=5&task=category

A Metaphysics Primer

Conversations with God for Kids [884]

Cosmic Harmony [885]

Culture of Life Institute [886]

David Wilcock: The Consciousness Field [887]

David Wilcock: The Source Field Investigations (SFI) Full Length Video [888]

Embracing the Contradiction [889]

Embodiment International [890]

Emerge and See: Waking Up In An Insane World [891]

---

[884] http://cwg4kids.com/
[885] http://www.cosmicharmony.com/index.htm
[886] http://www.cultureoflifeinstitute.org/
[887] http://stevebeckow.com/2011/01/david-wilcock-consciousness-field/
[888] http://www.youtube.com/watch?v=nR-klTa1y54&feature=player_embedded#!
[889] http://embracingthecontradiction.org/
[890] http://embodimentinternational.com/
[891] http://emergeandsee.blogspot.com/

A Metaphysics Primer

Emergent Mind [892]

Emissary of Light (James Twyman) [893]

Enlightenment Podcast [894]

Fetzer Institute [895]

Foundation for Conscious Evolution [896]

Foundation for Pluralism [897]

Freewill, Fate and Causality in Matrix Reloaded [898]

Generation 21 [899]

Global Consciousness Project [900]

---

[892] http://www.emergentmind.org/
[893] http://www.emissaryoflight.com/
[894] http://www.enlightenmentpodcast.com/
[895] http://www.fetzer.org/
[896] http://barbaramarxhubbard.com/con/
[897] http://www.foundationforpluralism.com/
[898] http://montalk.net/metaphys/70/freewill-fate-and-causality-in-matrix-reloaded
[899] http://www.g21.com/
[900] http://noosphere.princeton.edu/

A Metaphysics Primer

Global Mindshift [901]

Global Spirit [902]

How to Cultivate Compassion in Your Life [903]

Humanity's Team [904]

Institute for Sacred Activism (Andrew Harvey) [905]

Institute for Research on Unlimited Love [906]

Institute of Noetic Sciences [907]

Intergalactic Library [908]

Integral Institute [909]

---

[901] http://www.global-mindshift.org/
[902] http://www.globalspirit.org/
[903] http://www.wikihow.com/Cultivate-Compassion-in-Your-Life
[904] http://www.humanitysteam.org/
[905] http://www.andrewharvey.net/
[906] http://www.unlimitedloveinstitute.org/
[907] http://www.noetic.org/
[908] http://dhouchin.com/igl/LibraryFrame.htm
[909] http://www.integralinstitute.org/

Integrating Science and Mysticism [910]

International Association for Religious Freedom [911]

Interview with Dr. Masaru Emoto [912]

Journal of Consciousness Studies [913]

Kosmos [914]

Leading Edge International Research Group [915]

Living in Pure Awareness [916]

Metanexus Institute [917]

Mind and Life Institute [918]

---

[910] http://home.provide.net/~dougklim/ISMbook.html
[911] http://www.iarf.net/
[912] http://www.enwaterment.com/reiko-interview.html
[913] http://www.imprint.co.uk/jcs.html
[914] http://www.kosmosjournal.org/
[915] http://www.trufax.org/
[916] http://www.successconsciousness.com/index_00001e.htm
[917] http://www.metanexus.net/
[918] http://www.mindandlife.org/

A Metaphysics Primer

Mindfulness Journal [919]

Mindfulness Meditation Center [920]

Mystic Visions [921]

New Spirituality Network [922]

On Embodiment, Eros and Consciousness [923]

Oneness Minute [924]

Personal Authenticity Project [925]

Phoenix Centre for Regenetics [926]

---

[919] http://www.springerlink.com/content/121591
[920] http://www.mindfulnessmeditationcentre.org/
[921] http://www.aksworld.com/FreeReports/SpiritualMetaphysicalArticles.htm
[922] http://www.newspirituality.org/
[923] http://www.embodied-being.com/en/resources/articles/75-on-embodiment-eros-and-consciousenss.html
[924] http://www.onenessminute.org/
[925] http://personal-authenticity-project.com/markers-path-personal-authenticity
[926] http://www.phoenixregenetics.org/

A Metaphysics Primer

Principles of Spiritual Evolution (Part 1) [927]

Principles of Spiritual Evolution (Part 2) [928]

Principles of Spiritual Evolution (Part 3) [929]

Pure Awareness [930] [931]

Pure Awareness: A Meditation for Conscious Embodiment [932]

Quantum Think [933]

Science of Mind Foundation [934]

---

[927] http://montalk.net/metaphys/42/principles-of-spiritual-evolution-part-i
[928] http://montalk.net/metaphys/43/principles-of-spiritual-evolution-part-ii
[929] http://montalk.net/metaphys/56/principles-of-spiritual-evolution-part-iii
[930] http://pureawareness.org/
[931] http://pureawarenessbook.com/
[932] http://www.lifeformula.co.nz/marketplace/161-pure-awareness-meditation-conscious-embodiment
[933] http://www.quantumthink.com/default2.asp
[934] http://www.somfoundation.org/

A Metaphysics Primer

Science Without Bounds [935]

Speed of Light Films [936]

Spiral Dynamics Integral [937]

Spiritual Media Network [938]

Stages of Conscious Awakening [939]

Synergy Magazine: The Magazine Dedicated to Mindful Living [940]

Talking Dharma Project [941]

Teaching What We Need To Learn [942]

---

[935] http://www.adamford.com/swb/src/ScienceWithoutBounds.pdf
[936] http://speedoflightfilms.com/
[937] http://www.spiraldynamics.net/
[938] http://www.spiritmedianetwork.com/index.htm
[939] http://montalk.net/metaphys/117/four-stages-of-conscious-awakening
[940] http://www.synergymag.ca/
[941] http://www.orderofcompassion.com/talkingdharma/author/admin/
[942] http://teachingwhatweneedtolearn.com/

A Metaphysics Primer

Teachings of Osho [943]

The Academy for Future Science [944]

The Art of Being through Conscious Embodiment [945]

The Bigger Picture Website [946]

The Center for Compassion and Altruism and Education [947]

The Center for Integral Science [948]

The Compassionate Instinct [949]

The Dalai Lama Foundation [950]

---

[943] http://www.oshoteachings.com/
[944] http://www.affs.org/index.html
[945] http://www.awakening360.com/article/pilates-movement-fitness-awareness-yuki-the-art-of-being-conscious-embodiment
[946] http://www.vonward.com/
[947] http://ccare.stanford.edu/journal-articles
[948] http://www.integralscience.org/
[949] http://greatergood.berkeley.edu/article/item/the_compassionate_instinct/
[950] http://www.dalailamafoundation.org/dlf/en/index.jsp

A Metaphysics Primer

The Earth Charter Initiative [951]

The Energy Enigma [952]

The Essence of Reality [953]

The Forge Institute [954]

The Greater Good Science Center [955]

The Harmony Project [956]

The Headless Way [957]

The Isha System [958]

The Life and Works of Alan Watts [959]

---

[951] http://www.earthcharterinaction.org/content/
[952] http://www.energy-enigma.com/
[953] http://nehrer.net/
[954] http://www.theforge.org/site/content.php
[955] http://greatergood.berkeley.edu/
[956] http://www.theharmonyproject.org/index2.html
[957] http://www.headless.org/
[958] http://www.whywalkwhenyoucanfly.com/new/contenido.php?seccion=sistema_isha_intro
[959] http://alanwatts.com/

A Metaphysics Primer

The Lyricus Teaching Order (related to Wingmakers) [960]

The Network of Spiritual Progressives [961]

The Pineal Gland – The Bridge to Divine Consciousness [962]

The Sacred Geometry Stories of Jesus [963]

The Spiritual Caucus at the United Nations [964]

The Values Caucus at the United Nations [965]

Transitions (Denise Le Fay) [966]

Truth and Reality [967]

Uniting People [968]

---

[960] http://www.lyricus.org/
[961] http://spiritualprogressives.org/newsite/
[962] http://www.miraclesandinspiration.com/pinealgland.html
[963] http://www.jesus8880.com/
[964] http://www.spiritualcaucusun.org/
[965] http://www.valuescaucus.org/
[966] http://deniselefay.wordpress.com/
[967] http://www.spaceandmotion.com/
[968] http://www.unitingpeople.com/

A Metaphysics Primer

We Are Pure Awareness [969]

Wingmakers [970]

Wisdom Teachings with David Wilcock [971]

Virtue Science [972]

Vision in Action [973]

Vivid Life [974]

ZenJoyMeditation [975]

---

[969] http://thebuddhistblog.blogspot.ca/2007/05/we-are-pure-awareness.html
[970] http://www.wingmakers.com/
[971] http://www.gaiamtv.com/show/wisdom-teachings-david-wilcock?chan=HWilcock&utm_source=HDavidWilcock&utm_medium=Web&utm_campaign=10day
[972] http://www.virtuescience.com/
[973] http://www.via-visioninaction.org/
[974] http://vividlife.me/ultimate/
[975] http://www.zenjoymeditation.com/

A Metaphysics Primer

Hermeticism

The Hermetic tradition is a set of philosophical and religious beliefs, based primarily upon the writings attributed to Hermes Trismegistus, a wise sage and Egyptian priest, one whom is commonly seen as having been synonymous with the Egyptian God Thoth. [976]

There are three major works which are widely known texts for Hermetic beliefs; namely, [1] *The Emerald Tablet of Hermes Trismegistus*, a short work that coins the well known term in occult circles, *As above, so below*; [2] *The Corpus Hermeticum*, the body of work most widely known Hermetic text (composed of sixteen books that are set up as dialogues between Hermes and a series of others); [3] *The Kybalion: Hermetic Philosophy*, a book published in 1912 by three people calling themselves the Three Initiates. [977]

---

[976] http://www.golden-dawn.com/eu/displaycontent.aspx?pageid=115-hermetic-tradition
[977] http://www.golden-dawn.com/eu/displaycontent.aspx?pageid=115-hermetic-tradition

A Metaphysics Primer

As Above, So Below: Part 1 [978]

As Above, So Below: Part 2 [979]

7 Hermetic Aphorisms [980]

Corpus Hermeticum [981] [982] [983]

Emerald Tablet [984] [985]

Golden Dawn Library Books [986]

Hermetica [987]

---

[978] http://www.blavatsky.net/newsletters/as_above_so_below_part1.htm
[979] http://www.blavatsky.net/newsletters/as_above_so_below_part2.htm
[980] http://forums.riverofenlightenment.com/index.php?action=printpage;topic=2539.0
[981] http://www.sacred-texts.com/chr/herm/index.htm
[982] http://www.gnosis.org/library/hermet.htm
[983] http://www.world-mysteries.com/awr_6ch.htm
[984] http://en.wikipedia.org/wiki/Emerald_Tablet
[985] http://www.sacred-texts.com/alc/emerald.htm
[986] http://www.golden-dawn-canada.com/library.html
[987] http://en.wikipedia.org/wiki/Hermetica

A Metaphysics Primer

Hermetic Axioms [988]

Hermetic Fellowship Website [989]

Hermetic Philosophy: The Ancient and Eternal Wisdom [990]

Hermeticism [991]

Hermetic Kabbalah [992]

Hermetic Principles [993]

Kybalion [994]

Seven Rays [995]

---

[988] http://forum2.aimoo.com/DavidStClairForum/m/Category/Topic-1-423148
[989] http://www.hermeticfellowship.org/
[990] http://www.lightparty.com/Spirituality/HermeticPhilosophy.html
[991] http://en.wikipedia.org/wiki/Hermeticism
[992] http://www.digital-brilliance.com/index.php
[993] http://dailywicca.com/2011/11/26/hermetic-principles/
[994] http://en.wikipedia.org/wiki/Kybalion
[995] http://www.cdxviii.net/rays.html

A Metaphysics Primer

The Emerald Tablet [996]

The Emerald Tablet of Hermes: An Introduction to Hermetic Philosophy [997]

The Emerald Tablets of Thoth the Atlantean [998] [999] [1000]

The Hermetic Axiom and The Secret [1001]

The Hermetic Principles [1002]

The Kybalion [1003] [1004] [1005]

The Seven Ancient Principles of Hermes [1006]

---

[996] http://thepdi.com/Preview%20Emerald%20Tablet%20and%20Alchemy.pdf
[997] http://altreligion.net/?page_id=796
[998] http://www.horuscentre.org/library/Hermetism/The_Emerald_Tablets_Of_Thoth.pdf
[999] http://www.bibliotecapleyades.net/thot/esp_thot_1.htm
[1000] http://www.crystalinks.com/emerald.html
[1001] http://www.allconsidering.com/2008/hermetic-axiom-secret/
[1002] http://www.sunspiritgallery.com/hermetics.htm
[1003] http://www.ardue.org.uk/library/book8.html
[1004] http://www.sacred-texts.com/eso/kyb/
[1005] http://www.kybalion.org/kybalion.php
[1006] http://www.joy101.org/bc-03-7-hermetic-principles.html

A Metaphysics Primer

The Seven Hermetic Laws as stated in the Kybalion [1007]

The Seven Hermetic Principles [1008] [1009]

What Is Hermeticism? [1010]

Hermetic Transmutation

The goal of Hermetic practice is to transmute the base matter of the physical body into ever more refined and pure forms of energy and consciousness.

Freemasonry and the Hermetic Doctrine: Part 1 [1011]

Freemasonry and the Hermetic Doctrine: Part 2 [1012]

Freemasonry and the Hermetic Doctrine: Part 3 [1013]

[1007] http://processmediainc.com/titles/The%20Seven%20Laws.pdf
[1008] http://www.muhammadfarms.com/hermetic_principles.htm
[1009] http://www.corax.com/tarot/index.html?hermetic-principles
[1010] http://www.hermeticfellowship.org/HFHermeticism.html
[1011] http://calodges.org/ncrl/hermetic.htm
[1012] http://calodges.org/ncrl/hermes2.html
[1013] http://calodges.org/ncrl/hermes3.html

A Metaphysics Primer

Hermetic Alchemy [1014] [1015]

Hermetic Order of the Golden Dawn [1016] [1017]

Hermetic Philosophy [1018]

Hermetic Philosophy and Alchemy [1019]

Hermetic Science and the Alchemical Process [1020]

Isaac Newton [1021]

Mastering the Art of Polarity [1022]

Mental Transmutation: Le Kybalion [1023] [1024]

[1014] http://hermetic.com/caduceus/articles/2/4/hermetic-alchemy.html
[1015] http://tree.org/b11a.htm
[1016] http://www.golden-dawn.com/eu/displaycontent.aspx?pageid=115-hermetic-tradition
[1017] http://www.golden-dawn-canada.com/
[1018] http://www.mindspring.com/~pmarsh/pblesson2.htm
[1019] http://www.rexresearch.com/atwood/atwood2.htm
[1020] http://www.denverspiritualcommunity.org/Wisdom/OccultLawChpt4.htm
[1021] http://www.alchemylab.com/isaac_newton.htm
[1022] http://mindempowerment.net/blog/?p=64
[1023] http://www.rosicrucian-order.com/revista_kybal.htm
[1024] http://www.sacred-texts.com/eso/kyb/kyb05.htm

A Metaphysics Primer

The Goodness of Suffering [1025]

The Hermetic Teachings [1026]

The Hermetic Work of Paul Tisdell [1027]

The Mystery Experience (Timothy Freke) [1028]

David R. Hamilton, PhD. (author of How Your Mind Can Heal Your Body)

5 Beneficial Side Effects of Kindness [1029]

Compassion: The Elixir of Life? [1030]

Do Positive People Live Longer? [1031]

[1025] http://christian-hermetic.com/tag/alchemy/
[1026] http://www.realmagicstudies.com/RealMagicCourse/Hermetica.html
[1027] http://www.spirituallife.com.au/
[1028] http://www.themysteryexperience.com/
[1029] http://www.huffingtonpost.com/david-r-hamilton-phd/kindness-benefits_b_869537.html
[1030] http://www.huffingtonpost.com/david-r-hamilton-phd/compassion-the-elixir-of-_b_829610.html
[1031] http://www.huffingtonpost.com/david-r-hamilton-phd/positive-people-live-long_b_774648.html

A Metaphysics Primer

How Meditation Affects the Gray Matter of the Brain [1032]

Kryon (Channeled Material)

Activating the Third Layer of DNA [1033]

Against All Odds [1034]

All about God [1035]

Attributes of Ascension [1036]

Attributes of the Match Bearer [1037]

Attributes of the Shift [1038]

Back to Basics [1039]

[1032] http://www.huffingtonpost.com/david-r-hamilton-phd/how-meditation-affects-th_b_751233.html
[1033] http://www.kryon.com/k_chanelphilly03.html
[1034] http://www.kryon.com/k_channel09_montreal.html
[1035] http://www.kryon.com/k_chanelmoscow_2_07.html
[1036] http://www.kryon.com/k_chanelphilly.html
[1037] http://www.kryon.com/k_channel11_sacramento.html
[1038] http://www.kryon.com/k_channel09_moscow.html
[1039] http://www.kryon.com/k_chanelHarrisburg05.html

A Metaphysics Primer

Becoming Masters [1040]

Becoming Quantum [1041]

Choices [1042]

Co-Creation Explained [1043]

DNA Layer Nine (The Healing Layer) [1044]

DNA Revealed [1045]

Energetic Consciousness [1046]

How it Works [1047]

Human Evolution [1048]

[1040] http://www.kryon.com/k_chanelstaugustine06.html
[1041] http://www.kryon.com/k_channel09_sedona.html
[1042] http://www.kryon.com/k_channel09_seattle.html
[1043] http://www.kryon.com/k_chaneltoronto.html
[1044] http://www.kryon.com/k_channel10_Moscow1_.html
[1045] http://www.kryon.com/k_channel10_melbourne_1.html
[1046] http://www.kryon.com/k_channel10_berkeleysprings_.html
[1047] http://www.kryon.com/k_chanelmanhattan05.html
[1048] http://www.kryon.com/k_channel08_discovery.html

A Metaphysics Primer

It's in the DNA [1049]

Lightworker Frustrations, Part 2 [1050]

Lightworker Responsibilities [1051]

Meditation and Prayer [1052]

Needed Science for the Times [1053]

Perceptions of Masterhood, Part 1 [1054]

Perceptions of Masterhood, Part 2 [1055]

Perceptions of Masterhood, Part 3 (The Agreement) [1056]

Quantum Healing [1057]

[1049] http://www.kryon.com/k_channel08_kelowna.html
[1050] http://www.kryon.com/k_chanelnewport03.html
[1051] http://www.kryon.com/k_chanelresp05.html
[1052] http://www.kryon.com/k_chanelreno04.html
[1053] http://www.kryon.com/k_channel10_albuquerque.html
[1054] http://www.kryon.com/k_chanelhawaii103.html
[1055] http://www.kryon.com/k_chanelhawaii203.html
[1056] http://www.kryon.com/k_chanelidaho04.html
[1057] http://www.kryon.com/k_channel08_Vancouver.html

A Metaphysics Primer

The Challenge of Linearity [1058]

The Circle of Energy [1059]

The Cosmic Lattice, Part 1 [1060]

The Cosmic Lattice, Part 2 [1061]

The Eight Shifts in Enlightenment, Part 1 [1062]

The Eight Shifts in Enlightenment, Part 2 [1063]

The Golden Tray [1064]

The Great Scientific Bias [1065]

The History of DNA and the Human Race [1066]

[1058] http://www.kryon.com/k_chanellinear04.html
[1059] http://www.kryon.com/k_chanelsanfran.html
[1060] http://www.kryon.com/k_26.html
[1061] http://www.kryon.com/k_29.html
[1062] http://www.kryon.com/k_channel07_Mexico_01.html
[1063] http://www.kryon.com/k_channel07_Mexico_02.html
[1064] http://www.kryon.com/k_27.html
[1065] http://www.kryon.com/k_channel09_gaithersburg.html
[1066] http://www.kryon.com/k_channel09_portland.html

A Metaphysics Primer

The Humanization of God [1067]

The Incredible Human [1068]

The Interdimensional Universe [1069]

The Lemurian Connection [1070]

The Lightworker's Handbook [1071]

The Lineage of Spirituality [1072]

The Meaning of Enlightenment [1073]

The Perceptions of God [1074]

The Power of Compassion [1075]

[1067] http://www.kryon.com/k_channel11_New%20Jersey.html
[1068] http://www.kryon.com/k_channel08_Venezuela.html
[1069] http://www.kryon.com/k_chanelnewjersey03.html
[1070] http://www.kryon.com/k_chanelshastaB04.html
[1071] http://www.kryon.com/k_25b.html
[1072] http://www.kryon.com/k_channel09_delphi.html
[1073] http://www.kryon.com/k_chanelmoscow_1_07.html
[1074] http://www.kryon.com/k_channel10_portland_me_.html
[1075] http://www.kryon.com/Seattle00chanel.html

A Metaphysics Primer

The Quantum Factor (Physics with an Attitude) [1076]

The Recalibration of Dark and Light [1077]

The Recalibration of Knowledge [1078]

The Recalibration of the Human Being [1079]

The Recalibration of the Universe [1080]

The Recalibration of Wisdom [1081]

The Relationship to Gaia [1082]

The Secret of Mastery [1083]

The Seven Great Human Illusions of God [1084]

[1076] http://www.kryon.com/k_channel11_edmonton.html
[1077] http://www.kryon.com/k_channel11_San%20Antonio-12.html
[1078] http://www.kryon.com/k_channel11_Boulder-12.html
[1079] http://www.kryon.com/k_channel11_Red%20Deer-12.html
[1080] http://kryon.com/k_channel11_Patagonia%201-12.html
[1081] http://www.kryon.com/k_channel11_Lima-11.html
[1082] http://www.kryon.com/k_channel10_shasta_.html
[1083] http://www.kryon.com/k_channel10_Moscow2_.html
[1084] http://www.kryon.com/k_chaneledmonton06.html

A Metaphysics Primer

The Shift is Here [1085]

The Timing of the Great Shift [1086]

The Truth about DNA [1087]

The Unity of Humanity [1088]

The Way to God [1089]

The Winter of Spirituality [1090]

Through the Eyes of Ascension, Part 1 [1091]

Through the Eyes of Ascension, Part 2 [1092]

Un-defining the Spiritual Path [1093]

[1085] http://www.kryon.com/k_channel08_Chile.html
[1086] http://www.kryon.com/k_channel09_Madrid1.html
[1087] http://www.kryon.com/k_chanelDNA04.html
[1088] http://www.kryon.com/k_chanelVanc.html
[1089] http://www.kryon.com/k_channel08_Sedona.html
[1090] http://www.kryon.com/k_chanelwinter04.html
[1091] http://www.kryon.com/k_chanelgrandR03.html
[1092] http://www.kryon.com/k_chanelreno203.html
[1093] http://www.kryon.com/k_chanelsedona05.html

A Metaphysics Primer

What Does it Do? [1094]

Who You Really Are [1095]

Mayan Calendar

Serpent of Light: Beyond 2012 - The Movement of the Earth's Kundalini and the Rise of the Female Light, 1949 to 2013 [1096]

The Mayan Ouroboros: The Cosmic Cycles Come Full Circle [1097]

Metaphysical Media

Conscious Creation Journal [1098]

EnlightenNext Magazine [1099]

[1094] http://www.kryon.com/k_channel09_lagunahills.html
[1095] http://www.kryon.com/k_chanelcrystallake05.html
[1096] http://www.amazon.com/dp/1578634016
[1097] http://www.amazon.com/dp/1578635330/
[1098] http://www.consciouscreation.com/journal/
[1099] http://www.enlightennext.org/magazine/

A Metaphysics Primer

Gnosis Magazine [1100]

Healing Conversations with Lauren Galey [1101]

Indigo Sun [1102]

In Light Times [1103]

Innerchange Magazine [1104]

Kindred Spirit Magazine [1105]

New Frontier Magazine [1106]

News For The Soul [1107]

Nexus Magazine [1108]

[1100] http://www.lumen.org/
[1101] http://www.blogtalkradio.com/lauren-galey
[1102] http://www.indigosun.com/
[1103] http://www.inlightimes.com/
[1104] http://innerchangemag.com/
[1105] http://www.kindredspirit.co.uk/
[1106] http://www.newfrontier.com/
[1107] http://www.newsforthesoul.com/
[1108] http://www.nexusmagazine.com/

A Metaphysics Primer

OM Times [1109]

Presence Magazine [1110]

Silent Voices Magazine [1111]

Spirituality and Health Magazine [1112]

Theosophy Magazine [1113]

True Blue Spirit Magazine [1114]

Vitality Magazine [1115]

Metaphysical Study

A Journey into the Unseen [1116]

[1109] http://omtimes.com/
[1110] http://www.whispersofspirit.com/index.html
[1111] http://www.silentvoices.org.uk/
[1112] http://www.spiritualityhealth.com/
[1113] http://www.theosophycompany.org/pubs.html
[1114] http://www.truebluespirit.com/
[1115] http://vitalitymagazine.com/
[1116] http://i-am-a-i.org/

A Metaphysics Primer

Atlantic University [1117]

Book of Knowledge: The Keys of Enoch [1118]

Canadian Theosophical Association [1119]

Center for Sacred Sciences [1120]

Chakras Energy Healing Course [1121]

Endeavor Academy [1122]

Heartstorm Metaphysics Courses [1123]

Holistic Arts Institute [1124]

Holistic Healer's Academy [1125]

[1117] http://atlanticuniv.edu/index.html
[1118] http://www.keysofenoch.org/html/overview.html
[1119] http://www.theosophical.ca/main.shtml
[1120] http://www.centerforsacredsciences.org/
[1121] http://www.healing-journeys-energy.com/energy-healing-courses-chakras.html#axzz1pko8nPtj
[1122] http://www.endeavoracademy.com/
[1123] http://heartstorm.net/
[1124] https://holisticartsinstitute.com/
[1125] http://www.holistichealersacademy.com/

A Metaphysics Primer

Holistic Learning Centers [1126]

International College of Metaphysical Theology [1127]

International Quantum University for Integrative Medicine [1128]

Luna Holistic Home Study [1129]

Metaphysical Spirituality Program [1130]

Metaphysical Studies [1131]

Metaphysics Institute [1132]

Metaphysics: Multiple Meanings [1133]

Mindhance Learning Center [1134]

[1126] http://www.holisticlearningcenter.com/
[1127] http://www.metaphysicscollege.com/
[1128] http://iquim.org/
[1129] http://www.onlinehomestudies.com/
[1130] http://www.aiht.edu/catalog/metaphysical_spirituality.asp
[1131] http://www.metaphysical-studies.com/
[1132] http://www.metaphysicsinstitute.org/
[1133] http://www.websyte.com/alan/metamul.htm
[1134] http://www.mindhancelearning.com/

A Metaphysics Primer

Natural Energies College [1135]

Northern Star Academy of Holistic Studies [1136]

Online Energy Healing Courses [1137]

Online Esoteric Library [1138]

Online Papers on Consciousness [1139]

Reiki Blessings Academy [1140]

Sacred Spaces [1141]

School of Metaphysics [1142]

School of Multidimensional Healing Arts and Sciences [1143]

[1135] http://www.naturalenergies.com.au/certificate-metaphysicalstudies.htm
[1136] http://www.northernstaracademy.com/
[1137] http://www.healing-journeys-energy.com/energy-healing-courses-online.html#axzz1vEr7kqCs
[1138] http://www.hermetics.org/ebooks.html
[1139] http://consc.net/online
[1140] http://reikiblessings.homestead.com/
[1141] http://www.sacredspaceswa.com/
[1142] http://www.som.org/
[1143] http://www.smhas.com/

A Metaphysics Primer

Spencer Institute [1144]

Stonebridge Associated Colleges Distance Learning [1145]

The Ardue Library [1146]

The College of Metaphysical Studies [1147]

The Gnosis Archive [1148]

The Institute of Metaphysical Studies [1149]

The Metaphysical Community [1150]

The Mystery and the Mystic [1151]

The Salaam School of Wellness, Health and Wisdom [1152]

[1144] http://spencerinstitute.com/
[1145] http://www.stonebridge.uk.com/
[1146] http://www.ardue.org.uk/library.htm
[1147] http://www.cms.edu/home.html
[1148] http://gnosis.org/welcome.html
[1149] http://www.kathyoddenino.com/
[1150] http://metaphysicalsciences.ning.com/
[1151] http://www.ardue.org.uk/mystic.html
[1152] http://www.salaamartsandinspiration.com/

A Metaphysics Primer

The S.W.A.T. Institute [1153]

The Theosophical Society [1154]

Theosophy [1155]

Theosophy Library Online [1156]

Theosophy Talk [1157]

Theosophical Texts [1158]

Theosophy Watch [1159]

The Universal Light Institute [1160]

[1153] http://www.swatinstitute.com/index.html
[1154] http://www.ts-adyar.org/
[1155] http://www.blavatsky.net/blavatsky/secret_doctrine/secret_doctrine.htm
[1156] http://www.theosophy.org/
[1157] http://groups.yahoo.com/group/theos-talk/
[1158] http://www.austheos.org.au/clibrary/bindex-early-classics.html
[1159] http://theosophywatch.com/
[1160] http://www.universallight.org/

A Metaphysics Primer

The University of Arizona: Center for Consciousness Studies [1161]

The University of Science and Philosophy [1162]

Transformational Arts College of Spiritual and Holistic Training [1163]

University of Metaphysical Sciences [1164]

University of Metaphysics [1165]

Vesica Institute for Holistic Studies [1166]

Wisdom World [1167]

Yogananda Institute [1168]

[1161] http://www.consciousness.arizona.edu/
[1162] http://www.philosophy.org/
[1163] http://www.transformationalarts.com/
[1164] http://www.umsonline.org/
[1165] http://www.metaphysics.com/
[1166] http://www.vesica.org/
[1167] http://www.wisdomworld.org/
[1168] http://yoganandainstitute.org/

A Metaphysics Primer

Nondual Inquiry

Allspirit Nondual Quotations [1169]

Christian Nondualism [1170]

Christian Nonduality [1171]

Chuck Hillig [1172]

Definition of Nonduality: Interpretation and Practical Application [1173]

Dr. Greg Goode [1174]

Duality and Nonduality: Awakening to Unified Perspective [1175]

[1169] http://www.allspirit.co.uk/nondualquotes.html
[1170] http://www.members.shaw.ca/jgfriesen/
[1171] http://www.peacefulself.com/2008/06/christian-non-duality.html
[1172] http://www.chuckhillig.com/Home_Page.html
[1173] http://www.a-spiritual-journey-of-healing.com/non-duality.html
[1174] http://www.heartofnow.com/
[1175] http://www.esotericstudies.net/quarterly/Files060110/EQ060110-Brown.pdf

A Metaphysics Primer

Emptiness Teachings [1176]

Essays on Nonduality [1177]

Free Awareness [1178]

Jeff Foster [1179]

Jerry Katz on Nonduality [1180]

Living Realization [1181]

Natural Awakening: Nondual Training [1182]

Nondual Awakening and Discerning the Seer from the Seen [1183]

[1176] http://emptinessteachings.com/Emptiness.html
[1177] http://www.anintroductiontoawareness.com/Awareness/Essays/Essays.html
[1178] http://www.free-awareness.com/
[1179] http://www.lifewithoutacentre.com/
[1180] http://nonduality.org/
[1181] http://livingrealization.org/
[1182] http://www.nondualtraining.com/
[1183] http://realdharma.wordpress.com/2011/10/10/nondual-awakening-and-discerning-the-seer-from-the-seen/

A Metaphysics Primer

Non-dual Awareness [1184]

Nondual Roundtable: Part 1 [1185]

Nondual Roundtable: Part 2 [1186]

Nondual Science Institute [1187]

Nondualism in Christianity [1188]

Nonduality [1189]

Nonduality America [1190]

Nonduality, Maya and Spiritual Awakening [1191]

[1184] http://www.innerfrontier.org/Practices/NonDualAwareness.htm
[1185] http://nondualityamerica.wordpress.com/2011/03/07/in-the-round-nondual-roundtable/
[1186] http://nondualityamerica.wordpress.com/2011/06/18/in-the-round-nondual-roundtable-part-2/
[1187] http://nondual.net/
[1188] http://peterspearls.com.au/ndc.htm
[1189] http://www.wrmosb.org/nonduality/
[1190] http://nondualityamerica.wordpress.com/
[1191] http://www.successconsciousness.com/nonduality.htm

A Metaphysics Primer

Nonduality Magazine: Interview with Jerry Katz [1192]

Nonduality North [1193]

Nonduality Press [1194]

Over 200 Nonduality Blogs [1195]

Reflections of the One Life [1196]

Science and Nonduality [1197]

The Awakened Eye: Nonduality [1198]

The Non-dual Awakening of Ralph Waldo Emerson [1199]

[1192] http://www.nondualitymagazine.org/nonduality_magazine.2.interview.jerrykatz.htm
[1193] http://non-duality-north.com/
[1194] http://non-dualitypress.org/
[1195] http://nonduality.org/other-nonduality-blogs/
[1196] http://www.kiloby.com/index.php
[1197] http://www.scienceandnonduality.com/index.shtml
[1198] http://www.theawakenedeye.com/nonduality.htm
[1199] http://evolutionaryphilosophy.com/2009/02/07/the-non-dual-awakening-of-ralph-waldo-emerson/

A Metaphysics Primer

The Original Nonduality Website [1200]

The Transmission of Nondual Awareness [1201]

Undivided [1202]

Where do Christianity and Nonduality Meet? [1203]

Wisdom's Soft Whisper [1204]

Quantum Physics

Choosing From Infinite Thoughts Changes the Way We Experience Our Reality [1205]

Quantum Physics [1206]

Quantum Physics Made Relatively Simple [1207]

[1200] http://www3.ns.sympatico.ca/umbada/
[1201] http://diydharma.org/transmission-non-dual-awareness-ken-wilber
[1202] http://www.scienceandnonduality.com/index.shtml
[1203] http://www.youtube.com/watch?v=fvg2DgjVgbE
[1204] http://www.thewizardllc.com/satsang-radio-archives
[1205] http://www.infinite-manifesting.org/InfiniteThoughts.html
[1206] http://www.vision.net.au/~apaterson/science/physics_quantum.htm
[1207] http://bethe.cornell.edu/

A Metaphysics Primer

The Observer Effect [1208] [1209]

We Are the Observer Affecting Everything in Our Reality [1210]

Spiritual Endeavors

Any means that enables allows (enables) one to awaken to the intuitive awareness of unity, thereby further dissolving their attachment to egoic consciousness, can be referred to as a spiritual endeavor.

3 Tiny Habits to Enhance Your Mindfulness Practice [1211]

5 Minutes of Peace: Energy Chi for Beginners [1212]

5 Soul Thoughts For A Radiant Life [1213]

[1208] http://www.theobservereffect.com/home.html
[1209] http://www.vision.net.au/~apaterson/science/observer_effect.htm
[1210] http://www.infinite-manifesting.org/ObserverEffect.html
[1211] http://www.huffingtonpost.com/marguerite-manteaurao/mindfulness_b_1337948.html
[1212] http://www.huffingtonpost.com/2012/06/04/beginners-energy-chi-video_n_1424549.html?utm_hp_ref=mindfulness
[1213] http://www.huffingtonpost.com/william-horden/soul-thoughts_b_1503058.html

A Metaphysics Primer

5 Steps to Balance the Brain's Negative Bias [1214]

7 Easy Ways to Be Mindful Everyday [1215]

Adjusting Your Default Setting [1216]

Breathing: The Foundation of all Spiritual Endeavors [1217]

Cultivating Loving Kindness [1218]

Endless Satsang: Nirmala [1219]

Excavating the Heart through Buddhist Mindfulness Meditation [1220]

[1214] http://www.huffingtonpost.com/elisha-goldstein-phd/gratitude_b_1607672.html?utm_hp_ref=mindfulness
[1215] http://psychcentral.com/blog/archives/2012/06/09/7-easy-ways-to-be-mindful-every-day/
[1216] http://www.huffingtonpost.com/jon-kabatzinn-phd/mindfulness-b_1176966.html
[1217] http://simplydivinesolutions.com/blog/breathing-is-the-foundation-of-all-spiritual-endeavors/
[1218] http://www.huffingtonpost.com/david-nichtern/buddhism-beliefs-cultivat_b_577891.html
[1219] http://endless-satsang.com/
[1220] http://www.huffingtonpost.com/noah-levine/awakening-the-heart_b_852429.html

A Metaphysics Primer

For Relaxation, Try Chanting the Chakra Vowels [1221]

The Huffington Post: GPS For The Soul [1222]

The Huffington Post: Mindful Living [1223]

The Huffington Post: Spiritual Development [1224]

How Meditation Techniques Compare [1225]

How Mindfulness Meditation Can Help People with Rheumatoid Arthritis [1226]

How Mindfulness Rewires the Brain [1227]

[1221] http://www.huffingtonpost.com/claudia-ricci/chakra-chanting_b_1606147.html?utm_hp_ref=mindfulness
[1222] http://www.huffingtonpost.com/news/gps-soul
[1223] http://www.huffingtonpost.com/news/mindfulness
[1224] http://www.huffingtonpost.com/news/spirituality
[1225] http://www.huffingtonpost.com/jeanne-ball/how-meditation-techniques_b_735561.html
[1226] http://www.huffingtonpost.com/2011/12/28/mindfulness-meditation-rheumatoid-arthritis_n_1171685.html?utm_hp_ref=mindfulness#slide=309263
[1227] http://www.huffingtonpost.com/elisha-goldstein-phd/can-mindfulness-really-re_b_1017931.html

A Metaphysics Primer

How to Meditate [1228]

Is Compassion Meditation the Key to Better Caregiving? [1229]

Mindfulness as a Path to Personal Sustainability [1230]

Mindfulness Can Give Your Brain an Edge [1231]

Mindfulness Meditation Training Changes Brain Structure in Eight Weeks [1232]

Nonduality Satsang: Nova Scotia [1233]

Taking Your Seat: Simple Meditation Instructions For Ordinary People [1234]

[1228] http://www.huffingtonpost.com/sam-harris/how-to-meditate_b_861295.html
[1229] http://www.huffingtonpost.com/matthieu-ricard/could-compassion-meditati_b_751566.html
[1230] http://www.huffingtonpost.com/dr-terri-kennedy/mindfulness_b_1385730.html
[1231] http://www.huffingtonpost.com/david-nichtern/clarity-in-meditation_b_1000649.html
[1232] http://www.sciencedaily.com/releases/2011/01/110121144007.htm
[1233] http://nonduality.ca/
[1234] http://www.huffingtonpost.com/david-nichtern/taking-your-seat-simple-m_b_410303.html

A Metaphysics Primer

University of Metaphysical Sciences: Free Meditation Downloads [1235]

Understanding Meditation: How Attention Changes Our Brains [1236]

Want a Happier Brain? Try Mindfulness [1237]

What Is Mindfulness Meditation? [1238]

Why Mindfulness Meditation Makes Us Healthier [1239]

Why We Need To Teach Mindfulness in a Digital Age [1240]

[1235] http://www.umsonline.org/FreeMdtnDownloads.htm
[1236] http://www.huffingtonpost.com/michael-stanclift-nd/neuroplasticity_b_1131652.html
[1237] http://www.huffingtonpost.com/dan-goleman/mindfulness-brain_b_861228.html
[1238] http://www.huffingtonpost.com/ira-israel/what-is-mindfulness-medit_1_b_1428304.html
[1239] http://www.huffingtonpost.com/2011/11/02/mindfulness-meditation-health_n_1070101.html
[1240] http://www.pbs.org/mediashift/2012/04/why-we-need-to-teach-mindfulness-in-a-digital-age095.html

Symbols

Sacred Symbols [1241]

The Secret Language of Symbols [1242]

Synergy

Book 1: The Processes of Creation – Synergy [1243]

Entanglement [1244]

Greater Whole [1245]

Greatest Error [1246]

Light Wave Synergy: School of Evolutionary Fulfillment [1247]

[1241] http://www.world-mysteries.com/awr_7.htm
[1242] http://symboldictionary.net/?p=1914
[1243] http://thebibleforthenewage.com/education/bible-new-age/processes-creation-synergy/
[1244] http://dragonintuitive.com/entanglement/
[1245] http://dragonintuitive.com/greater-whole/
[1246] http://dragonintuitive.com/greatest-error/
[1247] http://lightwaveevolution.org/

Open to Synergy [1248]

Sanity Delusion [1249]

Self is Life [1250]

Synergy and Alchemy [1251]

The Synergy Principle: Human Action and Evolution of Consciousness [1252]

Wholeness of Synergy [1253]

The Laws of the Universe

12 Main Laws of the Universe and 21 Sub-laws [1254]

27 Mental Laws of the Universe [1255]

[1248] http://dragonintuitive.com/open-to-synergy/
[1249] http://dragonintuitive.com/sanity-delusion/
[1250] http://dragonintuitive.com/self-is-life/
[1251] http://www.eye-ris.org/SynergyAlchemy
[1252] http://www.newciv.org/ISSS_Primer/seminzi.html
[1253] http://dragonintuitive.com/wholeness-of-synergy/
[1254] http://www.altarearth.com/lawofattraction/the12universallaws/
[1255] http://timkuptz.wordpress.com/2007/11/12/27-mental-laws-of-the-universe/

A Metaphysics Primer

20 Primary Universal Laws [1256]

12 Universal Laws [1257]

One Mind, One Energy: The Power Is Within [1258]

The Laws of the Universe [1259] [1260] [1261]

The Master Key [1262]

The Master Key System [1263]

The Seven Natural Laws of the Universe [1264]

Universal Cosmic Law: The Seven Principles [1265]

[1256] http://www.peace.ca/universallaws.htm
[1257] http://www.one-mind-one-energy.com/12-universal-laws.html
[1258] http://www.one-mind-one-energy.com/universal-laws.html
[1259] http://www.trans4mind.com/healing/reality.html
[1260] http://www.ourglobalawareness.com/Laws_of_the_Universe
[1261] http://www.inwardquest.com/questions/419/what-are-all-the-laws-of-the-universe
[1262] http://www.ardue.org.uk/library/book25.html
[1263] http://www.masterkeysystem.tv/about-charles-haanel/
[1264] http://gittefalkenberg.wordpress.com/2010/02/28/the-7-natural-laws-of-the-universe/
[1265] http://www.pymander.com/AETHEREAL/PRINC~1.htm

A Metaphysics Primer

Universal Laws [1266] [1267]

Zero Point Energy [1268]

[1266] http://www.entrepreneursmindset.com/universallaws/
[1267] http://www.wiziq.com/tutorial/31210-Metaphysical-Tools-Universal-Law
[1268] http://www.crystalinks.com/zeropoint.html

About the Author

Michele Doucette is webmistress of Portals of Spirit, a spirituality website.

As a Level 2 Reiki Practitioner, she sends long distance Reiki to those who make the request, claiming only to be a facilitator of the Universal energy, meaning that it is up to the individual(s) in question to use these energies in order to heal themselves.

Having also acquired a Crystal Healing Practitioner diploma (Stonebridge College in the UK), she is guardian to many from the mineral kingdom.

She is the author of many spiritual/metaphysical works; namely, [1] *The Ultimate Enlightenment For 2012: All We Need Is Ourselves*, a book that was nominated for the AllBooks Review Best Inspirational Book of 2011, [2] *Turn Off The TV: Turn On Your Mind*, [3] *Veracity At Its Best*, [4] *The Collective: Essays on Reality* (a composition of essays in relation to the Matrix), [5] *Sleepers Awaken: The*

A Metaphysics Primer

Time Is Now To Consciously Create Your Own Reality, [6] *Healing the Planet and Ourselves: How To Raise Your Vibration*, [7] *You Are Everything: Everything Is You*, [8] *The Awakening of Humanity: A Foremost Necessity*, [9] *The Cosmos of The Soul: A Spiritual Biography*, [10] *Getting Out Of Our Own Way: Love Is The Only Answer*, [11] *Living The Jedi Way* and [12] *Vicarius Christi: The Vicar of Christ*, all of which have been published through St. Clair Publications.

In addition, she has written another volume that deals solely with crystals, aptly entitled *The Wisdom of Crystals*.

She is also the author of *A Travel in Time to Grand Pré*, a visionary metaphysical novel that historically ties the descendants of Yeshua (Jesus) to modern day Nova Scotia.

As shared by a reviewer, *Veracity At Its Best* "constructs the context for the spiritual message" imparted in *A Travel in Time to Grand Pré*.

Against the backdrop of 1754 Acadie, this novel, an alchemical tale of time travel, romance and intrigue, from Henry Sinclair to the Merovingians, from the Cathari treasure at Montségur to the Knights Templar, also blends French Acadian history with current DNA testing.

Together with the words of Yeshua as spoken at the height of his ministry, *A Travel in Time to Grand Pré* has the potential to inspire others; for it is herein that we learn how individuals can find their way, their truth(s), so as to live their lives to the fullest.

Several years in the making, she was also driven to write *Back Home With Evangeline*, the sequel to *A Travel in Time to Grand Pré*. It is here that Madeleine and Michel find themselves back in the twentieth century with a message that must be shared with the world. So, too, and even more importantly, must the message be lived, and experienced, by one and all.

So, too, is she the author of *Time Will Tell*, a uniquely moving tale that begins in the present day before weaving its way backward through time to connect a glowing thread of historic discoveries. Courtesy of past-life regression, Michaela (Dr. Mike) Callaghan, a brilliant metaphysical scientist, in the twenty-first century, discovers that she lived as a young, noble, Cathari herbalist healer, in the Languedoc area of France, during a time when political change was in the air.

When not working as a Special Education teacher, she continues to read, research and write, exploring her personal genealogies, all of which constitute her passion.

In the words of the Dalai Lama … *In order to be happy, one must first possess inner contentment; and inner contentment cannot come from having all we want; rather it comes from having and appreciating all we have.*

www.ingramcontent.com/pod-product-compliance
Lightning Source LLC
Chambersburg PA
CBHW070712160426
43192CB00009B/1164